LIBRARIANS' AGREEMENTS:

bargaining
for a
heterogeneous
profession

by
John W. Weatherford

The Scarecrow Press, Inc.
Metuchen, N.J., & London
1988

Library of Congress Cataloging-in-Publication Data

Weatherford, John W., 1924-
  Librarians' agreements.

  Bibliography: p.
  Includes index.
  1. Collective bargaining--Librarians--United States.
2. Librarians' unions--United States. I. Title.
Z682.2.U5W4 1988   331.89'04102'0973   87-35605
ISBN 0-8108-2073-0

Copyright © 1988 by John W. Weatherford
Manufactured in the United States of America

CONTENTS

I.	Introduction	1
II.	The Unit	7
III.	Opportunity	17
IV.	The Securities	23
V.	Money	43
VI.	The Boston Public Library	55
VII.	The University of California System	60
VIII.	The University of Florida System	69
IX.	Conclusion	79
X.	Bibliography	82

Appendix I: Agreement between City of Boston and Boston Public Library Professional Staff Association ... 97

Appendix II: University of California and University Federation of Librarians University Council--A.F.T. Agreement ... 141

Appendix III: Agreement between Board of Regents State University System of Florida and United Faculty of Florida ... 203

Index ... 299

I

INTRODUCTION

Much of the literature dealing with librarians' collective bargaining in the past fifteen years comprises studies of union organization or of librarians' views of its effect.[1] As agreements never tell the whole story of a bargaining relationship, these studies can be useful; but because they cannot tell the whole story either, agreements and other evidence are all the more important. Surveys of opinion may be sound scholarship based on scientific techniques, but the opinions themselves are not. No account has been taken of whether they are correct. Librarians' experiences as supervised or supervisors, union organizers or management team members, naturally color their views. One management style allows these team members to argue strenuously <u>in camera</u> for their views, and then requires them to support <u>fully</u> whatever decision is reached; another requires both private and public conformity. On the bargaining unit side, individual members are under less pressure to conform against their own opinions, but they are besieged by the union's version of events, particularly at that moment when the union and management teams have reached a table agreement, subject to ratification. Once the teams reach across the table to shake hands after they have initialled the last article, both teams have an interest in union ratification. Ratification by the management side should never be a problem. On the union side it is, often and inevitably. The union submits the tentative agreement to its ratifying body, and makes its case for the agreement. Although a ratifying body can be whatever the union constitution says it is, the practice among those that we are going to discuss is to consult the entire union membership. During

1

this process, management is careful to say only bland things, in order to give the union freedom to describe the agreement in whatever manner it judges most effective for achieving ratification. Unless something goes badly wrong during the life of the agreement, this description endures.

Much library literature on collective bargaining is addressed to librarians in the role of victim, underdog, or exploited employee, as workers needing to band together for security and recognition. Yet library literature on other subjects addresses librarians variously as professionals, as managers, as supervisors, and as persons whose interest in exploration is unclouded by their interest in security. Our writings about our profession, introspective and preaching to the converted, betray our uneasy knowledge that our status does not match the realities of our profession. Collective bargaining has the capacity to clarify some of these problems. It could reveal librarians not only as defensive beginners and inadequate bureaucrats, but also as creative beginners and managers. The library profession does not belong exclusively to any echelon, and we can only damage a profession that, like ours, is still struggling for external recognition if we define it as only present or potential bargaining unit members.

Readers aware of the strong emotional content of collective bargaining may be disappointed by the rather level treatment that it receives here. My only excuse is that I have concentrated on agreements, which are probably the least rhetorical and most dessicated of all the manifestations of collective bargaining. Think of the others: A knot of employees, moved by fear or a sense of injury, resolve to unionize. This commitment is an emotional one for them, however coolly they reach their resolve. Next they must win to their views those fellow workers that some agency has defined as forming a community of interest with them, in order to attain the election of a bargaining agent. This is an emotional experience both for the original knot and for the others, and it is a time of greater tension still if rival and dedicated unions contend for the right to represent them. Nor do passions subside at the next stage while union and management meet to bargain their wages, hours, and other terms and conditions of employment. Hanging over negotiations is the _ultimo ratio_ of the adversaries, the strike and the lockout; and what employee can avoid some stress in contemplating these? Nor do employees have a monopoly of emotional motivation. Owners

Introduction

and managers often react to the initiation of the new relationship with feelings of disillusionment and bitterness. They may feel, "If they want to play Union versus Management, I know the rules too." As other authors have put it, "They feel that the employees are ungrateful for management's attempts to improve working conditions. Managers feel hurt and consider employees disloyal to the goals of the organization."[2]

Although agreements are essential windows into collective bargaining, we should not rely exclusively on our view through them. Collective bargaining is a holistic relationship deeply affected by trust or mistrust, the skill of the negotiators, its familiarity or novelty on site, the local traditions and proclivities of union and employer, and the prosperity or grimness of the times. A long-established and trusting union-management relationship can well eventuate in an agreement that is traditional and sparse to the point of skimpiness, and that continues unchanged, but for economic provisions, over long periods. This sort of agreement has little else to say about the real relationship. No more do the agreements of parties whose modus operandi is regular cheating, violation, and litigation. It may be puzzling to read the ecstatic announcement of a union negotiator that "at last we have won recognition and respect," only to find that the vaunted agreement is as ordinary as they come; yet sometimes this homely pride means that some recognition and respect have been won that were not there before. One must be close indeed to the local issues to discern whether this kind of standard victory announcement is a routine bid for members' ratification or exulting over some advance, some breaking through into the adversary's conscious, that really did happen, that had been sorely missed before, and that will never be adequately expressed in the text of an agreement.

For negotiators drafting proposals and counterproposals for the table, ad hoc aids called clause finders are helpful. A clause can be successful in one agreement and a disaster in another because the interdependence of the parts of each agreement changes its effect. This is a book for those with a more general interest, and is not meant as a clause finder. It presents a few sample agreements with annotations, to preserve the practical flavor of entire agreements.

The selection of agreements in this book implies no

applause or denigration. They are meant only to be instructive. Municipalities are the greatest employer of librarians and their agreements number in the thousands.[3] One cannot read them all, but can easily choose a fairly typical example. No doubt somewhere in our towns and counties some clause spikes high above the mass for cleverness, but that would not be typical. The same holds for agreements covering school employees and public library employees. Agreements covering only public librarians are much less numerous; here the problem is not to find a typical example but one that has been made to differ from municipal employees' agreements especially to suit librarians. I am sorry to provide no agreements in which special librarians play an important part. Often they are the lone specimen of librarianship in their firm or a small part of a work force that may be either professional or service personnel. The agreements of college and university faculty, though most familiar to me, are the most difficult to select. The individualism of professors, their prodigality in examining routine matters de novo, and their urge to create an agreement fit for publication combine to produce agreements that are for the most part idiosyncratic even from campus to campus. I have chosen the University of Florida nine-campus system to represent faculty agreemants that cover librarians because it is large and deals with a broad spectrum of issues without many local peculiarities. Easiest of all to select have been the agreements of: university library employees and 2) university librarians, because so few of either exist. Among the former we may number the University of Chicago and Claremont Colleges; among the latter, Brandeis University and the University of California nine-campus system. The California agreement has been chosen because it is more closely tailored to academic librarians than that of Brandeis, but comparisons with Brandeis are drawn where instructive.

These selections have to do solely with the amount of interest an example might be expected to evoke, not with its value to those who made it. An agreement is the fixing of what ever arrangements union and employer have been able to make; a string quartet it is not. We can as students describe clauses as imaginative, dangerous, ambiguous, or just very commonplace. We are seldom near enough to say whether they actually work, and that is all their writers need care about.

NOTES

1. The past fifteen years have seen a number of studies of librarians' opinions of collective bargaining: In 1971, Joseph Vignone's Collective Bargaining Procedures for Public Librarians, Directors, and Board of Trustees Members, Scarecrow, 179pp. In 1975, Theodore L. Guyton, Unionization: The Viewpoint of Librarians, ALA, 204pp. In 1982, Bob Carmack and John N. Olsgaard, "Collective Bargaining among Academic Librarians: A Survey of ACRL Members," College and Research Libraries, 43:140-5, March 1982. Similar polling has appeared in a dissertation by James F. Wyatt, "A Study of the Attitudes of Academic Librarians, Library Directors and Academic Deans in Colleges and Universities of Eight Southeastern States towards Union Organization and Collective Bargaining for Academic Librarians," Florida State U., 1973, 183pp. Earlier literature appears to have been reviewed in an unpublished research paper by C.J. DiPerna, "Content Analysis of Articles Containing Reasons for and against Library Unions, 1917-1973," U. of N. Carolina, 1975, 132pp. Without implying any bias, one may cite a number of other works emphasizing union organizing, such as Archie Kleingartner and Jean R. Kennelly, "Employee Relations in Libraries: The Current Scene," pp. 1-22; and Don Wasserman, "Unionization of Library Personnel: Where We Stand Today," pp. 23-29 (both in Frederick A. Schlipf, ed., Collective Bargaining in Libraries, University of Illinois Graduate School of Library Science, 1975, 179pp.); and also Robert C. and Marjorie I. O'Reilly, Librarians and Labor Relations: Employment Under Union Contracts, Contributions in Librarianship No. 35, Greenwood Press, 1981, 191pp. The same vantage point characterizes studies dealing with the relations between unions and professional organizations by Katherine Todd, "Collective Bargaining and Professional Associations in the Library Field," Library Quarterly, 55:284-99, #4, 1985; by Joseph Krislov and Rhoda Channing, "Librarians and Independent Unions," pp. 475-487, and Dennis Chamot, "The Effect of Collective Bargaining on Employee-Management Relationships," pp. 489-515, of Margaret A. Chaplan's introduction to "Employee Organizations and Collective Bargaining in Libraries," Library Trends, 25:419-422, Oct. 1976. Similarly, Nancy E. Peace's special coverage of "Personnel and Employment: Collective Bargaining," pp. 219-220 of ALA Yearbook 1981, dealt with ALA's stance, the Social Responsibilities Round Table union task force, and unionization of librarians.

2. Robert D. Stueart and John Taylor Eastlick, Library Management, 2nd ed., Libraries Unlimited, 1981, p. 120.

3. In 1982 there were 3,301 county and 8,526 municipal bargaining units in the United States (not counting school districts, which provided another 15,918 units). Statistical Abstract of the United States 1986.

II

THE UNIT

A bargaining unit is a defined group whose community of interest allows them to be represented by a single, exclusive bargaining agent. The agent is a union. The difference is blurred by some writers on library unions, but unit and union should not be confused.[1]

One of the most important distinctions between unit and union lies in the degree of choice enjoyed by employees. In the United States, employees enjoy a well-protected, though regulated and periodic, choice of their union. They have much less choice of their bargaining unit. At the beginning of a formal bargaining relationship, employees are asked by the appropriate labor relations authority whether they desire collective bargaining, and if so which contending agent. For this purpose a governmental authority establishes a voting unit, as much like the eventual bargaining unit as possible. For both the voting and for the eventual unit, dubious inclusions and exclusions that are challenged by the employer or the interested union are decided by the authority.[2] The governmental authority is usually the National Labor Relations Board (NLRB) for private employers and its state counterpart for state and municipal employers, if the state has public employee bargaining legislation. Especially among public libraries confusion can arise as to who is the employer, and consequently what jurisdiction applies in a unit question. In various disputes of this sort courts have found that it is the city of Billings (Montana) and not its library trustees, and the Wayne county (Michigan) commissioners and not the library board, that are the employers of librarians.[3] On the

7

other hand, they have found that the library boards of the Buffalo and Erie county and the New York City public libraries are the employers and not the respective county and city governments. On these decisions hinge such questions as whether a union agreement is valid or void, whether a city can make rules affecting the compensation and agency shop responsibilities of library employees, and whether bargaining is governed by state or federal rules.[4]

The case of the Rosenberg Library, serving the public of Galveston (Texas) city and county, is a good example of this last effect. The union and librarians considered the Rosenberg Library to be a private employer and therefore under the protection of the federal NLRB; but the NLRB decided that at least the headquarters library was a political subdivision of Texas, where public employee bargaining is illegal.[5] A few states, like Texas, prohibit collective bargaining by their public employees (other than police and firefighters); many states have legislation permitting and regulating it, somewhat along federal lines; and the rest allow it passively according to the occasion.

In the last kind of situation, bargaining is voluntary on the part of the employer, and the bargaining unit like many other questions may be determined by negotiation. In any case, the desires of the individuals involved affect their inclusion or exclusion less than several other factors that govern the shaping of units, such as community of interest, viability, and effectiveness in bargaining. Of twenty-six states that have laws permitting and regulating bargaining in postsecondary education, for example, seventeen leave the final decision of unit determination to a state board, two permit it to be established by agreement between employer and union, and the rest are mute on the subject. Connecticut establishes two kinds of unit, professional and "classified," but allows professionals to vote on whether they are to enter a non-professional unit.[6]

The certification elections familiar in America usually determine not the composition of the unit, but whether a tentative unit is to bargain collectively or not, and if so what its agent should be. Once the unit has been established, it is difficult for those in positions that existed at the time to leave or enter it, though new accretions and reorganization can reopen the question of unit composition. Although the desires of the employees are stated by NLRB to be one of its criteria, unit determination is governed by a public policy that calls for harmonious and orderly labor relations. These require a stable unit based on community of interest rather than solicitude for dissident minorities. One might say of self-determined unit formation what Sir William Ivor Jennings said of self-determination in general: "On the surface it sounded reasonable: let the people decide. In fact it was ridiculous because the people cannot decide until somebody decides who are the people."[7]

Determinations of appropriate bargaining units can tell us about the nature of librarians' work in various environments. These are quite diverse. Contested unit determinations of the past twenty years have concerned librarians employed in radio and television studios, insurance companies, law offices, newspapers, hospitals, law firms, Catholic dioceses, Father Flanagan's Boys' Town, stock brokers, and of course public schools, public libraries, community colleges, and public and private colleges and universities. Let us look at the special librarians first, that is those employed in some operation other than public libraries and educational institutions. In six of eight disputed unit determinations, librarians were placed in bargaining units of either clerical or service and maintenance employees. In the seventh determination they were kept out of a professional unit of radio/TV producers and programmers. Only in the eighth were they kept out of a service and clerical unit because they were doing professional work.[8] Such have been the disputed cases involving special librarians. It is always possible that tribunals can make mistakes in such determinations, but it is even more likely that some librarians are not professionals in their positions. We must also be suspicious of the term "librarian" as it may be used outside public and educational libraries, for in the rest of the country's work places "librarian" is not an <u>appellation controlée</u>. Thus some of those whom the courts declined to call professional, librarians might not call librarian.

Public librarians can find themselves in one of three kinds of bargaining unit: municipal employees, public library employees, or sometimes, if there are enough of them, public librarians. Units of municipal employees customarily embrace everybody on the city or county payroll except supervisors, confidential employees, firemen, and police officers. Units of public library employees embrace everybody on the library payroll except supervisors, confidential employees, and guards. Units of public librarians are usually just that, sometimes defined as those with a library science degree. School and community college librarians and media specialists are generally included in the teachers' units.[9]

Academic librarians too now appear in three kinds of unit: faculty, library employees, and librarians. When <u>Collective Bargaining and the Academic Librarian</u> was published in 1976, the overwhelming majority of academic librarians who had collective bargaining were in faculty units.[10] Claremont College stood as the lone example of a unit of library employees, and there were no agreements with units of librarians alone. Since then, Brandeis and Boston Universities in 1978 and the University of California system in 1984 have acquired librarians' units. In the meantime, disputed unit determination cases continue to be studied on their individual merits. The librarians of Columbia Teachers' College were formed into a unit despite the employer's arguments for a faculty unit that would include them.[11] In the University of New Hampshire system the central governing board opposed the inclusion of librarians in that faculty unit, only to be overridden by the state education commission.[12] At Barber-Scotia College, the NLRB excluded the cataloger and a library technician from the faculty unit because there was no showing made that they were professional employees.[13] In these and other unit determinations neutral tribunals have drawn conclusions about the community of interest that binds librarians to a number of groups of employees such as clerical, faculty, professional, or service and maintenance, and have found librarians that fit each of these categories. The bases for such conclusions are not always the same. They have included the nature of the librarian's work, the similarity of fringe benefits, and the inconvenience of highly fragmented units.

As a result, agreements often do not recognize librarians as professional employees. In units covering municipal employees there is usually no recognition, formal or implicit, that librarians are professionals, unless one argues that being salaried rather than hourly somehow constitutes such a recognition. In schools and community colleges on the other hand they are treated like the schoolteachers with whom they have been included. In most unionized colleges and universities they form part of the faculty (even if second-class), and where they do not they are generally recognized as professionals. To the extent that academic librarians have achieved professional recognition it is not a goal for them. They have tended rather to seek faculty status, which they have come to see as more desirable whether they accept its full implications or not. The term "professional" might in academe seem like bureaucratese for "non-faculty." The University of California agreement deserves special attention because it treats librarians as more similar to faculty than any others who are not officially faculty, and continues pre-bargaining personnel procedures somewhat parallel to those of faculty, even though unit determination has separated them. In sum, what is viewed in academe as a rather minimum recognition of status is still an unachieved longing in most public libraries.

Bargaining units have a geographical dimension as well, consisting of a single library or of a city-wide, county-wide, or state-wide system, each affecting the employees' environment. Even if the unit is coterminous with a pre-existing management organization, it can cause a concentration power through central bargaining.

Thus important effects flow from the composition of the unit. It may deliver or secure to librarians in schools, colleges, universities, and a minority of public libraries official recognition of their professional or faculty status. For the rest, it has done no such thing. What is the best unit composition for librarians? One made up solely of librarians ought to provide the highest sensitivity to their special aspirations and concerns, and a large and diverse unit to submerge them in a heterogeneous group whose community of interest ignores them. The two models exist in tension.[14]

Probably nothing in the formation of bargaining units has a greater effect on librarians' sense of identity than the rule excluding supervisors. In federal and some state jurisdictions this exclusion applies to all supervisors; in others, supervisors may have a unit of their own if those they supervise are not in it.[15] Librarians with titles suggesting that they are supervisors do appear in nonsupervisory units, but that is probably because they do not meet the labor relations test of supervision, whereby they must at least have the power effectively to recommend the hiring, discipline, and discharge of another.[16] It is not enough to be a mentor or timekeeper, to relay directives, or to revise another's cataloging.

Thus in disputes the head librarian of the Capital Times newspaper, the head librarians of Bradford College and the Catholic University Law School, and the director of learning resources of Mount Vernon College were found not to be supervisors.[17] These are the exception, however, and the following were, as true supervisors, excluded from the unit: the head librarians of the Bulletin and Arkansas Gazette newspapers, the co-ordinator of library services of the Delaware (Pennsylvania) Community College, department heads in the libraries of New York University, Rensselaer Polytech, Fordham, and Claremont Colleges; the circulation/reserve, biomedical, education/psychology, and documents librarians, the heads of serials cataloging and law technical services, and the assistant head cataloger at the University of Chicago; the head librarians at Point Park and Florida Southern Colleges and the University of San Francisco; and six assistant librarians at Northeastern University.[18] Most exclusions of supervisors go undisputed and simply appear in recognition articles.

One of the reasons supervisors are excluded from a unit is the danger that they might be the employer's instruments in illegally dominating or assisting the union. When the University of Chicago met with a union committee seeking to organize the librarians, the committee included some supervisors. Supervisors also participated in union recognition picketing, and one attended a union convention as a delegate. Their activities constituted an unlawful interference and assistance by the university in union activities.[19]

So many librarians supervise somebody that, in federal jurisdictions such as Claremont Colleges and Brandeis Univeristy, unit determination can exclude roughly half the librarians. To what degree does this formal dichotomy divide the profession? Library literature has yet to deal with this question despite its manifest interest in librarians' opinions of collective bargaining.

Unit determination among private sector academic librarians encountered a special complication in 1980 when the U.S. supreme court ruled that the faculty of Yeshiva University, because they determined essential policies of the university such as curriculum, admissions, and graduation requirements, were managerial employees and therefore excluded by the National Labor Relations Act from collective bargaining.

The Unit

The decision applies only to NLRB jurisdiction and so far has not affected any state college or university faculties. Since then, some faculties have been found to be managerial, some not, but time has not diminished the importance of the Yeshiva decision. Soon after the Yeshiva decision was delivered, my article in Library Journal predicted that it would drive a wedge between academic librarians and faculty members at some universities, even though at that time nearly all faculty bargaining units included librarians.[20] The Yeshiva tests applied to faculty show that librarians seldom qualify as managerial employees. In denying bargaining to the Boston University faculty unit, which included non-supervisory librarians, the NLRB and supreme court cited the authority of faculty members in "grading, teaching methods, graduation requirements, and student discipline," as well as a major role in faculty personnel actions.[21] The librarians were already in a unit of their own, and they do not wield the authority that made the Boston University faculty managerial employees. Where faculty members cannot bargain collectively because of their managerial duties, most librarians would still be eligible to do so because they do not possess the prerogatives that make them managerial employees.

Some academic librarians seek full faculty status including the same role in governance as their classroom colleages. If the realities of this status matched its outward appearance, that is, if the librarians truly and effectively exercised the prerogatives that the faculties of Boston, Yeshiva, and some other private colleges and universities exercise, they too would become ineligible for collective bargaining. In the private sector collective bargaining is not a means at all, but a hindrance to librarians seeking the powers of faculty governance. If librarians at such institutions do not have these powers, and can constitute a viable unit alone or with other non-faculty employees, collective bargaining is still open to them.

The kind of bargaining unit that holds librarians affects not only their working environment but their identity. The community of interest that forms the basis of unit determination very often embraces a wide variety of municipal employees whose work is not even education, let alone librarianship. Then again, even librarians' units split librarians along supervisory lines. Some librarians may, to be sure, give their best attention to their profession or to their unit without neglecting the other.

NOTES

1. Bernard D. Meltzer and Stanley D. Henderson, Labor Law: Cases, Materials, and Problems, 3rd ed., Boston, 1984, p. 380.

2. An example of the difference between responsibility and supervision at the Illinois State Library is to be found in 80 LA 34 (1982).

3. AFSCME vs City of Billings, Montana, 93 LRRM 2753 (1976); Wayne County Library Board vs Wayne County Board of Commissioners, 97 LRRM 2304 (1977).

4. Erie County vs Buffalo and Erie County Public Library Board of Trustees, 74 LRRM 2450 (1970); New York Public Library vs New York State Public Relations Board, 87 LRRM 2632 (1974) and 90 LRRM 2463 (1975).

5. American Libraries, 14: 506, Sept. 1983, describes the dispute that initiated the case. The decision is in 116 LRRM 1050 (1984) but was not reported in American Libraries. See also Martin Schneid, "Recognition and Bargaining Units," in Frederick A. Schlipf, ed., Collective Bargaining in Libraries, University of Illinois Graduate School of Library Science, 1975, pp. 43-53, for an explanation by an NLRB official.

6. Julia Newcomer and Elvis C. Stephens, "A Survey of Patterns of Unit Composition at Public Higher Education Institutions Involved in Collective Bargaining," Journal of Collective Negotiations in Higher Education, 11:89-112, no. 2, 1982.

7. Quoted in The Spectator, 257:18, Sept. 27, 1986. For unit formation, see John E. Abodeely, The NLRB and the Appropriate Bargaining Unit (Report No. 3 of Labor Relations and Public Policy Series), University of Pennsylvania, 1971, pp. 65-86.

8. Librarians included in clerical or service units: Ohio Casualty Ins. Co. (1969) 71 LRRM 1089; Arkansas Gazette (1975) 89 LRRM 1443; Backus Hospital (1975) 90 LRRM 1696; Jewish Hospital of Cincinnati (1976) 91 LRRM 1499;

Baptist Memorial Hospital (1976) 93 LRRM 1454; Stroock & Stroock & Lavan (1980) 105 LRRM 1609. Librarians excluded from clerical units: Witter, Dean & Co. (1974) 87 LRRM 1479; Kanawha Valley Memorial Hospital (1975) 89 LRRM 1451. Librarians excluded from production-programming unit: WTAR Radio-TV (1967) 67 LRRM 1062.

9. Daniel Barron and F. William Summers, "The School Library Media Professional in the Negotiations Process," School Library Media Quarterly, 12:265-8, Summer 1983.

10. John W. Weatherford, Collective Bargaining and the Academic Librarian. Scarecrow Press, 1976, pp. 32-43. In the same year, Gwendolyn M. Cruzat also pointed out the predominance of faculty units containing librarians, their lack of choice of bargaining unit, and the essentially union behavior of the AAUP, NEA, and AFT: "Collective Bargaining in Academic Librarianship." Wayne State University Ph.D. Dissertation, 1976. 76 pp.

11. Teachers College, Columbia University (1977) 94 LLRM 1397.

12. University System of New Hampshire (1977) 94 LRRM 2919.

13. Barber-Scotia College (1979) 102 LRRM 1330.

14. For a prominent union leader's cogent summary of the role of high-school media librarians in bargaining, see Albert Shanker, "Neither Fish nor Fowl," Illinois Libraries, 60:571, Sept. 1978. More recent commentaries from the schools are Donald G. Turner, "Negotiation in Public Education: State of the Art," School Library Media Quarterly, 12:279-85; and Daniel Barron and F. William Summers, "The School Library Media Professional in the Negotiations Process," School Library Media Quarterly, 12:265-8, Summer 1983.

15. Meltzer, Op.cit., 712ff.

16. Abodeely, op.cit., 207.

17. Capital Times (1978) 97 LRRM 1124; Bradford College (1982) 110 LRRM 1055; Catholic University (1973) 82 LRRM 1385; Mt Vernon (1977) 95 LRRM 1349.

18. Bulletin (1976) 94 LRRM 1259; Arkansas Gazette (1975) 89 LRRM 1443: Delaware CC (1975) 92 LRRM 2615; NYU (1975) 91 LRRM 1165; Rensselaer Polytech (1975) 89 LRRM 1844; Fordham (1974) 87 LRRM 1643; Claremont (1972) 81 LRRM 1317; Chicago (1973) 83 LRRM 1678; Point Park (1974) 85 LRRM 1542; Florida Southern (1972) 80 LRRM 1160; USF (1973) 84 LRRM 1403; Northeastern (1975) 89 LRRM 1862.

19. University of Chicago Library, (1973) 83 LRRM 1678.

20. John W. Weatherford, "Collective Bargaining and the Academic Librarian, 1976-79," Library Journal, 107:481-2, Feb. 15, 1980.

21. (1986) Decisions and Orders of the National Labor Relations Board, v. 281 no. 115.

III

OPPORTUNITY

The most common opportunity to be found in agreements is promotion. The promotion familiar in labor relations is an upward movement within the organization to a position of greater skill and responsibility, usually accompanied by a higher functional title and improved compensation. The number of such opportunities is limited by the structure of the organization, so that there must be a vacancy into which to promote before there can be a promotion. Among municipal and public library employees agreements most commonly deal with timely posting of promotion opportunities so that employees can apply before external candidates and discuss the application with friends and family. Seniority is usually stated to be one of the criteria for promotion, and if an internal and external candidate are equally qualified preference is given to the former.

Promotion in agreements resembles layoff and recall. Instead of bumping a junior, a senior employee bids for the desired vacancy, and the decision rests on combinations of qualifications, ability, and seniority. Disputes center on seniority versus the other considerations. Published arbitrations in 1984 held for seniority in five of eight cases.[1] Promotions based on seniority conflict with affirmative action where management has chosen or been forced to set racial or sexual quotas in promotion. The issue is discussed further in Securities.

Academic promotion has an altogether different meaning. At some universities it is a hard-won recognition of achievement and promise, and at others a concession that a certain number of years have passed since appointment or the last promotion. In either case, it brings a higher title of rank and a modest (usually 5%) addition to base salary, but without affecting the faculty member's duties and responsibilities. At some universities, however, promotion to the rank of assistant or even associate professor is prerequisite to tenure. Because there is no connection between academic promotions and organizational structure, there need be no limit to them, though some institutions maintain quotas as a means of budget control.[2] Academic librarians' promotions may be expressed as faculty ranks (e.g., assistant professor), as parallels to such ranks (e.g., assistant librarian), or simply as numbers (e.g., I through IV).

Because promotion often requires added skills, training and educational opportunity are closely related to it, and education can lift one out of the organization altogether. The education and training opportunities offered in agreements tend to be combinations of the following:

1. Time for workshops and conferences,

2. Reimbursement of conference and workshop expenses,

3. Staff and professional development programs,

4. Salary increases for formal education units completed,

5. Reimbursement for tuition and related expenses for courses,

6. On-job training for the next level up. Except for the last, applicants may under some agreements have to show the relevancy of the opportunity to the job. Re-training is rather a security than an opportunity, aimed at giving new skills to persons whose old skills are no longer wanted. When eligibility for retraining is connected to seniority, its role as a security is even plainer.

Educational opportunities exist outside union environments, especially in colleges and universities, but agreements remain our best source for them. Librarians may wish to glean ideas from others' agreements. Among municipal employees, those in Oakland, California, are eligible for leaves to attend conferences if they are job-related. Expenses may or may not be reimbursed. Oakland does, however, pay part of the tuition for academic courses (75% if the student makes an A, 50% if a C). Madison Heights, Wisconsin, pays up to $200 a year towards tuition if the course is job-related. Contra Costa county pays up to $600 a year per employee for career development training. Huntington Beach, California, offers a pay incentive at the rate of one dollar a month per credit hour earned, up to 8.25% of base pay. Although these are only examples of educational opportunities to be found in municipal employees' agreements, perhaps half of them have no educational provisions at all. So it is too with public library agreements. The public librarians of Buffalo and Erie County can get three and a half hours off per course per week after they have earned twelve credit hours. Brooklyn Public Library in 1984 agreed to appoint a training officer to develop training programs connected with promotions.[3]

By 1979-80, 29% of university agreements dealt somehow with professional development.[4] As some such benefits preceded collective bargaining we cannot suppose that they must appear in agreements to exist. A recent study indicates that librarians who have collective bargaining are neither more nor less engaged in professional development activities than the others.[5] Among the librarians of Boston University seeking to organize in 1979, one of the union organizers gave professional development as one of the principal concerns.[6] The Brandeis agreement gives librarians the opportunity to audit courses or to take them for credit at a 50% discount. Moreover, one employee per semester may receive 3.5 hours a week leave to take a course deemed suitable for professional development. Brandeis librarians, with approval of their supervisors, may audit Brandeis courses free, and with the approval of the personnel office may take courses for credit at 50% discount. One librarian per semester may take three and a half hours per week off work to attend a course for professional development relevant to the job.

At some universities and colleges, agreements provide educational opportunities for the families of employees. The Brandeis agreement allows librarians with five years' employment to send their children through four years of undergraduate study at Brandeis for a 75% reduction in tuition; wives of librarians with one year's employment enjoy a 50% reduction for such courses.

Though all leaves and hours are economic matters, their interest to librarians lies also in their function as an opportunity to advance in their careers, through education or promotion. The main variables of vacations are their length, how much can be accumulated, when they can be taken, and what happens to unused vacation at termination. The annual accrual of vacation varies from six days a year to thirty. Often the carry-over is limited to the following year. It may depend on longevity, in civil service systems as well as in such agreements as that of the Santa Monica municipal employees, whose maximum accumulated vacation grows from thirty to fifty days according to length of service. Vacation time growing with longevity is a familiar civil service feature preceding collective bargaining. The proper time to take vacation is subject to the convenience of the employer. Occasionally an agreement provides that postponements for the employer's convenience are not to deprive an employee of the full amount of vacation earned. This proviso is probably unnecessary barring some local misunderstanding, and most libraries do not have it. The employer's convenience does however sometimes force employees into competing for the most desirable vacation weeks. In public libraries and among municipal employees it is common for the agreement to resort to seniority to resolve such conflicts. Sometimes minimum vacation is established, to make it clear that employees are not to take, say, ninety minutes' vacation every now and then. A few libraries require that vacation be taken all in one piece, but usually there are no such restrictions, because requiring the supervisor's permission suffices to handle such problems. Unused vacation that does not exceed a certain stated limit on accumulation is usually paid off in cash upon the departure of the librarian.

Holidays are usually seven or eight specified days when employees are not required to work. Generally these are also days when the work place is closed, but sometimes the library is kept open with a skeleton staff, and compensatory time off is given those working on holidays, at rates varying from equal to double time. Usually holidays falling on Sunday are granted on the Monday; a little less often holidays falling on Saturday are granted on the Friday. Homogenized anniversaries such as "Presidents' Day" occasionally appear. The following are the usual holidays granted, though probably no single agreement grants them all: New Year's Day, Martin Luther King Day, Lincoln's Birthday, Washington's Birthday, Good Friday, Memorial Day, Independence Day, Labor Day, Rosh Hoshanna, Yom Kippur, Columbus Day, Veterans' Day, Thanksgiving, and Christmas. Sometimes the employee's birthday is added to these, or one to three wild-card holidays of the individual's choice.

Professional development and educational opportunities can lift an employee out of his or her unit and even out of the organization. Within the unit, though, the promotion opportunities that trainees might hope this preparation would open can prove disappointing. If seniority is treated with substantially greater respect than training or ability in promotion decisions, the value of the development and educational benefits diminishes markedly.

NOTES

1. 84 LAIS 1007, 1023, 1053, 1283, 2094, 2111, 2162.

2. John W. Weatherford, Collective Bargaining and the Academic Librarian, Scarecrow, 1976, pp. 52-54.

3. Larry Brandwein, "Coexistence to Cooperation," Library Journal, 109:1999-2000, Nov. 1, 1984.

4. John Andes, "A Decade of Development in Higher Education Collective Bargaining: Changes in Contract Content," Journal of Collective Negotiations in the Public Sector, 11:289, #4, 1982.

5. William Caynon, "Collective Bargaining and Professional Development of Academic Librarians," College and Research Libraries, 43:133-139, March 1982. Caynon found that collective bargaining had no effect, good or bad, on the professional development and activities of librarians. His is a statistical study and he presumably was speaking of statistical effect and not causality. One might, without contradicting him, set up models, one of which is a previously underachieving population of librarians whom collective bargaining had delivered from stultifying conditions and thus elevated to the level of some other group of librarians whose more stimulating

environment they had no reason to alter by collective bargaining. In local situations opportunities for professional and educational development have been sought and attained at the bargaining table. Without further study along the lines sketched by Cayman, we do not know how significant this model is.

    6. Rosemary Gallagher interviewed in <u>American Libraries</u>, 10:575, Nov. 1979.

IV

THE SECURITIES

Of the myriad securities one might desire, we are concerned here only with those that lie within the power of bargaining to provide. Some of these have become so well established that they no longer create anxiety. Employees are paid on pay day. Their checks are never (well, hardly ever) a surprise. Their health coverage is not dropped in April to balance a July-to-June budget. These securities are often part of an individual employment contract, whether written, oral, or implied. Yet anxieties remain. Employees do not like to be discharged from their jobs, not even laid off. They might rather not be subject to disciplinary rules, but they especially wish them to be fair in content and application. They hope to work safe from injury. They want security from unfair discrimination, and from that special form of discrimination, harassment. It is these desires that lie alongside money at the heart of collective bargaining.

It is hard to imagine a greater security than a long term contractual guarantee of one's pay and position regardless of performance or the employer's financial situation. America's unions cannot obtain so absolute an undertaking, any more than its civil service systems do. Employers can retrench for any of several reasons; unions bargain how retrenchment is to affect the employees in their care. Except in college and university faculty agreements, which have inherited the superior protection of tenure, the central feature of this process is seniority.

In its simplest form, seniority would so govern the

employer's reduction of the work force that the newest employees in the unit would be terminated first, and the senior remainder would continue unmolested in any way by the retrenchment. This simplest form probably does not exist, because the random dismantling of some operations and preservation of others would fatally disrupt the employer's organization. To avoid this disruption and still preserve the principle of seniority, standard agreements do not directly attack management's right to eliminate <u>positions</u>, but provide that the <u>persons</u> terminated be those with least seniority. Under this familiar arrangement, when the employer retrenches positions, a senior employee occupying a condemned position can take a surviving position if it has a junior occupant. The person so dislodged can seek the same salvation. and so on, until only the most junior are left to be laid off. For employees this graphically termed "bumping" has the advantage of making their lives during retrenchment a little more predictable; at such trying times, some know the seniority list almost by heart. Seniority and bumping also insulate the employee from any reprisal or prejudice on the part of the employer. Logically enough, recalling laid-off employees is governed by inverse seniority.[1]

  The employer's view of this process may be quite different, and include visions of disastrous bumpings. A promising young employee with a good and recent education has been trained, at some expense and because of her aptitude and promise, in new technologies. (I make her female to add to the point). She and her position are important to the employer. In the next retrenchment she is bumped by a senior employee whose education is neither good nor recent and whose training has all led up to mending, labelling, and filing, which he performs well (as might be expected after fifteen years' application). This offensive scenario can occur whenever seniority is allowed to fill the more important position with the less able employee. To reduce this kind of damage to the operation, the employer may bargain language that requires not seniority alone but appropriate skills and aptitudes for bumping, and sets up cells within which seniority is contained, so that for instance a cataloger could not bump a reference librarian or vice versa regardless of seniority. Agreements employ phrases such as "appropriate skills and aptitudes" or "competence to do the work" to describe the factors to be weighed against seniority when conflict arises between the two principles. Each and every one of these conflicts is highly important to at least two employees, and sometimes to the employer. Any vagueness in the agreement combines with the high personal importance of each such dispute to generate numerous arbitrations. As seniority is a concrete and numerically-expressed factor, and skill, competence, and aptitude are not, it is not surprising to find seniority winning more than half the arbitrations where the two concepts are weighed.[2]

Academic librarians with real faculty status have (or are eligible for) tenure. Tenure has over the decades proved more secure than seniority. As a result, university faculty agreements often do not trouble to have seniority provisions. It is still true that "there is hardly an employee with greater formal security than the tenured professor."[3] So far, membership in a faculty is the only way to assume the burdens and guarantees of tenure, for the librarians' units of Brandeis University and the Universities of Chicago and California do not have it. An added degree of security pertains in universities that have incorporated into their own policies the principles set forth in 1940 by the American Association of University Professors (AAUP). These exempt faculty members from economic retrenchment except in case of "financial exigency." In the course of time, courts have given the term a meaning closer to financial "disaster," so that it is very difficult to show the exigency prerequisite to discharging a tenured faculty member.[4] Of course the AAUP can not legislate, but institutions that have incorporated its standards in their policies are bound by them because they are bound to follow their own policies.

The AAUP principles preceded faculty bargaining by nearly thirty years, and today universities subscribing to them may or may not have a collective bargaining relationship with their faculties. On the other hand, colleges and universities have sometimes bargained with their faculty unions agreements that violate various AAUP principles. The conditions for dismissing a tenured professor under AAUP principles do not include failing to pay union dues or service fees, but a number of faculty agreements that include librarians stipulate that payment of these fees is a condition of continuing employment of faculty bargaining unit members, including tenured librarians and professors. If the university had earlier incorporated AAUP principles into its policies, the agreement has superseded this part of them.

Union security clauses backed by sanctions are even more common outside faculty agreements. A majority of unit members may cheerfully bear union fees and the way they are enforced. Because some union security clauses do appear as a threat to the security of some individuals, this is a good place to describe the various ways in which employers and unions agree to enforce the payment of money by employees to unions for union services. Historically, the most draconian of these was the "closed shop," which excluded from employment all who were not members of the union. A slightly more permissive version, the "union shop," allowed nonunion persons to take a job but required them after a short time to join the union or lose the job. Among those that are the subjects of this book, both versions are illegal. "Agency shop" is legal. This requires bargaining unit members who are union members to pay union dues, and bargaining unit members who are not union members to pay a fee to the union to compensate for the services it has constructively rendered employees as their agent. Agency shop clauses in agreements enforce collection either by making payment a condition of continued employment, or by imposing on the member a civil liability to pay, or sometimes by involuntary deduction from his or her paycheck. Further developments in agency shop are discussed in the chapter on Money.

The effects of layoff can be softened by: a) banking on normal attrition, b) polling employees to find whether any might be willing to retire or to reduce their pay and schedules temporarily or indefinitely, and c) retraining employees whose present skills are no longer needed. These palliatives are often suggested but not required in agreements. In anxious times, much hope is pinned on retraining, probably more than it can bear. Retraining cannot help if the employer's object is to reduce the total number of employees. It may or may not help if the employer's object is to move resources from an operation based on older skills to one based on newer. An important consideration for the employer is whether the cost of re-training is greater or less than the alternative costs of bumping, severance pay, and unemployment insurance levies. The effectiveness of retraining programs depends, too, on whether aptitude or seniority governs the selection of the trainees.[5]

Traditionally unions have bargained not only to soften the impact of layoffs on employees but to prevent the erosion of the unit. Often, as in the Fresno county library, agreements call for the employer to give the union ten days' notice so that they can meet and confer on the effect on members of the unit of an external contract. If the Los Angeles county library transfers out any functions presently performed by its librarians' unit, it has agreed to "encourage utilization of affected employees by the new employer," or if possible, to place the affected members elsewhere in the library or in county employment, or to train the member for a new position. These provisions cannot be taken in isolation. If they are accompanied by layoff clauses expensive to the employer, some of the financial advantage of farming out functions disappears. Nobody can tell how many employers have contracted out because of a union, or for that matter how many have refrained for the same reason.

In thousands of libraries certain kinds of contracting out are unquestioned. Thirty or forty years ago, internal binding shops gave way to contracts with external firms. Automatic order and approval plans have consumed much of the book selection work that twenty years ago was wholly in the hands of local talent. Although librarians' work may still locally include establishing main entries and assigning subject headings and classifications to books, as well as keeping up with subscriptions and delivery of serials, this local work has been markedly eroded by technological contracting out in the form of bibliographic utilities, networks, and computer subsystems, all of which affect the kind and number of employees needed in libraries. Yet librarians, if we are to judge by library literature, have been keen on these developments rather than hostile. The only nationally published exceptions have been the opposition by some AFSCME union librarians to a government decision in 1983 to contract out many operations of federal libraries to private information enterprises, and a similar dispute over contracting out by the U.S. Naval Academy.[6]

Most leaves are a form of security, and in agreements they are an undertaking by the employer to tolerate absences for certain reasons. One reason can be a conflict of two duties, for example the duty to work and the duty to serve on a jury. Provision for jury leave with pay is practically universal in agreements. Less often leave is also given to employees answering subpoenaes. Some employees must use personal leave if they are principals in the litigation.

Military, national guard, and reserve leave are equally familiar. In some cases they are supplemented by a war clause protecting the seniority of reservists called to active duty in war time.

Bereavement or funeral leave usually amounts to three or four days. Agreements sometimes define those immediate family members for whose death the leave is available. Under some agreements, the employee must actually attend the funeral to earn the leave.

Occupational assault leave appears occasionally. At the Buffalo and Erie County libraries, absences during the month after a job-related assault are paid leaves and are not counted against the employee's sick leave.

Sick leave is so familiar to employees that they may regard their own system as standard. Beyond their considerable uniformity, we do find variations. The essential characteristics of sick leave are the rate at which it accrues, the maximum amount allowed, the convertibility of unused leave, and the conditions of its use. After a probationary period ranging from a few weeks to a year, sick leave accrues at rates of from twelve to 160 days a year. These accrual rates do not represent as great a cost as the range might suggest, because as the number of days of potential incapacity goes up the proportion of actual lost time goes down. This proportion is not especially costly to the employer, nor important to the fortunate majority of employees, but it is vital to a few. The employer's costs rise, however, if the annual accruals are allowed to accumulate. If only a few employees are incapacitated for two weeks in one year, how many more will be incapacitated for two weeks over a two-year period? Or over five years? How much this cost will rise we cannot closely predict, because it is affected by several variables such as the rate of turnover among the employees. Employers attach importance to this contingent cost and usually impose some maximum on the amount of sick leave that an employee may carry over from year to year. Most of these maximum accumulations range from 42 to 380 days.

It takes little agility for the healthy person to start regarding aid to the sick as a tax on the well, and from there it is a short step to seek to minimize the tax. Unused sick leave thus becomes a property right in the minds of even conscientious employees. Why should they be penalized for being well? Especially if it is the result of clean living? Why should they go to work with sniffles when the hypochondriac at the next desk exploits the same condition to stay at home? From an employer's viewpoint, if these feelings are given no consideration they will become a morale problem. Many agreements therefore provide rewards for unused sick leave. It may be exchangeable for other benefits at various ratios ranging from even trade to one dollar of exchange benefit for every six dollars of unused sick leave. The benefit may be cash at retirement or retirement time credit, or, as in the Detroit Public Library, a choice of several applications, such as weddings, moving, legal matters, funerals, and public transit failures.

Sickness or temporary disability resulting from pregnancy is not a novel use of sick leave. Yet a woman may be kept from work not by traditional definitions of disability, but by danger of miscarriage; her inability to work can exceed the period usually allowed for sick leave; or, arguably, her need extends beyond mere disability. In many agreements we find that sick leave is available only for disabilities, including those occasioned by pregnancy. In others, sick leave is applicable to pregnancy per se without any requirement to show disability. Sometimes maternity leave can be taken from sick leave and necessity leave, or in combinations with leave without pay. A pregnancy-related disability before childbirth is generally grounds for sick leave.

Childbearing and a cluster of related needs for leave are not well suited to simple sick leave, judging from the changes in how it is treated in agreements. We now find not only sick leave but pregnancy, maternity, infant care, parental, paternal, abortion, and adoption leaves. Here and there (as among the Wisconsin teachers and Gladstone, Oregon, municipal employees) the agreement expressly allows a pregnant woman to work until she is unable to do so. Elsewhere (as in Contra Costa County, California) the employer could require her to take leave. After childbirth an employee may of course suffer continued disability, but normally the mother's need to remain at home arises from infant care rather than disability. Infant care leaves are without pay and their maximum lengths vary from four to twelve months. The chief benefit of a leave without pay is some assurance of a job at its end, and the Gladstone agreement moreover promises return to an equal or better job. The Pregnancy Discrimination Act of 1978 provides that "women affected by pregnancy, childbirth, or related medical conditions shall be treated the same for all employment-related purposes...."[7] In 1983 the supreme court made the act apply to men, in the sense that disability benefits for pregnant employees would have to be the same for male employees' spouses.[8] A California law requiring employers to give pregnant women up to four months' unpaid leave and then reinstate them was overturned by the U.S. supreme court in 1984.[9] Disability attendant on an abortion expressly qualifies for sick leave in Gladstone and Contra Costa agreements, but it may in practice do so elsewhere as well. Leave without pay for adoption is provided in the Wisconsin teachers' and Buffalo public library's agreements.

Parental leave is available without pay to Wisconsin's school teachers for six months with the possibility of an extension of another six. This is not to be confused with paternity leave as the term is used in the Rapid City public library agreement, where a father can take three to eight days' sick leave if his wife is in hospital for childbirth. Marriage is probably not a prerequisite for maternity leave, but the Gladstone agreement expressly states that it is not. Whether marriage affects eligibility for parental or paternal leave is unclear so far.

Agreements seldom curtail the employer's right to have a physician of the employer's choice ascertain that the person taking sick leave: a) was truly ill and b) is fit to return to work. False use of sick leave is grounds for discipline or discharge. In Madison Heights, for instance, a first offense may bring ten days' suspension, and a second, dismissal. Sometimes, as at Santa Ana, sick leave is not granted for self-inflicted injuries, or for injury or illness resulting from the employee's wilful misconduct or work on another job. Sick leave can usually be taken not only for disability but for exposure to contagious disease.

Some agreements deal at least partially with conflicts of leaves. If I am ill during my vacation, is that time sick leave or vacation? What if my unit are allowed to make holidays of their birthdays and mine falls on Christmas? What if I also get sick on Christmas? Such doubts can cause unnecessary aggravation, and are easily resolved before misunderstanding can arise.

Leave without pay may not sound like much of a favor, but it brings with it the possibility of returning to one's position at the end of it. It is not always truly without pay, for certain retirement and insurance coverages may continue throughout, and certainly if the leave falls under the Pregnancy Discrimination Act.

Although clauses named "Discipline and Discharge" may sound threatening, they subject these managerial acts to some regular system. By requiring certain kinds of reasons, prohibiting others, and setting up a clear procedure, they provide an important security. The difference between conditional or probationary employees and regular employees lies in the burden of proof required for their discharge, but a skillful union representative can sometimes shift the burden of proof onto the employer even for probationary employees. The distinction is less clear now than formerly, owing to court decisions and legislation eroding the doctrine of employment at will.[10] Moreover, a probationary employee falling into any of the classes protected by a nondiscrimination law or agreement has access to a hearing on that issue. Finally, the terms "probationary" and "conditional" imply that certain goals or criteria exist, the achievement of which will normally assure the new employee graduation to regular status. These factors, especially in combination with a short probation period, make the probationer more secure than one hired explicitly at the pleasure of the employer. Six months is a common probation period in industrial-model agreements. Employers might well prefer periods that reflect the different lengths of time required to discern the promise of, say, a typist, a librarian, and a police officer.

As a ground for disciplining or discharging employees, "just cause" covers a wide variety of reasons. Though not perfectly defined, it is a familiar term in labor relations. The employer has to show that the delinquency was the employee's, and that its effect was harmful enough to lead to discharge or to the discipline imposed. The proof need rest only on the preponderance of the evidence.[11] Where there is little doubt about the delinquencies, their harmfulness becomes the main issue and the union seeks, sometimes successfully, to have discharge reduced to discipline, or to show that the effect was so trivial as to call for no action at all.[12] There are several sanctions short of discharge, and when they are applied in a logical order they constitute progressive discipline. Thus a supervisor can progress from helpful hints to balder statements to oral reprimand to written reprimand, and thence to suspension without pay for a certain time. It is not necessary to pass through every stage to apply progressive discipline. Some arbitrators care whether these steps are taken as a bona fide effort to improve the employee, as opposed to formalities observed so as to accomplish a good clean termination; other arbitrators do not care, if strict construction of the agreement does not require them to do so.[13] As a practical matter, positive disciplinary measures can sometimes salvage a potentially useful employee, and if these matters do not lie in the normal competencies of supervisor or manager the employee is in some organizations referred to counselling or support groups. Chronic absenteeism, the most common disciplinary cause, is both a problem in itself and a symptom of others, such as depression and drug abuse. Counselling programs are sometimes an area of constructive co-operation between management and union.[14] Librarians seldom appear in the literature of discipline and discharge, for besides absenteeism the offenses producing the bulk of such cases are sabotage, harassment of fellow employees, assault on foremen, horseplay, fighting, and walking off work.

How do agreements bring security against unfair discrimination? Most of the protections provided in the discrimination articles of agreements are also provided by law. The Civil Rights Act of 1964 prohibits discrimination on the basis of race, sex, religion, color, or national origin, and these prohibitions are repeated and sometimes broadened in municipal ordinances and the laws of 45 states. The Age Discrimination Act of 1978 prohibits discrimination based on age; the Rehabilitation Act of 1973 discrimination against "otherwise qualified" handicapped persons; and the Pregnancy Discrimination Act of 1978 discrimination against pregnant women. The Labor Relations Act of 1935 has long prohibited discrimination on the basis of union activity. States also have varieties of legislation with the same purpose. Each or all of these kinds of discrimination may also be prohibited to the employer and the union in an agreement, though the agreement normally provides complainants the machinery to proceed against only the employer and not the union. It must also be remembered that agreements do not protect applicants from employment discrimination, since they are not employees and therefore not in the bargaining unit.

The main advantage to the employee in having these guarantees in the agreement is that he or she can have a complaint of discrimination treated as a grievance that goes to arbitration, a process usually more expeditious and less costly than resort to the courts. A complainant can still go to court if disappointed in the arbitration, and this is an area in which judicial deference to arbitration is not usual. Agreements cannot deprive the complainant of his or her day in court, but many (e.g. that of the University of California librarians) abort discrimination grievances if the complainant goes to court before arbitration is completed.[15]

Handicapped persons have been called "perhaps the most forgotten minority in this country," not least because of unresolved ambiguities in the legislation.[16] Must an employer put a totally deaf librarian at a reference desk, for example? Is AIDS a handicap? What handicaps are not protected, if any? As usual, too, we must remember that states have their own handicap discrimination laws, the scope of which sometimes goes beyond the federal. The University of California agreement includes medical condition and mental handicap with the usual protected handicaps. No easy, universal test lies at hand for deciding whether rejection of a handicapped person is the kind of discrimination that is prohibited. A partial test is to ask whether the person, but for the handicap, is otherwise qualified to do the job. Although this is common enough to have won the name "but-for" or "bfoq" test, it is not always conclusive.

Whatever the whole extent of sex discrimination, agreements can effectively address unfair impairments of opportunity, compensation, and working conditions. As the chapter on opportunities indicates, these opportunities are mostly promotion, training, and education. The chapter on money addresses the question of unfairly discriminatory compensation. There remains a form of sex discrimination that affects working conditions, sexual harassment.

One study of sexual harassment has stated that thirty to ninety percent of working women have experienced it in some form.[17] Most cases have now fallen into "working condition" harassment and the less common "quid pro quo" harassment. It is a statutory offense in federal and other jurisdictions, but is seldom specifically named in agreements, although the agreement of the University of California librarians offers an aggrieved person the option to resort to the institution's sexual harassment complaint procedures. The offenders may be supervisors or they may be fellow-workers in the same or another bargaining unit. Whoever the offending employee may be, the employer is more likely than not to be held responsible. Employers who discipline or discharge union employees for sexual harassment are of course subject to grievance, and arbitrations appear to address these issues rather than the employer's responsibility for a sexual harassment.[18] Clients too can commit sexual harassment. No agreement can make clients behave, but some might in the future address measures the employer should take.

The identification of "sexual preference" or "sexual orientation" as a prohibited basis for discrimination is recent and still unusual in agreements, though it appears in the Boston Public Library and some California agreements, and as a stated policy of Central Michigan University outside its agreements. Unlike most groups mentioned in antidiscrimination articles, this has no specific federal statute to protect it. In some communities municipal ordinances now forbid discrimination by the city against its employees and applicants because of their "sexual preference" or "sexual orientation." Some of these are being challenged in the courts.[19] In communities that have no such ordinance, or where the ordinance faces a dubious future, this clause assumes added importance as the only special protection available to homosexual employees. It is for homosexual persons that the ordinances and agreement clauses are meant, though either of these phrases is broad enough to offer shelter to other preferences and orientations as well.

Some discrimination articles, for example that of the University of California librarians and some others in Florida and California, prohibit discrimination on the basis of citizenship. Aliens, as a result of a long series of court decisions beginning in 1886, are now largely protected from blanket discrimination in time of peace, except when citizenship is essential to the performance of the job. Public employers are more circumscribed in this respect than private employers. Moreover, "Only lawful immigrants have full constitutional protection, including protection from employment discrimination."[20] It is therefore possible for an agreement to give an alien employee protections that the law does not; on the other hand the Immigration Act of 1986 makes the employer liable for employing illegal immigrants. Discrimination based on national origin is usually illegal, and discrimination articles sometimes include national origin as well.[21]

"Blacks," write E.J. Josey and Marva L. DeLoach, "remain underrepresented in librarianship. Progress towards eradication of this inequality has been slow and uneven."[22] The effect of underrepresentation gives blacks a set of problems and goals quite distinct from those of women, who as we shall see in discussing money, attribute some of their problems in the profession to their being overrepresented. This difference is reflected in Library Literature, in which, to take only the last six years, articles under "Women librarians" outnumber those under "Black librarians" by 92% to 8%, a proportion roughly the same as that of the two groups in librarianship.[23]

Some employers have adopted affirmative action plans more detailed and concrete than most, particularly setting quotas affecting retention and promotion. It is not difficult to see, considering the recency of affirmative action hirings, that the beneficiaries would lack seniority and that the first severe round of layoffs would thus wipe out most or all of the gains achieved by the affirmative action hirings. For the same reason, promotions heavily dependent on seniority simply do not fall to recent appointees, whatever campaign recruited them. Employers and unions sometimes agree to forego some seniority as a joint effort towards affirmative action. Alternatively, employers sometimes settle with some agency (e.g., the EEOC) by establishing quotas for retention and promotion, and thereby unilaterally weaken the seniority system. Both of these courses have led to litigation, in which the courts have made a further distinction, between affirmative action quotas that stem from an employer's established guilt and represent either a directed or a negotiated settlement, and affirmative action quotas set up voluntarily by the employer, from such motives as conscience, public and market relations, or avoidance of future litigation. The validity of affirmative action plans that bypass seniority has depended in part on whether they were responses to proved discrimination. At this writing, supreme court decisions have resolved some but not all of the questions raised by this conflict of principles.[24]

Safety in the work place was an important concern of

labor unions in the nineteenth century, as it still is. This
concern has given rise to much state and federal legislation,
culminating in the Occupational Safety and Health Act of 1970,
variously re-stated in turn by a number of states. The Act
has led to the promulgation of standards by the U.S. department of labor, the latest of which, issued in 1986, is the
"Right to Know" that certain materials are potentially hazardous to health. The terrible and all-too-visible manglings
that gave industrial safety urgency in the nineteenth century
have given place to subtler perils now that we know how to
produce and use enormously more complex materials. Although libraries are still safer to work in than mines, trawlers,
or grain mills, the department of labor's list of the hazardous
materials that we now have a right to know about includes
such familiar library goods as glue and toner: not to be
shunned, but used with ventilation and ordinary sense. It
is not surprising then to find that few if any library agreements have a strong safety article. One writer predicts that
a growing use and suspicion of video display terminals will
work its way into the agreements and grievances of employees
who regularly work with them.[25]

Many agreements prohibit discrimination against employees because of their union activities. This kind of discrimination is prohibited in the private sector by the National
Labor Relations Act of 1935, and in many state public employee relations acts. A recent study of NLRB cases argues
that at least that agency applies the statutory protection inadequately.[26] Even a belief that this were true would of
course motivate a union to include such protection in the
agreement.

What security can come from promises that need not be
kept? Binding arbitration is the principal means of enforcing
the terms of an agreement, and it is the most fundamental
difference between having an agreement and not having one.
Employees who do not have collective bargaining may enjoy
high security, good pay and benefits, ample educational,
promotion, and development opportunities, a clear-cut handbook of procedures and work rules, and even a formal grievance procedure, and yet lack resort to binding arbitration.
Commercial non-labor contracts sometimes have arbitration
provisions, and there is nothing to prevent individual employment contracts or non-union company policy from providing
arbitration. Certain individuals can have arbitration in Texas,
for example, where public employee collective bargaining is

illegal. Yet in the main stream, grievance arbitration and collective bargaining go side by side.

Arbitration in this context means the interpretation of the labor agreement by a neutral person. The occasion for arbitration is a grievance that has not been otherwise resolved. Contrary to popular belief, an arbitrator's duty is not to give justice but to interpret the agreement; not to mediate or conciliate unless especially charged to do so, but to decide between the two parties. The neutrality of the arbitrator is assured in part by various selection procedures which often include the presentation of an initial list of which all but one are eventually vetoed by the parties. The list is usually drawn up by a neutral body such as the American Arbitration Association. When collective bargaining first came to faculty in higher education, some persons on both sides feared that without vigilance on their part the institution might be molded by the new relationship to an industrial model in which faculty members could no longer play their wonted role. As one protection, they agreed (as in the CUNY agreements of 1969 and later) to list in the agreement itself a panel of potential arbitrators whose familiarity with academic life made them acceptable. As another protection, the CUNY and some other agreements provided that an arbitrator was not to exercise or supplant academic judgment in reaching a decision. The librarians of the University of California have inherited this two-tier system, either as a vestige or a renewal of their quasi-faculty status.

In any event, the arbitrator draws his or her charge and authority solely from the agreement, which simultaneously gives the arbitrator full power to settle a dispute and prohibits him or her from altering the terms of the agreement itself. Some agreements expressly exclude certain of their provisions from arbitration, for example overtime, merit pay, and educational benefits. Often the first question for the arbitrator to decide is the arbitrability of the issue. Within the areas assigned to them, arbitrators exercise great power. Although they cannot compel testimony, they can place witnesses under oath. In practice a union or management seldom appeals successfully from an arbitrator to a court except in discrimination cases, for it is the preference of courts to defer to arbitration rather than re-examine it. In general they will interfere only if the arbitration is contrary to law, or if the arbitrator exceeded the power assigned by the agreement, or if the agreement delegated power that its makers had no right to delegate. Arbitrators are not bound by previous arbitration decisions regarding other agreements, though over the years they have developed patterns, definitions, and principles on which they rely.[27]

The way to arbitration is a grievance, which is essentially an allegation that the agreement has been violated. It is almost always the employer who is alleged to have done so, because usually only the union or the employee can grieve, and only the employer can be held responsible. Agreements define grievance and sometimes also define those who have standing to grieve. the latter helps prevent busybodies and chronic pitiers from gorging the grievance machinery with complaints of what they believe to be wrongs suffered by a co-worker. In defining grievance, agreements sometimes add to the grounds, extending them from "violation" to include "misinterpretation" and "misapplication" of the agreement as well. Faculty union agreements sometimes extend the grounds further. Some AAUP agreements such as that at the University of Cincinnati make alleged violations of academic freedom grievable, and Oakland University does not define its grievances at all. Otherwise, grievance procedures vary little according to the unit they cover. Thus the Brandeis librarians and the Brandeis nonprofessional library employees have identical grievance procedures in their respective agreements, and these in turn resemble school and maintenance grievance procedures all over the country.

Some grievance procedures are faster and more efficient than others, regardless of the units they serve. They commence with a local, informal stage. If they are not resolved at that stage, they proceed to a higher and more formal one. Where a library is part of a larger geographical system (for instance, a city government) a certain stage takes the grievance out of the library and into the employer's central organization (often the personnel office). From there the decision to go to arbitration usually rests with the union and the employer. Throughout the grievance process, the stages are subject to time limits. These are usually expressed as numbers of days, and litigation appears year after year over what a particular agreement meant when it used the term "day." Where effective peer evaluation occurs, it is quite common for grievances to be lodged by a disappointed employee technically against the employer but practically against the peers, who are fellow-members of the bargaining unit.

The classic securities of collective bargaining live on. In times of retrenchment, layoffs afflict the least senior in a manner that increases predictability and insulates the employees from either reprisal or good management on the part of the employer. Discipline and discharge too conform to procedures and standards that usually accord due process. Union concern wins strong safety clauses for employees in dangerous situations, less so for those considered at less risk, such as librarians. More novel dangers, such as client assault, chemicals, and radiation, have so far received little attention in agreements.

What has changed in the past twenty years or so is the growth of a rival security industry, operated by state and federal governments. Many of the securities offered in agreements are now provided by government agencies as well, though sometimes less effectively.

NOTES

1. Elkouri and Elkouri, op.cit., pp. 551-609.

2. For a curious and complex bumping context between a "seasoned non-pro" and a new MLS, see "Norwalk Nonpro Gets Job Created for M.L.S. Grad," Library Journal, 104:670, March 15, 1979; and "Norwalk Union Backs Pro Bumped by Nonprofessional," Library Journal, 104:1410-1411, July, 1979. This second title notwithstanding, the union successfully backed first the non-professional contender, and then a generally favorable employment for the MLS. The employer had described the qualifications for the position as an MLS "or" equivalent experience. The "or" effectively leaves the question of the equivalency of experience to an MLS in the hands of minor officials in affirmative action and personnel departments.

3. John W. Weatherford, Collective Bargaining and the Academic Librarian, Scarecrow, 1976, p. 46.

4. George L. Joughin, Academic Freedom and Tenure, A Handbook of the American Association of University Professors, University of Wisconsin Press 1967. 343 pp. The decision in Chicago Teachers v. Hudson is conveniently summarized in The Arbitration Journal, 41:68-9, Sept. 1986.

5. How the Xerox Corporation dealt with shifts in demand for skills is described in Richard A. Morano and Norman Deets, "Professional Retraining: Meeting the Technological Challenge," Training and Development Journal, 39:99-101, May 1985.

6. "Contracting Out Federal Library Operations," Library Journal, 108:618-622, April 1, 1983; "OMB Revises Contract Policy on Library Operations," American Libraries, 14:636, Nov. 1983; and "Kitsap Library in Washington Runs a Federal Library on Contract," Library Journal, 108:778, April 15, 1983. A recent survey of the status of contracting out in the private sector is provided by Mark A. Ellmore, Jr., "Subcontracting: Mandatory or Permissive Subject of Collective Bargaining? Labor Law Journal, 36:773+, Dec. 1985.

7. Reva B. Siegel, "Employment Equality Under the Pregnancy Discrimination Act of 1978," Yale Law Journal, 94:929-956, March 1985.

8. Theresa Johnson, "The Legal Background and Implications of Pregnancy Benefits," Labor Law Journal, 35:352-9.

9. Siegel, op.cit., note 21.

10. R.M. Smith, "Exceptions to the Employment-at-Will Doctrine," Labor Law Journal, 36:875-91, Dec. 1985; and J. Stieber, "Recent Developments in Employment-at-Will," Labor Law Journal, 36:557-63, Aug. 1985.

11. Elkouri and Elkouri, op.cit., p. 62.

12. Ibid., p. 630.

13. Ibid., p. 631.

14. Thomas R. Knight, "The Impact of Arbitration on the Administration of Disciplinary Policies," Arbitration Journal, 39:43-56, March 1984; and Allan W. Ferrant, "Dealing with Problem Employees," Supervision, 46:3-5, Oct. 1984. For related counseling of employees, see Stephen J. and Sharon Brookens Holoviak, "The Benefits of In-House Counseling," Personnel, 61:53-59, July-Aug., 1984.

15. For recent developments regarding sex discrimina-

tion, see Marcia Cohen, "Sex Discrimination," Labor Law Journal, 36:67+, Feb. 1985. How labor grievance arbitrators handle discrimination complaints is discussed favorably by Vern E. Hauck, "The Efficacy of Arbitrating Discrimination Complaints," Labor Law Journal, 35:175-181, March 1984; but two different views on how much support the courts give arbitrators in discrimination cases appear in Elvis C. Stephens, "Why Courts Overrule Arbitrators' Awards," Labor Law Journal, 36:108+, Feb. 1985; and Elaine Gale Wrong, "Courts' Review of Arbitration Awards in Discrimination Grievances," Labor Law Journal, 37:123-126, Feb., 1986.

16. "Employment Discimination Against the Handicapped and Section 504 of the Rehabilitation Act: An Essay on Legal Evasiveness," Harvard Law Review, 97:996-1015, Feb. 1984; more recently, David A. Larson, "What Disabilities Are Protected Under the Rehabilitation Act of 1973?" Labor Law Journal, 37:752-66, Nov. 1986 adds subsequent cases, which still leave much unresolved.

17. Jo Cates, "Sexual Harassment: What Every Woman and Man Should Know," Library Journal, 110:23-9, July 1985.

18. For sexual harassment as a form of sex discrimination, see Margaret Garvey, "The High Cost of Sexual Harassment," Personnel Journal, 65:75-84, Jan. 1986; Patricia Theiler, "Power Play," Common Cause, 12:30-33, Jan.-Feb. 1986; and Frances S. Coles, "Sexual Harassment: Complainant Definitions and Agency Responses," Labor Law Journal, 36:369-376, June 1985. The last, though centering in California, is a useful gathering of surveys of victims. This problem as it is manifested in libraries is treated in a very practical manner by Jo Cates, op.cit.

19. For a balance of legal and social considerations regarding discrimination against homosexuals, see "The Constitutional Status of Sexual Orientation: Homosexuality as a Suspect Classification," Harvard Law Review, 98:1285-1309, April 1985; and Business Week, p 126+, Nov. 26, 1984.

20. Daniel J. Hoffheimer, "Employment Discrimination Against Resident Aliens by Private Employees [sic]," Labor Law Journal, 35:142, March 1984.

21. For the employment status of aliens, see Charles

O. Agege, "Employment Discrimination Against Aliens: The Constitutional Implications," Labor Law Journal, 36:87-94, Feb. 1985, a useful though hortatory historical survey; in the private sector which is less common for librarians, Avak Keotahian, "National Origin Discrimination in Employment," Employment Relations Law, 11:467-492, Winter 1986.

22. E.J. Josey and Marva L. DeLoach, "Discrimination and Affirmative Action: Concerns for Black Librarians and Library Workers," in John Harvey and Elizabeth M. Dickinson, Librarians' Affirmative Action Handbook, Scarecrow 1983, pp. 177-99.

23. Library Literature for 1980-1985 inclusive.

24. "Court Takes Broad New Look at Affirmative Action Issue," Congressional Quarterly, pp. 2104-8, Oct. 19, 1985, draws the issues together conveniently, although subsequent decisions have made it a little stale. Another useful, and later, commentary on the cases is in Bill Wagner, "Affirmative Action at the Crossroads," ABA Journal, 72:38-41, May 1, 1986. The dissonance between ordinary seniority provisions and anti-discrimination law is still only partly settled. For recent discussions see M.J. Fox, Jr. and Allen R. Nelson, "Defining a 'Bona Fide' Seniority System Under Title VII of the Civil Rights Act of 1964," Journal of Collective Negotiations in the Public Sector, 14:111-125, no. 2, 1985; and George M. Sullivan and William A. Nowlin, "The Clarification of Firefighters v. Stotts," Labor Law Journal, 37:788-803, Nov. 1986.

25. Gail E. Brooks, "How Have Unions Addressed the Issue of VDT Users' Health and Safety?" Labor Law Journal, 37:668-75, Sept. 1986. See also Lawrence E. Dube, Jr., "OSHA's 'Right to Know' Comes to the Workplace," Labor Law Journal, 36:696+, Sept., 1985.

26. William N. Cooke, "The Rising Toll of Discrimination Against Union Activists," Industrial Relations, 24:421-442, Fall, 1985.

27. Elkouri and Elkouri, op.cit., pp. 1-43.

V

MONEY

Agreements deal comprehensively with salaries and most fringe benefits unless, as sometimes happens in the public sector, management has no legal control over the purse strings.

The employer uses money to have functions performed, and the employee performs functions to get money. These motives are not absolute, but a matter of priorities. It can be argued, as Sever and Westcott do, that librarians get less money because its priority is lower among them:

> The librarian, given the pay scales endemic to libraries, probably is not motivated by money as much as other job and professional rewards.[1]

The employer tends to want a close link between the performance of the functions it desires and the money it dispenses, the closer the better:

> The authority to make a commitment to specific rewards needs to be given to the first line supervision level.... library management should be wary of any action which may lead to undermining belief in a direct connection between performance and reward.[2]

To be sure, some public employers, or at least their managers, have a relaxed view of this connection; but those who have performance goals show interest in rewarding the employee who achieves them. Performance rewards in libraries generally take the form of merit pay. How these rewards are distributed varies. Merit pay may be given to the tenth, say, whose performance is outstandingly good, or alternatively to all but the tenth whose performance is outstandingly bad. It can be so small as to be a mere symbol, or large enough to constitute a powerful economic incentive. It can be a permanent augmentation of salary, or more commonly a bonus representing one year's reward. Some California library agreements add to the salaries of those who are bilingual. Within these communities, "bilingual" usually menas Spanish-speaking. Obviously library service is enhanced if a librarian knows the first language of any of the library's non-English-speaking public. Saying "bilingual" when one means Spanish and not Finnish is one of those linguistic casualties of bargaining, like saying "sexual orientation" when one means homosexuality and not paedophilia. Whether the bilingual increment in this context might be regarded as also a form of affirmative action depends on whether there are local market factors that make the increment necessary to obtain bilingual librarians.

Unions have as one of their main goals to optimize the total compensation of the bargaining unit and not to reinforce links between performance and reward.[3] Several devices reduce this linkage: step-system salary and wage tables tied rigidly to formal work classifications, payment for time spent rather than piece-work, seniority in its many ramifications, salary "equity" redistributions, and grievance machinery. Unions do not give a high priority to merit, and for some it is anathema. Market factors interest them as a gauge and rationale for union goals in seeking compensation for the bargaining unit, but not as a means of importing an elite to take jobs otherwise awaiting present members.

The numerical majority comprising the less well-paid members of the unit gain by egalitarian redistributions of compensation. These the union seeks to achieve by "cost of living" additions, and by statistically-based "equity" additions which, when demystified, are seen to be seniority rewards. Both of these augmentations are called "adjustments," though there is rarely if ever provision to adjust for the downside during the life of the agreement.

Unions and even many employers have assumed that employees have some claim to maintain at least last year's standard of living, since the decline in the value of money is not the fault of any individual, and when the employee agreed to work for a stated amount of money it stood at a higher value. Unions have won wide acceptance of the Bureau of Labor Statistics' <u>Consumer Price Index</u> (CPI) as the definitive gauge of what is melodramatically called the "cost of living." In its "CPI (U)" the bureau monitors the prices of various items thought to constitute the regular purchases of an urban worker, each item being weighted according to its proportion of this worker's total basket of goods.[4]

From merely applying the CPI to wages in bargaining some industries graduated to applying it automatically through a cost of living adjustment (COLA). The pertinence of this "basket" declines for those who are much poorer or richer. The former's basket, for example, would probably not hold an automobile. The latter's basket would hold items not in the bureau's contemplation, for we can assume neither that those earning two or three times as much as the bureau's worker eat two or three times as many eggs, nor if they eat the same number that they pay two or three times as much per egg. For example, a rise in housing costs is not bad news for those who are large or small landlords on the side. Holders of bonds and other securities, and those at a certain phase of building pension funds, usually experience an offsetting interest benefit during inflation. It is rather undiscriminating of employers and unions to compensate them for an event that has increased their net worth. Cost-of-living increases, though facially egalitarian, may favor the upper end of the unit, even allowing for the fact that the basket holds no educational expenses. The preponderance in agreements of compensation systems that disconnect performance from reward suggests that unions more conscientiously and effectively represent the interests of their constituents than do public employers, whose constituents are after all only those who pay taxes or tuition to them.

Equal pay for equal work enjoys a legal status that equal pay for equal (or "comparable") worth does not. A classic case, to illustrate the former, involved "custodians," all male, who received higher pay then "housekeepers," all female, an illegal distinction because they all did equal work despite their titles.[5]

Some disparities between the sexes pervade nearly all

kinds of libraries, though only that in school libraries is very large. Some relation between this disparity and the proportion of women is, however, apparent (see table on page 47).

The comparable worth doctrine would extend the principle so as to require equal pay for jobs of "comparable worth," or more accurately, roughly equal worth. We librarians, and probably many others too, have used equal worth, in conversation or in the privacy of our thoughts, to form our opinions on how we or the profession ought to be paid. We may have selected for our invidious comparisons plumbers or policemen. John Berry's gorge rose at quarterbacks in his editorial on comparable worth.[6] To the extent that we have felt wronged in such disparities we have made judgments about the worth of these other callings. Before the appearance from 1964 on of the various antidiscrimination statutes and rules, such speculations as these simply led us to feel that we needed more effective efforts to demonstrate our true worth. Since these developments, many have drawn the further conclusion that such disparities in pay have arisen not from ignorance of our worth but from a deeper and more subtle devaluation of our work because it is largely performed by women, whose historical standing in the labor market has been inferior. However novel the observations may seem, the phenomenon observed is of ancient provenance according to anthropological examples cited by advocates of the doctrine.[7]

Any pay improvements brought to librarians by comparable worth would benefit male librarians as much as females, for the generic penalty has fallen on both sexes. Herein lies its essential difference from equal pay for equal work, which eliminates unjustified pay disparities between sexes and races within the library (or other lines of work). Librarianship began as a male occupation, then swung overwhelmingly to females, and was on its swing back from them when equal worth, long an articulated issue, arose as a manifestation of sex discrimination.

Opponents of the equal worth doctrine question the assumptions about worth that the doctrine makes. Let us go back to our earlier invidious comparisons and our assumption that a just world would pay us more than plumbers. Plumbers might hold a different view. How are such dissensions over worth resolved? They have heretofore been resolved by the

LIBRARIANS' MEDIAN PLACEMENT SALARIES, UNITED STATES[8]

1981

Kind of Library	No. of Women	No. of Men	Women's Median Salary	Men's Median Salary	Percent Female	Lag in Women's Salary
Public	382	66	14,000	14,610	85%	4%
School	293	32	15,004	18,500	90%	23%
Academic	278	80	14,500	15,000	78%	3%
Special	320	49	16,000	16,000	87%	0%
Mean					85%	8%

1984

Kind of Library	No. of Women	No. of Men	Women's Median Salary	Men's Median Salary	Percent Female	Lag in Women's Salary
Public	330	80	16,500	17,200	80%	4%
School	199	17	19,000	20,000	92%	5%
Academic	268	123	17,300	17,800	69%	3%
Special	286	60	20,000	19,000	83%	-5%
Mean					79%	2%

free market in labor, which deals not only with plumbers and librarians but with the more egregious and revolting cases of "soap" stars and quarterbacks. The labor market must seem unfair to many, but what mechanism could substitute for its brutal truths? If the doctrine came to form the basis of a bureaucracy, as other egalitarian interventions have done, it could well hamper the present ability of librarians to ascend alongside the rising technology of their world. How many years would it take a government agency to establish the official "worth" of a tool and die cutter after technological developments have altered the original facts and made the government study obsolete before its issuance? Why would librarians be any different? Ten years ago, librarians were offended by the recommendations of Hay Associates, the management consultants, for New Jersey librarians,[9] which they regarded as more demeaning than their status quo; now they welcome Hay Associates for their recommendation regarding San Jose librarians.[10] If we have felt uneasy with the evaluations of librarians by management consultants and by the office of management and budget, why are we so confident that evaluation by minor civil servants in a bureau of comparable worth assessment would improve our status?

Comparable worth has been officially adopted by twelve states for their public employees.[11] Its destiny in the courts is quite unknown at this writing, but the main question there is whether pay differences that ignore the doctrine constitute illegal discrimination under Title VII of the Civil Rights Act of 1964. If they do, presumably the government establishment that handles discrimination will expand to handle comparable worth and apply the criteria of skill, problem-solving, working conditions, and accountability to positions under their various jurisdictions.

Even if they do not, comparable worth is now fair game in bargaining, at least in the public sector. One has at the bargaining table ultimately only reason and force. Comparable worth is a rationale no less valid for such purposes than many other arguments that are brought forth at the table. It is also a cause that can easily appear as reason versus hoary injustice. This scenario might be expected to gain sympathy among the neutral public, who sometimes become important in public sector bargaining, and to galvanize potential union members who may have become jaded with other union causes.[12]

Is comparable worth "in reality only available to women? To white women? And if not, why have black workers--both men and women--not taken up the cause of comparable worth to improve their employment situation?" asks a former EEOC attorney. It is, she concludes "because of the specific employment situation of white women today--high job segregation and low wages--[that] wage comparability is, for the moment, primarily a theory for white women. As black and other minority women merge into that job structure ... their interest in wage comparability is likely to grow.... because it is unlikely that black men would want to stay in 'traditional' black male jobs, and because the other employment problems of black men are so pressing, wage comparability is not a theory which will find appeal among black male workers," though she suggests ways in which they can make it an issue.[13]

Where, as in municipal employees' bargaining units, examples of seeming comparable worth unfairness appear, it is easier to observe the data even though it is difficult to evaluate it. If there are such problems within the same bargaining unit they are also a problem for the union as well as the employer. In San Jose, whose municipal employees union went on strike over comparable worth and thereby gained an extra fourteen percent or so for certain workers including librarians, the highest paid librarian is now the highest paid member of the municipal employees' bargaining unit.[14] The same is true, however, of East Detroit and Scituate, without an articulated comparable worth rationale. In the municipal employees' units where librarians seem to trail, it is often the building and other craft trades that lead: the historical heritage of earlier union work. Sometimes too we can see market influences, as when accountants lead librarians. When we find units in which refuse collectors, meter readers, and (in Bristol) even the library's maintenance supervisor are rated above the highest librarian in the unit, we can readily see how librarians become depressed and frustrated by their own intuitive evaluations of their work and that of their co-members.

Some literature has grown up in recent years around the question of whether librarians gain more money by way of collective bargaining than without it. The question may seem absurd to those who engage in it for precisely that reason, yet the answer is not simple. Even the question must be chosen carefully. For example, "Do librarians make more after adopting collective bargaining than they did before"? elicits different information from "Do librarians with collective bargaining make more than those without it?" Serious but partial studies over the past decade have attacked this problem and concluded variously that libraries with unions have paid experienced librarians more than those without; that there is no statistically significant difference in pay between those with and without unions; and that there is a slight but significant difference.[15]

These authors have shown courage in attacking this problem, which is a knotty one. What does "with unions" mean? Their mere presence or the existence of a bargained agreement? What is the value of total compensation, since the growth and importance of fringe benefits has made mere salaries less meaningful? How should one weigh compensation at a nonunion library if, as some argue, the presence of unions elsewhere in the community has raised its level? Have unions settled for less than the employer was planning to give, as trustee Albert Mayer reported hearing?[16] What would be revealed by a longitudinal study of not only union and nonunion but preunion institutions? How much is compensation affected by the mere geographical factors that accompany union concentration (e.g., urban versus small-town environments)? Because supervisors are usually excluded from units, the librarians remaining in them may be expected to earn somewhat less than the national averages for librarians remaining in them a caveat for everybody who compares union and non-union salaries. In a profession so heavily female, can the effects of unionization be distinguished from those of other pressures making for equal pay?[17]

A study of higher education institutions (perhaps an applicable parallel) indicated that faculty unionization during the first two years brought significantly greater pay increases which then declined for at least the next four years, in some cases becoming inferior to nonunion compensation in the sixth year. The history of collective bargaining among university faculty is still too short to generalize extensively from longitudinal studies.[18] Whatever happens over time, the initial year of faculty bargaining has brought especially sharp rises in the compensation of academic librarians.[19]

When estimates of compensation with and without unions

are close, the amount of union dues or service fees enters
the question, not when they are $25 a year, but when they
approach or exceed $300. The hitherto slight difference
between dues and service fees should increase as recent
court decisions have made the distinction important. Dues
are paid for full membership in the union. As this membership must be voluntary under our constitution, all who pay
dues do so voluntarily. Unions however have to serve and
represent not only their dues-paying members but all other
members of the bargaining unit. To cover the cost of serving and representing those who do not pay dues, the union
may levy service fees as a substitute for dues. How to collect these fees from reluctant employees is addressed in most
agreements. Common methods are: a) payroll deduction,
b) to agree that an employee will be terminated, at the union's
request, for non-payment; and c) to agree simply that employees owe a fee to the union, which can then sue to collect it if the employee will not pay. As the union has in
the past set the amount of service fees, it is not sheer coincidence that they have equalled or come close to the amount
of the dues. Recent court decisions now permit unions to
enforce service fees only for the costs of collective bargaining, grievance adjustment, and contract administration. It
is no longer enough for the union to declare what these
amount to, or to set up a body of its own selection as an
appeal board, or to use the disputed money for its own purpose pending appeal. Dissident or doubtful bargaining unit
members now have a right to due process in determining how
much they should pay the union for its specific, assigned
services.[20]

Unless compensation for librarians is artificially raised
or depressed, it should roughly reflect the market for them.
An intermediate term projection of jobs available for librarians
(leaving out schools) was 5,891 for 1987 and 5,827 for 1990.
The supply, in another intermediate projection (again omitting
schools), was 4,600 for 1987 and 4,900 for 1990 (all but 600
in either year having degrees from ALA-accredited programs).
On its face, this is a 19% balance in favor of librarians.
Whether this will be a real advantage depends on how librarians' services are valued by their various publics and the employers who represent these publics. The favorable balance
in 1983 was 29%.[21] Market influences on the creation and
compensation of librarians need further study.

The mechanics by which agreements set salaries can be described quickly. Agreements can set base salaries by tabulation or by formula. Tables establish wages and salaries according to employment class or level, and often additionally by amount of service within a class. The tables may be the creation of bargaining, or may be built upon pre-existing scales such as a civil service list. Formulae change one's previous salary by stating certain factors in the agreement: a set number of dollars, or a percentage of the previous salary, or various combinations of the two. Upon either of these mechanisms more purposeful influences can be made to operate, such as merit, market, equity, and cost of living.

NOTES

1. Shmuel Sever and Fred Westcott, "The Motivational Basis for Compensation: Strategies in the Library Environment," College and Research Libraries, 44:228-35, May 1983.

2. Ibid.

3. Charles Craypo, The Economics of Collective Bargaining: Case Studies in the Private Sector, BNA, 1986, pp. 61-64.

4. U.S. Dept of Labor. Bureau of Labor Statistics. CPI Detailed Report. Latest issue examined, Sept. 1986.

5. Equal Pay Act of 1963.

6. "Comparable Worth: A Legal and Legislative Primer," Association Management, 37:58-9+, May 1985; further information in 37:70, Dec. 1985. The article lists pros and cons. For a librarian's advocacy of the doctrine, see Katherine Phenix, "Women Predominate, Men Dominate: Disequilibrium in the Library Profession," Bowker Annual 1984, pp. 82-9. A skeptical view of the doctrine is well summarized in Ken Jennings and Robert L. Willits, "A Neglected Consideration in Sex Based Wage Discrimination Cases," Labor Law Journal, 37:412-22, July 1986.

7. Association Management, loc. cit.

8. John Berry, "The Value of 'Women's Work'," Library Journal, 109:1784, Oct. 1, 1984.

9. "N.J. College Librarians May Lose Faculty Status," Library Journal, 95:4088, Dec. 1, 1970; and "N.J. Librarians Ask Status Fight Aid," Library Journal, 96:1556, May 1, 1971.

10. Russell Fischer, "Pay Equity and the San Jose Strike," Library Journal, 106:2079-85, Nov. 1, 1981.

11. This is just what happened at Yale in 1984. Crocker Coulson, "Labor Unrest in the Ivy League," Arbitration Journal, 40:53-62, Sept. 1985. See also Fischer, op.cit., and L.R. Pearson, "Library Workers Lead Strikers in Comparable Pay Strike," American Libraries, 12:397, July-August 1981.

12. Judy Scales-Trent, "Comparable Worth: Is This a Thing for Black Women?" Women's Rights Law Reporter, 8:51-8, Winter, 1984-85. See also E.J. Josey and Marva L. DeLoach, "Discrimination and Affirmative Action: Concerns for Black Librarians and Library Workers," in John Harvey and Elizabeth M. Dickinson, Librarian's Affirmative Action Handbook, Scarecrow 1983, pp. 177-199, supporting the point that employment and entry are the greater immediate problem for black librarians.

13. Fischer, op. cit. The figures are not from the article but from the San Jose agreement for 1982-83.

14. Carol Learmont and Stephanie Van Houten, "Placements and Salaries, 1981," Bowker Annual, 1983, pp. 279-94. Also published in "Placements and Salaries, 1983," Library Journal, 109:1805-11, Oct. 1, 1984.

15. Bowker Annual, 1986, p. 321.

16. Mary Rosenthal's study is most convenient because she thoroughly summarizes the earlier studies: "The Impact of Unions on Salaries in Public Libraries," Library Quarterly, 55:52-70, Jan. 1985. An earlier effort can be found in Marilyn A. Oberg, Mary Blackburn, and Joan Dible, "Unionization: Costs and Benefits to the Individual and the Library," Library Trends, 25:435-499, Oct. 1976.

17. The anecdote is from Albert I. Mayer, "Unions: Plus or Minus?" Wilson Library Bulletin, 54:242-3, Dec. 1979.

18. Baker, H. Kent, "The Short and Long Term Effects of Collective Bargaining on Faculty," Journal of Collective Negotiations in the Public Sector, 13:235-50, #3, 1984.

19. John W. Weatherford, Collective Bargaining and the Academic Librarian, Scarecrow, 1976, pp. 26-9.

20. The latest and most pertinent U.S. supreme court decision at this writing is Chicago Teachers Union No. 1, AFT, AFL-CIO, et al. v. Hudson et al., decided unanimously March 4, 1986. For a summary up to its time, see William H. Foeller, "Employer Preferences and Public Sector Union Security," Journal of Collective Negotiations in the Public Sector, 13:203-10, #3, 1984; and more recently (but preceding the Chicago Teachers decision) Jan W. Henkel and Norman J. Wood, "Restrictions on the Uses of Union Dues: A Threat to Public Sector Unions?" Journal of Collective Negotiations in the Public Sector, 15:41-51, #1, 1986.

21. Michael D. Cooper, "Projections of the Demand for Librarians in the United States," Library Quarterly, 54:331-67, #4, 1984; and Nancy A. Van House, "Projections of the Supply of Librarians," Library Quarterly, 54:368-95, #4, 1984. See also Mary Jordan Coe, "Personnel and Employment: Compensation," A.L.A. Yearbook, 1983, pp. 205-6; Suzanne Hildebrand, "Women in Librarianship, Status of," A.L.A. Yearbook, 1983, pp. 277-9; and Lance Query, "Personnel and Employment: Compensation," A.L.A. Yearbook, 1984, pp. 220-1.

VI

THE BOSTON PUBLIC LIBRARY

[The following commentaries apply to the agreement in Appendix I.]

Boston Public Library
   and
Boston Public Library Professional Staff Association
   1980-82

Article II. Non-Discrimination.

    Both the employer and the union have undertaken not to discriminate against employees on any of the grounds mentioned, but as the grievance process in this agreement is expressly confined to complaints against the employer, the agreement offers no remedy for discrimination by the union. It would be a most unusual agreement that did so. There are still many unsettled questions as to what constitutes unfair discrimination (e.g., compulsory retirement ages, handicap hiring, linguistic disability as discrimination based on national origin), and only time is likely to build up a body of decisions to enlighten us. The addition of "sexual preference" is recent and still uncommon. Discrimination articles are discussed in the chapter "Securities."

Articles III and IV. Dues and Service Fee Deductions.

    See the chapter "Environment."

Article V. Management Rights.

In general this is a standard statement of management's rights, which can be found, with changes in detail and sequence, in most agreements.

The employer's right to contract out work otherwise performed by the bargaining unit may be addressed in a separate clause, or, as here, as part of management rights. What has been bargained is the impact of this contracting-out on the employees who have been doing that work. Under this agreement, if the work taken away is only part of the employee's position, he or she may retain the position, and in any case has a claim to similar vacancies if qualified. There is no reason to suppose that this clause was written to address any specific library contracting-out; such provisions are usual in municipal and many other employees' agreements. For contracting out, see the chapter "Securities."

Article VI. Discipline and Discharge.

This agreement covers "pre-professional" employees who are library school students. Their probation ends four months after graduation, and they then get a regular position if there is a vacancy. See the chapter "Securities."

Article VII. Grievance.

See the chapter "Securities." This library is an agency of city government, and at Step 3, the last before arbitration, the City of Boston takes over.

Article VIII. No Strike.

Boston Public's librarians, like the great majority of librarians, are public employees, falling within one of many state jurisdictions. Eight states as of 1984 had legislation permitting strikes by public employees, but not Massachusetts. (See Robert D. Pursley, "An Analysis of Permissible Strike Authorization among Public Workers," Journal of Collective Negotiations in the Public Sector, 13:259-276, #3, 1984.) Why have such a provision in an agreement then? The no-strike clause is primarily for the employer's benefit, though it can be reassuring for employees who hope there will be no strikes. The clause would still be an enforceable part of the agreement if, say, a state were to repeal its no-strike legislation. Historically, the no-strike clause is the union's trade to gain the right to grieve to arbitration.

Section 2 requires the union to disavow wild-cat strikes and discourage them as best it can; and section 3 provides that if the union lives up to this undertaking it will not be liable for damages done by the wild-cat strikers. There is nothing here to prevent peaceful picketing by the union or individuals; peaceful picketing is constitutionally protected as a form of free speech. If another union sets up a picket line around the library, it is uncertain when librarians would or would not be required to cross it; deliberate ambiguity is embodied in the word "reasonable."

Strikes in support of collective bargaining objectives began in the private sector, and were a simple tit for tat in which labor's only leverage was to withhold service and thus reduce the employer's profits until the employer was motivated to grant concessions. In the public sector the relation between strikers and management is less simple, for the management has no profit to be threatened. What is threatened is some segment or other of the public, and the hope of the union is that public employers will reach agreement with the strikers when the pressure applied on them by a deprived public makes it likely that there will be some adverse political consequence of not reaching agreement. The public employer is after all not spending his or her own money, but that of the taxpayer. This fact may make the public employer's task easier, but still the taxpayers who clamored for settlement are quite capable of resenting the cost of the concessions they urged.

Although this relationship is familiar to readers, it helps to explain the relative power of various kinds of employee, and the reflection of that power in strikes. The services of garbage collectors (whether they are called Sanitary Technician III or not) will be more quickly and pungently missed by the general populace than those of the best librarians.

Article IX. Stability of the Agreement.

Section 1 is meant to avoid confusion resulting from

side agreements by (perhaps unauthorized) representatives of union and management, or the oral understandings and "gentlemen's agreements" that tend to crop up as the representatives of the two sides get to know each other over the years. Section 2 protects the agreement from erosion by neglect or contrary practice.

The very important question of laying off employees has somehow found its way into this article; other than its editorial location it is a standard layoff and recall provision based on seniority and qualification: see the chapter "Securities."

Article X. Hours of Work and Overtime.

Most work weeks vary between 35 and 40 hours. The librarians have more freedom to trade hours and relieve each other than is found in municipal employees' agreements. Some of them are needed during most hours of library service, which far surpasses the work week. Overtime, because it is extremely common in municipal employee agreements, is not unusual in public libraries, though virtually unknown among librarians covered by faculty agreements.

Article XI. Vacancies.

Opportunities for promotion or transfer within the library system are posted internally for the benefit of any librarians who wish to apply. Section 2 makes it clear that seniority is an important element, because qualifications and ability can often be argued to be "relatively equal," and the employer's judgment to the contrary can be alleged to be "arbitrary, capricious, or unreasonable." See the chapter "Opportunities."

Article XII. Temporary Service in a Higher Position.

Article XIII, Holidays.
Article XIV, Annual leave (Vacation).
Article XV, Sick leave.

Article XVI, Other leaves of Absence.
and Article XVII, Leave without pay.
 See the chapter "Leaves."

Article XVIII. Professional Staff - Management Committee.

Joint union-management committees are a fixture in industrial, municipal, school, and public library agreements, and can frequently be found in university agreements. They are a normal mode of communication between the parties, and when successfully conducted can prevent day-to-day labor relations problems from building into crises. They are not to be confused with professional participation in governance.

VII

THE UNIVERSITY OF CALIFORNIA SYSTEM

[The following commentaries apply to the agreement in Appendix II.]

University of California
and
University Federation of Librarians AFT
1 July 1986 - 30 June 1988

Article I. Recognition.

The recognition reiterates the inclusion by the California Public Employment Relations Board (PERS) of all nine campuses in a single bargaining unit. The University system is in some respects highly centralized, and central bargaining can be a powerful magnet for further concentrating the management of the nine institutions. Several of the clauses will be seen to tend this way.

The exclusion of student assistants from the bargaining unit is the practice among universities, though those with faculty units have not found such an express exclusion necessary. Unlike most (but not all) faculty agreements, this includes temporary employees. "Potential career status" refers to library school students who are trainees and therefore another group of temporary employees included in the unit.

The two parties can agree to modify the unit within PERB rules. If management wishes to introduce a new kind of librarian, it gives notice to the union, which may wish to argue the matter and appeal to PERB.

The inclusions are described from a pre-existing personnel office list; the exclusions are the groups customarily exempt from collective bargaining.

This agreement does not specifically identify the supervisors exempted. The Brandeis University agreement lists at least some of its exempt supervisors: the university librarian, associate, and assistant, the department heads, six section heads, and two others, creating an exempt group of over a dozen out of twenty-eight librarians.

Article II. Nondiscrimination.

This is not a blanket undertaking by the University to refrain from discriminating against any of the groups mentioned, but rather to apply the agreement equally to all, subject to existing regulations. Citizenship, mental handicap, and medical condition are among the grounds included here but not in the Boston Public Library agreement.

Elsewhere in the agreement there are certain limitations on grievability. The last sentence ensures that this clause will not be a way to grieve the ungrievable.

Article III. Professional Activities and Development.

Regular university admissions requirements for courses are made non-grievable. Grievances are allowed over the Professional Activities and Development article, but the arbitrator is told again not to substitute his or her judgment for the academic judgment of the university. Brandeis offers tuition discounts not only for its librarians but for their children and spouses, as private colleges and universities are more likely to do. Brandeis also offers paid leave of 3.5 hours a week to one librarian per semester to take courses for professional development; competition for such a leave is resolved by considering the value of the course, the applicant's work record, and seniority.

Article IV. Process for Promotion and Advancement.

Pre-existing peer review systems continue on each

campus as before, but the agreement now imposes some procedural uniformity, setting a relative time-table and defining adequate notice. Sections 5 and 10 refer to the confidentiality of peers' evaluations vis à vis the candidate. Since this process is largely ungrievable, it is unlikely that an arbitrator would expose the communications submitted in confidence. The candidate must certify his or her satisfaction that procedures have been properly followed, and this requirement applies also to any added material the review committee might later gather. Section 9 allows a candidate to challenge for cause the presence of another librarian on his or her review committee; it does not state how much weight is given such a challenge.

Most of the peer review procedures were created locally and before collective bargaining. Whether they are written by librarians or professors, such documents are seldom written with an arbitrator in mind. As a result, arbitrations based on such essays are more a gamble than usual. This clause excludes nearly the entire peer review process from grievance and arbitration. See the chapter on securities for the treatment of peer review by some other universities.

Promotion in the Brandeis library has the sense of moving into a higher vacancy rather than its academic sense in the California library.

Article V. Personnel Files.

This ensures the librarian a right to view and copy all non-confidential materials in his or her file. Materials confidential vis a vis the employee would be pre-employment evaluations (if these are kept) and peer evaluations. The agreement alone cannot prevent the subpoena of peer evaluations, of course. Anonymous communications are not permitted in the file. A librarian may request the removal or correction of anything from his or her file, but the decision rests with management. The file is closed to all but the employee, management personnel having business with it, and a designee of the employee's, such as a union representative. Although the agreement does not say so, presumably other file materials can be open to the subject yet confidential vis a vis his or her peers--sick leave records, for instance.

Article VI. Transfer and Reassignments.

Librarians who voluntarily or involuntarily move from one of the nine campuses to another or from one job title to another within the bargaining unit retain all their accruals of leave and seniority. Otherwise, all that management promises is to discuss an involuntary transfer with the person being transferred, and not to use a reassignment as a corrective action.

Article VII. Layoff.

This is a familiar sort of layoff provision, except for the final section of this article, keeping the arbitrator from substituting his or her judgment for the academic judgment of the university, and for the provision allowing the university to ignore seniority for affirmative action reasons. Otherwise, seniority governs layoff unless the skill that management wishes to retain is "essential" to the operation of the library, and the person to be thus retained possesses that skill to a "substantial" degree above senior employees. How "essential" the skill is, and how "substantial" its possession, might depend on the employer's "academic judgment," but it is all likely to be argued before an arbitrator if only to determine arbitrability.

The right of laid-off temporary librarians to re-employment expires on the date that their temporary employment would have expired if they had not been laid off.

Brandeis provides for layoff according to qualifications, experience, performance, and seniority within job classifications. The exclusion of the arbitrator from substituting his or her judgment for that of the university is in the arbitration article. The Brandeis agreement does not provide an exception to protect affirmative action appointments from seniority.

Article VIII. Health and Safety.

This article is purely informational. The employer and the union agree that safety is a good thing. The employer agrees to do whatever it would have to do anyway. The article ends with an admonition to employees to be careful and to report unsafe conditions.

Article IX. UFL Rights.

Article X. Release Time.

Article Xi. Dues Deduction.

   This article simply provides for dues deduction from payroll checks when, and only so long as, employees so desire. See Russell Fisher's interview with Philip Hoehn, <u>Wilson Library Bulletin</u>, 58:274-7, Dec. 1983, who explains that the state of California does not permit compulsory union service fee charges, and allows no more than a maintenance of membership clause requiring union members to continue as members of their union for the duration of the agreement. This agreement does not have a maintenance-of-membership clause.

Article XII. Salary.

Article XIII. University Benefits.

   The University of California system is very large, and it is not surprising or in any way undesirable that a relatively small group like its non-supervisory librarians should ride along on the benefits of a larger sub-division of system employees, in this case the "non-Senate academic employees." If the university ever does choose to add or substract benefits for only the librarians, it has undertaken here to meet and confer with the union. The librarians of Brandeis, a much smaller institution, also ride on the institution's general benefits. At both, disputes over insurance coverage and benefits are not grievable.

Article XIV. Fee Waiver

Article XVI. Management Rights.

This is a strong management rights clause, although they all tend to look somewhat overwhelming to rank and file unit members. The Boston agreement proclaimed management's right to do many reasonable things; this agreement does not require them to be reasonable. Moreover, these management rights are specifically exempted from grievance and arbitration. This is somewhat unusual, and it is uncertain what its effect would be.

Article XVIII. Leaves of Absence.
Article XIX. Sepcial Leaves of Absence.
Article XX. Sick Leave.
Article XXI. Vacation.
and Article XXII. Holidays.

See the chapter "Leaves."

Article XXIII. Indemnity.

Article XXIV. Corrective Action, Dismissal, Release.

This is the discipline and discharge article, dealing with regular and "potential career status" librarians and then for temporary librarians. The former are subject to written reprimand, suspension, or dismissal for just cause. When a temporary librarian is terminated before the end of his or her fixed term, the action is called a release; of course no action at all is required to terminate a temporary employment at the end of its term. A temporary librarian released before term has a right to an informal hearing.

Paragraph E provides for expedited discipline consisting of five days' or less suspension without pay. Greater suspensions require written notice with reasons, and have their own informal appeal procedure, in lieu of the informal stages of the grievance procedure. Those who are not temporary librarians may appeal from this informal stage to the first formal stage of grievance.

Brandeis simply requires a librarian seeking arbitration

of discipline or discharge to prove that the employer's judgment in applying it was arbitrary and capricious.

Article XXV. Grievance Procedures.

The article imposes some order and discipline on the conduct of grievances: time limits, the exclusion of new allegations after entry into the first formal stage, and the citation in the written grievance of the four essential elements (D.d.). In general, preparation for a grievance is to be on the grievant's own time.

Librarians complaining of sexual harassment may elect the university's sexual harassment complaint procedure instead of the informal stages of grievance. If they do, they can bring a union representative with them.

The numerous state and federal laws covering various kinds of discrimination have created numerous tribunals to which persons can resort. Whatever resort the agreement provides, it cannot deprive the librarians of access to these tribunals, nor protect the employer from multiple jeopardy. Paragraph I does however abort a grievance if the grievant files the same complaint elsewhere.

Article XXVI. Arbitration.

This article resembles many others except for its provisions establishing a regular panel of potential arbitrators, offering an option for expedited arbitration, limiting the award of back pay, and barring the arbitrator from substituting his or her judgment for the academic judgment of the university.

Brandeis also bars the arbitrator from substituting his or her judgment for that of the university, but does not refer to it as "academic."

Article XXVII. Concerted Action.

This is the no-strike, no-lockout clause. It also prohibits any sympathetic activity, such as respecting another union's picket line, that would interfere with the operation of the university. Brandeis has a similar article. The affirmative anti-strike action required of the union is similar to that in the Boston Public Library agreement.

Article XXVIII. Severability.

Paragraph A is a standard provision protecting the rest of the agreement if part of it proves invalid.

Article XXIX. Waiver.

Provisions such as that in paragraph A are called zipper clauses. Employers have a continuous duty to bargain with their unions. To avoid destabilizing consequences that neither party may desire, they agree that they have bargained everything that either of them wished, and that the agreement is the result of all of that bargaining even if not all of the issues appear in the agreement. Normally, a novel issue unforeseen by the parties during bargaining might suffice to invoke this "duty to bargain," but not in this agreement.

Provisions such as that in paragraph B appear in various versions only in academic agreements, and not in all of those. In university faculties, a rich growth of traditional procedures and policies has grown up over many years before collective bargaining arrived on campus. These are recognized in the University of California faculty agreement, and librarians' counterpart procedures and policies are similarly recognized in this agreement. The university makes these procedures policy by incorporating them into the manual, just as the university makes the agreement itself policy by ratifying it. The mere fact that the librarians' existing procedures and policies are so treated in the agreement attests to the similarity of these librarians to faculty, even though they were formed by the state into separate units. These other procedures and policies are not grievable or arbitrable under the agreement. They contain an internal appeals mechanism, and employ terms and concepts unfamiliar to a labor arbitrator. Anyone drafting a document that is likely to be taken to arbitration ought to write it with arbitrators in mind. Here, however, leaving certain personnel matters in an academic enclave immune to arbitration represents an unorthodox and significant devolution of power and responsibility by the union. Whether these arrangements can survive governmental demands for precision and disclosure only time will tell.

Paragraph B includes a reference to LAUC (Library Association of the University of California), a professional association that for many years has addressed the standards of the profession and the aspirations of its members, and that at one time was reckoned a candidate to be their bargaining agent. Its activities have set it far apart from ACRL (the Association of College and Research Libraries) or ALA (American Library Association). The Library Association of the City of New York (LACUNY) more closely resembles LAUC, but the CUNY (City University of New York) faculty agreement never gave LACUNY the recognition that the University of California librarians' agreement has given LAUC.

The Brandeis agreement has no provision equivalent to XXIX.B.

Article XXX. Duration of Agreement.

This two-year agreement is the second negotiated between these parties. Often a first agreement covers one year, and subsequent agreements, as the parties come to know the issues, stretch to three years; in this case, however, the first and second agreement were both for two years. Paragraph B provides some relief from the rigors of the zipper clause: In the second year of the first agreement, either party could reopen negotiations on economic articles ("economic reopeners") and up to three other articles ("wild cards"). This second agreement adds one wild card for each party. This agreement expires on its final date. Some other agreements continue beyond their "final" dates until they are replaced by a new agreement.

Nota Bene.

The policies and procedures mentioned in XXIX.B. appear at the end of the agreement booklet for information and convenience only, and form no part of the agreement. For us, of course, they are no less instructive.

VIII

THE UNIVERSITY OF FLORIDA SYSTEM

[The following commentaries apply to the agreement in Appendix III.]

Agreement between Board of Regents State University System of Florida and United Faculty of Florida, 1985-1988.

Preamble.

The parties both describe and recommend the continuation of the academic governance machinery of the universities in the state system. The preamble offers reassurance that the traditional roles of senates, departments, and faculties will continue side by side with those of the union and the regents. It addresses two distinct faculty anxieties: 1) Will faculty members whose power base is in the union displace those based in the senate and departments? and 2) Will the great power of those at a central bargaining table erode or perhaps even erase the autonomy of the individual universities in the system? The phrasing and style are probably quite suitable to convey these reassurances to faculty members familiar with the system. They might puzzle an arbitrator, but then the preamble has been made non-grievable.

Article 1. Recognition.

The details of the unit recognized appear in Appendix A, below. The provisions regarding board meetings are in the spirit of Florida's "sunshine" act providing for open and accessible meetings of public bodies. Paragraph 1.4 partially protects the universities from unfair labor practice charges for meeting with groups such as senate committees, and reiterates that the union is the only agent for changing bargainable terms.

Article 2. Consultation.

This schedules quarterly consultation meetings between union representatives and management at both the system and campus levels. Union-management joint committees for consultation during the life of the agreement are almost universal.

Article 3. UFF (United Faculty of Florida) Privileges.

We must view the large number of faculty members released to do union work in the perspective of the Florida system, which is one of the largest in the country. Those released receive regular salary increases, but their work with the union is not evaluated for, say, tenure or promotion.

Article 4. Reserved Rights.

This is not a long list of management rights. The theory of reserved rights is that management has all the legal rights that it does not specifically give up in bargaining, and that is asserted here.

Article 5. Academic Freedom.

The style of this article reverts to that of the preamble. Unlike the preamble, this article is subject to grievance and arbitration. Academic freedom does not have a berth of its own in American law because it is part of those protected by the first amendment. Academic freedom arose in countries such as Germany and Spain, where it was distinct from and superior to the liberties enjoyed by the populace.

Article 6. Nondiscrimination.

The first paragraph is a general statement of intent

The University of Florida System 71

regarding sexual harassment and affirmative action and is
not grievable. The second lists prohibited gounds for discrimination.
This agreement adds veteran status, political
affiliation, and marital status to the usual grounds, and incorporates
by reference a Florida statute prohibiting discrimination
based on union activity. These all hereby become
grievable, though here again the grievance is aborted if the
complaint is taken through another channel. As in the Boston
Public Library agreement, both management and the union
agree that neither will engage in the prohibited discrimination.
The two agreements provide recourse against management
but not the union.

Paragraph 6.3 leaves unanswered the question of
whether the employee must demand only specific, named documents
or can require a certain amount of searching and compiling
on the part of the employer.

Article 7. Minutes, Rules and Budgets.

These are all public information and the only additional
requirement is their placement in libraries.

Article 8. Appointment.

Besides the usual advertising by which universities
seek to fill positions, vacancy notices are to be posted throughout
the Florida system. For purposes of appointment, the
article identifies further groups protected from discrimination,
for instance local residents and spouses of employees.
A clause-finder would probably miss this addition to the antidiscrimination
terms. Paragraph 8.3 is intended to eliminate
any misunderstanding among new employees about their jobs.

Paragraph 8.4 opens an opportunity for librarians
(among others) to convert to an academic year, subject to
the approval of the local university on a case-by-case basis.
Those who succeed convert from a nominal twelve to a nine
month work year at 18.2% salary reduction; this reduction is
exactly pro rata if we allow for the four weeks' vacation that
twelve-month employees receive.

Paragraph 8.6 was written for the case of classroom

teachers, and plainly not in contemplation of a librarian converting to the academic year.

Article 9. Assignment of Responsibilities.

Part of this article, on the other hand, was written for librarians. The Washington formula suggests a funding level for book purchases.

An unusual and important feature of this article subjects a work assignment to binding arbitration if the employee thinks it is either arbitrary or unreasonable. Appendix H provides a grievance procedure peculiar to this issue, and the "neutral umpire" is selected from a previously agreed panel. It is nonetheless final and binding arbitration. Often the grounds of grievances are "arbitrary and capricious" or "arbitrary and unreasonable." Here the substitution of "or" for "and" might make even a reasonable arbitrary decision grievable.

Article 10. Annual Employee Performance Evaluation.

For teachers, performance evaluation includes visits to classrooms by evaluators. The use of classroom visits for evaluation occurs also at CUNY and a number of universities with and without collective bargaining. Elsewhere it is sometimes resisted as an affront to academic freedom. The criteria for evaluation for promotion and tenure are familiar: teaching effectiveness, scholarly and creative activity, and service to the university and community. Although librarians are also subject to evaluation, this article too was obviously written for classroom teachers and not librarians.

The rest of the article deals with the problem of evaluating a teacher's oral English language proficiency. We already know from Article 6 that there is to be no discrimination against employees because of their national origin. Florida, as one of the states where lack of English proficiency has attracted attention, has also set standards and tests to determine it. These scores must be used rather than any subjective judgment, although it is left to the supervisor's judgment to call for testing in the first instance. Librarians, it appears, are not required in the agreement to have this proficiency. Teachers who do not pass the test are not discharged but sent from the classroom to some other work. Where do they go? To the library?

Article 11. Personnel Evaluation File.

These provisions do nothing new or unusual regarding the location, contents, and availability of an employee's personnel file. It does make an instructive reference to the file's "integrity," which is lost if custody is interrupted and the folder is passed around from committee member to committee member away from the supervision of somebody responsible for the file. It would be interesting to know how many libraries really protect the integrity of personnel files.

Article 12. Reappointment.

This establishes the length of notice to which regular employees are entitled if their appointments are not to be renewed. Before earning tenure, regular employees have only a term appointment (usually one, two, or three years), with no assurance of a further appointment. This is common in universities with and without bargaining, and represents a critical distinction between pre-tenure and probation. This article does however require the employer to furnish written reasons for the refusal to reappoint; and as these are grievable in this agreement the distinction is growing blurred. In just this case, an employee is able to grieve to arbitration alleged violations of not only the agreement but the constitutions of the United States and Florida.

Layoff differs materially from refusal to reappoint, not least in the minds of prospective employers, who are likely to consider layoff no stigma but otherwise wonder why the candidate was not reappointed by the previous employer. Layoff also implies some conditional undertaking, however hedged, to rehire the employee. This article assures the employee that if the circumstances call for layoff the employer must treat it as such and not simply solve the problem by non-reappointment.

Article 13. Layoff and Recall.

Tenured faculty enjoy some protection from layoff, at

the expense of the untenured, but only within a layoff group (see the chapter "Securities").

Conflicts between seniority and affirmative action have led to some important litigation in the country, but this agreement reduces the problem by allowing the employer to modify layoffs to conform to affirmative action goals. The employer has broad discretion in choosing which of two equally qualified employees are to be laid off, but must use certain specified factors in doing so. One of these is seniority.

For two years after layoff, a laid off employee may be asked back if a similar position becomes available at the same university. If the employee turns down the invitation, that is the end of his or her recall rights.

Article 14. Promotion Procedure.

As the chapter "Opportunities" points out, academic promotion is wholly different from industrial promotion. "Potential for growth" and "past performance" play a primary role here, as opposed to ability to do the job. In academe, the work is no different after promotion. Seniority plays no part in Florida system promotions, though it sometimes does in those of other unionized universities. The employer however sets the criteria, notifying the union of modifications so that they can be discussed. The employer must furnish written reasons for denial of a promotion.

Article 15. Tenure.

The pre-tenure period here is an option of five or six years, during which eligible teachers and librarians strive to meet the tenure criteria as they existed at the time of hiring. During this period, too, these employees are given "appraisals" of their progress (if any) towards tenure. Appraisals serve to aid the candidate in his or her efforts, but the candidate may also wish to use them as evidence for tenure. Once tenured, the employee can be terminated only through layoff or for just cause. The employer in this agreement does not need to show financial exigency to effect layoffs (see the chapter "Securities").

Article 16. Termination and Other Action.

Non-academic agreements would call this article Discipline and Discharge, and the two have many similarities. Yet pre-tenure faculty, as we have seen, have term appointments, and if a term appointment is simply not renewed its holder is not "terminated" in any way that invokes this article and the employer therefore does not have to prove incompetence or misconduct when declining to renew a term appointment.

Article 17. Leaves.

The chapter "Leaves" covers nearly all of this article. As is usual at universities, those with academic year appointments do not earn annual leave. This difference was taken into account in calculating salary conversions between academic and calendar year appointments under Article 8.4. Sabbatical leaves are treated below (Article 22).

Child care leave (17.12) enables a parent of either sex to take six months without pay to care for a new-born or newly-adopted child.

Article 18. Copyrights and Patents.

Universities in and out of bargaining develop policies to deal equitably with faculty members' rights to profit from their own writing or invention. The problem of equity arises when, as often happens, the institution has made some material contribution to them. The Florida system has put its policy in the agreement, but its gist is to leave the details to individual negotiation between the faculty member and the institution.

Article 19. Conflict of Interest/Outside Activity.

Universities wrestle with these complexities in and out of bargaining, in and out of agreements. Some conscientious and able faculty members and librarians engage in outside business activity or consultation. Sometimes their involvement keeps them up with their field of expertise in a way that no other activity can, and can moreover enhance the reputation of the university. At other times, the outside enterprise overshadows what was supposed to be the principal employment, that at the university, without enhancing either the employee's expertise or the university's reputation. Outside activity is only one kind of conflict of interest. Causing the university to purchase something that would bring the employee profit or a commission would be a more clearly unethical conflict. Disputes over possible conflicts of interest are grievable in this agreement. Florida is not alone in also having statutes dealing with these matters.

Article 20. Grievance Procedures and Arbitration.

This article contains a few restrictions that are not typically found in grievance and arbitration provisions. The arbitrator cannot award re-appointment for a missed time limit unless the grievant can show that an opportunity for other employment was lost because of it. The arbitrator is also told not to award punitive damages nor damages retroactive to more than thirty days before the filing of the grievance, nor to substitute the arbitrator's judgment for the administrator's. A Florida statute makes available to either party a judicial review of arbitrability, either prior to an actual grievance hearing or after the arbitrator's decision. Paragraph 20.21 expresses the doctrine, "Obey now, grieve later," which is more often implied than expressed.

Article 21. Other Employee Rights.

This miscellaneous article includes the only safety provision, several informational items, and an opportunity to take most courses tuition-free at each of the nine universities in this system.

Article 22. Professional Development Program and Sabbaticals.

The professional development leave is meant only for those outside the tenurable and tenured class. It is one semester at full pay for about 5% of this group each year. All members of the unit may have some study leave: paid leave if the study is required by the employer, unpaid or vacation time otherwise.

Sabbatical leaves in the agreement are essentially the same as those in many universities without collective bargaining. What is unusual in this article is its commitment to grant half-pay full-year sabbatical leaves to all elgible applicants, and a minimum of sixty full-pay half-year sabbaticals. Employer contributions to retirement and insurance continue during these leaves.

For retraining, the system may make use of any of these programs, including the free tuition in the previous article.

Article 23. Salaries

Article 24. Fringe Benefits.

Article 25. Insurance Deduction.

Article 26. Payroll Deduction.

Article 27. Maintenance of Benefits.

Article 28. Miscellaneous Provisions.

These include the no-lockout-no-strike provision and some legal tidying-up. Further, if the employer creates a new job class the parties may confer regarding it, but whether it is to be in or out of this bargaining unit will be decided by the state employee relations commission. An individual employee who does not like his or her job classification may complain about it but not grieve.

Article 29. Severability.

This provides a little more detail than usual, but like all severability clauses preserves the agreement even if parts of it are found or made illegal.

Article 30. Amendment and Duration.

This agreement extends for three years, but the economic parts of it must be renegotiated annually.

Article 31. Totality of Agreement.

This compares closely with other zipper clauses we have seen.

Article 32. Definitions.

Even if it is a dust bin of afterthoughts, the definitions clause resolves critical ambiguities. Now, when we read in the grievance article that formal grievances must be filed within twenty-five days, we know that the clock keeps ticking through Sundays, holidays, and summer term. In other agreements the clock is equally likely to stop on some of these days.

Appendix H. Memorandum of Understanding.

Article 9 gives special treatment to disputes over assignments of duties, and in this appendix the parties have set up the arbitration mechanism exclusively available for such disputes. To minimize the disruption that a delay might cause, this mechanism moves much faster than the main grievance and arbitration procedures. Deadlines are shorter and the "neutral umpire" from a pre-agreed panel is chosen and ready sooner.

IX

CONCLUSION

These agreements suggest that on balance collective bargaining can deliver firm improvements for librarians in many common situations. Bad situations can be made better, some problems solved, and troublesome anxieties allayed in these agreements. The librarians on the spot must judge how they are served, even if their choices of basic bargaining environment are more constricted than some writers suggest. The beginning librarian's only practical choice is to go to work in a unionized or nonunionized organization. How often, if ever, this consideration affects today's graduates might lend itself to a short study to accompany other surveys of librarians' opinions. Even the employed librarian's choices are circumscribed, for one union certification election can last decades, stretching beyond the retirement of all the original participants. Ordinarily only successful decertification petitions reopen the choice of agent or of whether to have collective bargaining at all, and these occasions are rare. Thus librarians only occasionally affect the shape and size of the bargaining unit. They can sometimes influence the substance of an agreement. The responsiveness of the agreement to their desires depends jointly on the importance of librarians within the bargaining unit and on the importance of the unit to the employer.

A comparison of agreements demonstrates both real and potential differences arising from the composition of the unit. Agreements for academic librarians alone differ from those for faculty in which librarians are included, and both differ markedly from other librarians' agreements. On the other hand, the similarity between municipal employees' and public librarians' agreements suggests that the latter group have had either little opportunity or little need to shape them to professional aspirations. The familiar joint union-management committees meeting during the life of the agreement can be useful in developing professional opportunities, but they are likely to be more successful if dominated by librarians than if they represent a heterogeneous collection of municipal employees: unit composition all over again, in different guise.

Recognition of the needs and worth of librarians is an essential ingredient in their relations with their employers and unions alike. About 86% of librarians are women. Some "women's issues" (e.g., affirmative action, fair pay, facially neutral discriminations, harassment) have led to extensive legislative change, but agreements can still deal with them more effectively and promptly. Seniority does not discriminate against women in librarianship, as it does in male-dominated jobs, but it can muffle the effect of training and development programs if slavishly followed. Librarians have five or six years of university, but that is only half the distinction it was twenty years ago. These facts should generate rising interest in professional development and educational opportunities. One instrument for recognition is the agreement. In reality, most of them accord librarians no formal recognition of professional status: they are not called professionals, and neither their educational opportunities nor their other treatment differ from those of other municipal workers in the unit. There is nothing to prevent some such recognitions being made in an agreement if the union and employer have enough interest and confidence in librarians' claims to work them in.

Compensation itself is a recognition of sorts, more general in its statement but highly legible to the public and to the librarian. Librarians can make few generalizations about the relationship between unionization and compensation, unless it were to observe that the most gainful situation is to be a librarian in a faculty union in its first year or two of bargaining. Among municipal employees librarians are at or near the top of their units in compensation, but of course that may not be enough, and the exceptions are startling. What accounts for these apparent anomalies? Professionals who earn more than librarians have skills for which there is a market in the private sector. In the public sector, com-

Conclusion

pensation levels are more artificial and perhaps more vulnerable to long accepted but obsolescent and even prejudicial values. Hence the faith of many librarians in the doctrine of comparable worth. The problem remains familiar, to persuade others of the worth of a librarian's work. No checklist of skills, working conditions, and accountability will enable either outside consultants nor inside bureaucracies to judge the worth of librarians without understanding the effect of what they do, and that requires a successful experience in using information. That is our old problem, not a new one. If we solved it, we might make friends with the open market, and walk among the other professions without crutches.

The major security in agreements is a grievance process culminating in binding arbitration. The real effect of an agreement containing binding arbitration rests not on the number of grievances lost or won, but on the invisible influence its provisions exert over the behavior of both parties. Experienced union and management officials usually know what will and will not prevail in arbitration, and tailor their daily actions accordingly, while the agreement lies in its file cabinet. There are apparently enough purblind martinets in administration to ensure years of collective bargaining, and though unions have been declining in the private sector they have been rising in the public. The number and firmness (or rigidity) of rules are a matter of fine judgment in a humanistic organization. Neither administrators nor union representatives always take to a supple management style, and for them the greatest security and comfort dwell in the most detailed regulations. For wedding unionists who like to dot their i's to administrators who like to cross their t's, there is no yenta to rival bargaining, no certificate like an agreement.

Some librarians have agreements, and others will never have any because they are supervisors or managers. The former gain nothing by calling themselves "real" or "working" librarians. It is not persuasive to argue for the professional status of librarians and then define them as persons who do not supervise anybody. If the bargaining unit comes to be regarded as defining the profession, then the governors of institutions will perforce look to non-librarians for any managing that is to be done, thus placing a ceiling over the careers of able and creative librarians who might have found their best expression at that level, and in a larger perspective stunting librarianship as an influence in events where it might be central.

X

BIBLIOGRAPHY

A.L.A. Personnel Manual. A.L.A., 1977. 39 pp.

Abodeely, John E., The NLRB and the Appropriate Bargaining Unit (Report No. 3 of Labor Relations and Public Policy Series), University of Pennsylvania, 1971, pp. 65-86.

Adams, Mary L., "A Comparison of Librarians' Status Between Academic Institutions with and without Collective Bargaining Units." U. of Missouri PhD Thesis, 1975. 119 pp. Abstract only consulted.

Agege, Charles O., "Employment Discrimination Against Aliens: The Constitutional Implications," Labor Law Journal, 36: 87-94, Feb. 1985.

Andes, John, "A Decade of Development in Higher Education: Changes in contract Content," Journal of Collective Negotiations in the Public Sector, 11:285-96, #4, 1982.

Aussieker, William, "The Changing Pattern of Faculty Strikes in Higher Education," Journal of Collective Negotiations in the Public Sector, 14:349-57, #4, 1985.

Baker, H. Kent, "The Short and Long Term Effects of Collective Bargaining on Faculty," Journal of Collective Negotiations in the Public Sector, 13:235-50, #3, 1984.

Ballard, T. H., "Public Library Unions: The Fantasy and the Reality," American Libraries, 13:16-17, Nov. 1982.

Bibliography

Barron, D. D., and F. W. Summers, "The School Media Professional in the Negotiation Process," School Library Media Quarterly, 11:265-96, Summer 1983.

Berry, John, "The Value of 'Women's Work'," Library Journal, 109:1784, Oct. 1, 1984.

Billings, R. G., Professional Negotiations for Media/Library Professionals, District and School, Association for Educational Communications and Technology 1980, 90 pp.

Brandwein, Larry, "Coexistence to Cooperation," Library Journal, 109:1999-2000, Nov. 1, 1984.

Brooks, Gail E., "How Have Unions Addressed the Issue of VDT Users' Health and Safety?" Labor Law Journal, 37: 668-75, Sept. 1986.

Cain, A. Sue And James E., "Equal Rights--By State?" Labor Law Journal, 35:714-17, Nov. 1984.

Carmack, Bob, and John Olsgaard, "Collective Bargaining Among Academic Librarians: A Survey of ACRL Members," College and Research Libraries, 43:140-8, March 1982.

Cates, Jo, "Sexual Harassment: What Every Women and Man Should Know," Library Journal, 110:23-9, July 1985.

Caynon, William, "A Study of the Effect of Collective Bargaining on the Professional Development and Activities of Academic Librarians." PhD Thesis, Indiana University, 1980. Abstract only consulted.

_____, "Collective Bargaining and the Professional Development of Academic Librarians," College and Research Libraries, 43:133-9, March 1982.

Chaplan, Margaret A., ed, "Employee Organizations and Collective Bargaining in Libraries," Library Trends, (preface) 25:419-422, Oct. 1976.

Coe, Mary Jordan, "Personnel and Employment: Compensation," A.L.A. Yearbook, 1983, pp. 205-6.

Cohen, Marcia, "Sex Discrimination in Academic Employment:

Judicial Deference and a Stricter Standard," Labor Law Journal, 36:67+, Feb. 1985.

Coles, Frances S., "Sexual Harassment: Complainant Defense and Agency Responsibility," Labor Law Journal, 36:369-76, June 1985.

"Comparable Worth: A Legal and Legislative Primer," Association Management, 37:58-9+, May 1985.

"The Constitutional Status of Sexual Orientation: Homosexuality as a Suspect Classification," Harvard Law Review, 98:1285-1309, April 1985.

Cooke, William N., "The Rising Toll of Discrimination against Union Activists," Industrial Relations, 24:421-42, Fall 1985.

Cooper, Michael D., "Projections of the Demand for Librarians in the United States," Library Quarterly, 54:331-67, #4, 1984.

Coulson, Crocker, "Labor Unrest in the Ivy League," Arbitration Journal, 40:53-62, Sept. 1985.

"Court Takes Broad New Look at Affirmative Action Issue," Congressional Quarterly, pp. 2104-8, Oct. 19, 1985.

Crawford, Miriam I., "The Case for Affirmative Action in Libraries," in John Harvey and Elizabeth M. Dickinson, eds., Librarians' Affirmative Action Handbook, Scarecrow, 1983, pp. 16-63.

Craypo, Charles, The Economics of Collective Bargaining: Case Studies in the Private Sector, BNA 1986. 259 pp.

Cruzat, Gwendolyn, "Collective Bargaining in Academic Librarianship," PhD Thesis, Wayne State University, 1976. 76 pp. Abstract only consulted.

Davis, Charles, "Equity vs Fairness: The Impact of State Collective Bargaining Policies on the Implementation of Affirmative Action Programs," Journal of Collective Negotiations in the Public Sector, 13:225-34, #3, 1984.

DiPerna, C. J., "Content Analysis of Articles Containing Reasons for and against Library Unions, 1917-1973." U. of North Carolina, 1975, 132 pp.

Dube, Lawrence E., Jr., "OSHA's Hazard Communication Standard: 'Right to Know' Comes to the Workplace," Labor Law Journal, 36:696+, Dec. 1985.

Ehrenburg, Ronald G., Daniel R. Sherman, and Joshua L. Schwarz, "Unions and Productivity in the Public Sector: A Study of Municipal Libraries," Industrial and Labor Relations Review, 36:199-213, Jan. 1983.

Elkouri, Frank and Edna Asper, How Arbitration Works. BNA, 1974. 819 pp.

Ellmore, Mark A., Jr., "Subcontracting: Mandatory or Permissible Subject of Collective Bargaining?" Labor Law Journal, 36:773+, Dec. 1985.

"Employment Discrimination Against the Handicapped and Section 504 of the Rehabilitation Act: An Essay on Legal Evasiveness," Harvard Law Review, 97:996-1015, Feb. 1984.

Ferrant, Allan W., "Dealing with Problem Employees," Supervision, 46:3-5, Oct., 1984.

Fischer, Russell, "Pay Equity and the San Jose Strike," Library Journal, 106:2079-85, Nov. 1, 1981.

_____, "Collective Bargaining for Librarians," Wilson Library Bulletin, 58:274-7, Dec. 1983.

Fisher, Eunice M., Collective Bargaining for Librarians: A Personal Perspective," Illinois Libraries, 64:1210-15, Dec. 1982.

Foeller, William H., "Employee Preferences and Public Sector Union Security," Journal of Collective Negotiations in the Public Sector, 13:203-210, #3, 1984.

Fox, M. J., and Allen R. Nelson, "Defining a Bona Fide Seniority System Under Title VII of the Civil Rights Act of 1964," Journal of Collective Negotiations in the Public Sector, 14:111-25, #2, 1985.

Gallagher, Rosemary, interviewed in American Libraries, 10:575, Nov. 1979.

Garvey, Margaret S., "The High Cost of Sexual Harassment Suits," Personnel Journal, 65:75-84, Jan. 1986.

Gaston, Cheryl L., "An Idea Whose Time Has Not Come: Comparable Worth...," Population Research and Policy Review, 5:15-29. #1, 1986.

Guyton, Theodore L., Unionization: The Viewpoint of Librarians. ALA 1975. 204 pp.

Hauck, Vern E., "The Efficacy of Arbitrating Discrimination Complaints," Labor Law Journal, 35:175-81, March 1984.

Heim, Kathleen M., and Katharine Phenix, On Account of Sex, an Annotated Bibliography on Women in Librarianship, 1977-1981. ALA 1984. 188 pp.

Henkel, Jan W., and Norman J. Wood, "Restrictions on the Uses of Union Dues: A Threat to Public Sector Unions?" Journal of Collective Negotiations in the Public Sector, 15:41-51, #3, 1986.

Hildebrand, Suzanne, "Women in Librarianship, Status of," A.L.A. Yearbook, 1983. pp. 277-9.

Hoffheimer, Daniel J., "Employment Discrimination Against Resident Aliens by Private Employees," Labor Law Journal, 35:142-7, March 1984.

Holoviak, Stephen J., and Sharon Brookens, "The Benefits of In-House Counselling," Personnel, 61:53-9, July-Aug. 1984.

Hunt, M. A., and M. Mosley, "Impact of Collective Bargaining on Media Programs in Southern Florida," Florida Media Quarterly, 8:9-13, Fall 1982.

Jaffe, M. E., "Public Librarians Unite!" Public Libraries, 21:4, Spring 1982.

Jennings, T., "CUNY Librarians and Their Union," Bookmark, 40:221-4, Summer 1982.

Johnson, Theresa, "The Legal Background and Implications of Pregnancy Benefits," Labor Law Journal, 35:352-9, June 1984.

Josey, E. J., and Marva L. DeLoach, "Discrimination and Affirmative Action: Concerns for Black Librarians and Library Workers," in John Harvey and Elizabeth M. Dickinson, Librarians' Affirmative Action Handbook, Scarecrow, 1983, pp. 177-199.

Joughin, George L., Academic Freedom and Tenure, A Handbook of the American Association of University Professors. University of Wisconsin Press, 1967. 343 pp.

Kearney, Richard C., "Public Employment, Public Employee Unions, and the 1980's," School Library Media Quarterly, 111:269-78, Summer 1983.

Keotahian, Avak, "National Origin Discrimination in Employment," Employee Relations Law Journal, 11:467-92, Winter 1986.

Kleingartner, Archie, and Jean R. Kennelly, "Employee Relations in Libraries: The Current Scene," in Frederick A. Schlipf, ed., Collective Bargaining in Libraries. University of Illinois Graduate School of Library Science, 1975. 179 pp.

Knight, Thomas R., "The Impact of Arbitration on the Administration of Disciplinary Policies," Arbitration Journal, 39:835-41, Nov. 1985.

Kohl, John P., "Equal Employment Opportunity in America," Labor Law Journal, 36:835-41, Nov. 1985.

Labor Arbitration Information System, Labor Relations Press, Ft Washington, Pa., 1984.

Labor Relations Reference Manual. BNA, Washington, D.C., vol. 1- , 1937- .

Leap, Terry, Jozetta H. Srb, and Paul F. Peterson, "Health and Job Safety: An Analysis of Arbitration Decisions," Arbitration Journal, 41:41-52, Sept. 1986.

Learmont, Carol, and Stephanie Van Houten, "Placements and Salaries, 1981," Bowker Annual, 1983. pp. 279-94.

_____, and _____, "Placements and Salaries, 1983," Library Journal, 109:1805-11, Oct. 1, 1984.

Lilore, D., Local Unions in Public Libraries. Library Professional Publications 1984. 134 pp.

Livingston, B., "Collective Bargaining Hailed," Library Journal, 105:1124, May 15, 1980.

Martin, Lowell A., Organizational Structure of Libraries, Scarecrow, 1984. 294 pp.

Mayer, A. I., "Unions: Plus or Minus?" Wilson Library Bulletin, 54:242-3, Dec. 1979.

McKinney, T. Charles, "Fair Representation of Employees in Unionized Firms: A New Direction from the Supreme Court," Labor Law Journal, 35:363-700, Nov. 1984.

Meltzer, Bernard D., and Stanley D. Henderson, Labor Law: Cases, Materials, and Problems, 3rd ed., Boston: Little Brown, 1984. 1386 pp.

Mika, Joseph J., "Patterns of Collective Bargaining... in Academic Institutions of Pennsylvania," PhD Thesis, University of Pittsburgh, 1980. 267 pp. Abstract only consulted.

Monat, Jonathan S., and Angel Gomez, "Decision Standards Used by Arbitrators in Sexual Harassment Cases," Labor Law Journal, 37:712-18, Oct. 1986.

Morano, Richard, and Norman Deets, "Professional Retraining: Meeting the Technological Challenge," Training and Development Journal, 39:99-101, May 1985.

Neely, Anthony, "The Government Role in Rooting Out, Remedying Discrimination," National Journal, 16:1772-5, Sept. 22, 1984.

Newcomer, Julia, and Elvis C. Stephens, "A Survey of Patterns of Unit Composition at Public Higher Education Institutions Involved in Collective Bargaining," Journal of Collective Negotiations in the Public Sector, 11:89-112, #2, 1982.

Bibliography

"1984 Salary Survey Update," Special Libraries, 75:338-40, Oct. 1984.

Nolan, Denis R., and R. L. Abrams, "The Future of Labor Arbitration," Labor Law Journal, 37:437, June 1986.

Oberg, Marilyn A., Mary Blackburn, and Joan Dible, "Unionization: Costs and Benefits to the Individual and the Library," Library Trends, 25:435-49, Oct. 1976.

O'Reilly, Robert C. and Marjorie I., Librarians and Labor Relations: Employment Under Union Contracts. Greenwood Press, 1981, 191 pp.

Ogden, Warren C., et al., "The Survival of Contract Terms," Labor Law Journal, 36:688+, Sept. 1985.

Peace, Nancy E., "Personnel and Employment: Collective Bargaining," A.L.A. Yearbook, 1981, pp. 219-20.

Pearson, L. R., "Library Workers Lead Strikers in Library Comparable Pay Strike," American Libraries, 12:397, July-August 1981.

Phenix, Katherine, "Women Predominate, Men Dominate: Disequilibrium in the Library Profession," Bowker Annual 1984, pp. 82-9.

Puddington, Arch, "Seniority: Not for Whites Only," New Perspectives, 16:8-13, Fall 1984.

Pursley, Robert D., "An Analysis of Permissible Strike Authorization Among Workers," Journal of Collective Negotiations in the Public Sector, 13:259-76, #3, 1984.

Query, Lance, "Personnel and Employment: Compensation," A.L.A. Yearbook, 1984. pp. 220-1.

Rosenthal, Mary, "Impact of Unions on Salaries in Public Libraries," Library Quarterly, 55:52-70, Jan. 1985.

_____, "Library Unions in Minnesota," Minnesota Libraries, 27:102-9, Winter 1982-83.

Scales-Trent, Judy, "Comparable Worth: Is This a Thing for

Black Women?" <u>Women's Rights Law Reporter</u>, 8:51-8, Winter, 1984-85.

Schlipf, Frederick A., ed., <u>Collective Bargaining in Libraries</u>. University of Illinois Graduate School of Library Science, 1975. 179 pp.

Schneid, Martin, "Recognition and Bargaining Units" in Frederick A. Schlipf, ed., <u>Collective Bargaining in Libraries</u>, University of Illinois School of Graduate Science, 1975, pp. 43-53.

Sever, Shmuel, and Fred Westcott, "The Motivational Basis for Compensation: Strategies in the Library Environment," <u>College and Research Libraries</u>, 44:228-35, May 1983.

Shanker, Albert, "Neither Fish nor Fowl," <u>Illinois Libraries</u>, 60:571, Sept. 1978.

Siegel, Reva B., "Employment Equality Under the Pregnancy Discrimination Act of 1878," <u>Yale Law Journal</u>, 94:929-56, 1985.

Smith, R. M., "Exceptions to the Employment-at-Will Doctrine," <u>Labor Law Journal</u>, 36:875-91, Dec. 1985.

<u>Statistical Abstract of the United States 1986</u>. U.S. Government Printing Office.

Stephens, Elsie, "The Professional Status of Librarianship Revisited," <u>Journal of Library Administration</u>, 7:7-12, Spring 1986.

Stephens, Elvis C., "Why Courts Overrule Arbitrators' Awards," <u>Labor Law Journal</u>, 36:108+, Feb. 1985.

Stieber, J., "Recent Developments in Employment-at-Will," <u>Labor Law Journal</u>, 36:557-63, Aug. 1985.

Stueart, Robert D., and John Taylor Eastlick, <u>Library Management</u>, 2nd ed., Libraries Unlimited, Littleton, Colo., 1981. 191 pp.

Sullivan, George M., and William A. Nowlin, "Critical New Aspects of Sex Harassment Law," <u>Labor Law Journal</u>, 37:617-24, Sept. 1986.

Theiler, Patricia, "Power Plays," Common Cause, 12:30-3, Jan.-Feb. 1986.

Tidwell, Gary L., "The Meaning of the No-Strike Clause," Personnel Administrator, 29:51-3+, Nov. 1984.

Todd, Katherine, "Collective Bargaining and Professional Associations in the Library Field," Library Quarterly, 55:284-99, #4, 1985.

————, "Librarians in Labor Unions," Journal of Collective Negotiations in the Public Sector, 14:255-67, #3, 1985.

Turner, Donald G., "Negotiation in Public Education: State of the Art," School Library Media Quarterly, 11:279-85, Summer 1983.

U.S. Dept of Labor. Bureau of Labor Statistics. CPI Detailed Report, Sept. 1986.

Van House, Nancy A., "Projections of the Supply of Librarians," Library Quarterly, 54:368-95, #4, 1984.

Van Zant, Nancy Patton, ed., Personnel Policies in Libraries. Neal-Schuman, 1980. 133 pp.

Vignone, Joseph A., "An Inquiry into the Opinions and Attitudes of Public Librarians, Library Directors, and Library Board Members Concerning Collective Bargaining Procedures for Public Library Employees in Pennsylvania." PhD Thesis, University of Pittsburgh, 1970. 204 pp. Abstract only consulted.

————, Collective Bargaining Procedures for Public Library Employees: An Inquiry into the Attitudes of Public Librarians, Directors, and Board of Trustees Members. Scarecrow, 1971. 179 pp.

Wagner, Bill, "Affirmative Action at the Crossroads," A.B.A. Journal, 72:38-41, May 1986.

Wasserman, Don, "Unionization of Library Personnel: Where We Stand Today," in Frederick A. Schlipf, ed., Collective Bargaining in Libraries. University of Illinois School of Library Science, 1975, 179 pp.

Weatherford, John W., Collective Bargaining and the Academic Librarian, Scarecrow, 1976. 147 pp.

_____, "Collective Bargaining and the Academic Librarian, 1976-79," Library Journal, 107:481-2, Feb. 15, 1980.

Weibel, Kathleen, and Kathleen Heim, The Role of Women in Librarianship, 1876-1976. Oryx Press, 1979, 510 pp.

Weiler, Paul, "Striking a New Balance: Freedom of Contract and the Prospects for Union Representation," Harvard Law Review, 98:351-420, Dec. 1984.

Witt, Elder, "The Court Takes a Broad New Look at Affirmative Action Issues," CQ Weekly Report, 43:2104-5, Oct. 19, 1985.

Wrong, Elaine Gail, "Courts' Review of Arbitration Awards in Discrimination Grievances," Labor Law Journal, 37:123-6, Feb. 1986.

Wyatt, James F., "A Study of the Attitudes of Academic Librarians, Library Directors, and Academic Deans in Colleges and Universities in Eight Southeastern States towards Union Organization and Collective Bargaining for Academic Librarians." PhD Thesis, Florida State University, 1973. 191 pp. Abstract only consulted.

AGREEMENTS CONSULTED

Colleges and Universities:

Faculty including librarians:

Adelphi, 1976
Bard, 1974
Boston State College, 1975
Central Michigan, 1984-87
City University of New York, 1978-80
Eastern Michigan, 1978-81
Ferris State, 1976
Fitchburg State, 1976
Florida Board of Regents, 1985-88

Bibliography

    Goddard, 1978-80
    Hofstra, 1976
    Illinois Board of Governors, 1979-82
    Kent State, 1978-80
    Lowell State, 1976
    Minnesota State University Board, 1979-81
    Monmouth, 1976
    New Jersey State College System, 1976
    Oakland, 1976-79
    Pennsylvania State College System, 1985-87
    Pittsburg (Kansas) State, 1979-80
    Rider, 1979-82
    Rutgers, 1979-81
    State University of New York, 1976
    Southeastern Massachusetts, 1976-80
    Temple, 1976
    University of Bridgeport, 1978-81
    University of Cincinnati, 1979-81
    University of Massachusetts, 1980-83
    University of Rhode Island, 1975
    Western Michigan, 1978-81
    Wayne State, 1978-80
    Worcester State, 1975

Faculty without librarians:

    Fairleigh Dickinson, 1976
    Saginaw Valley, 1976-78
    University of California, Santa Cruz, 1985-86
    University of Connecticut, 1979-80
    University of Delaware, 1975
    University of Maine, 1979-81
    University of Hawaii, 1981-83
    Wentworth, 1978-80
    Youngstown, 1977-81

Librarians only:

    Brandeis, 1978-80
    University of California System, 1986-88

Non-faculty professionals, including librarians:

    University of Connecticut, 1979-82

Library employees including librarians:

   Claremont Colleges, 1974

Schools:

Schools including media librarians:

   Wisconsin Board of Education, 1981-83

Public Libraries:

Public librarians:

   Boston, Mass., 1980-82
   Buffalo and Erie County, N.Y., 1981-83
   Detroit, Mich., 1980-83
   Santa Monica, Calif., 1980-83

Public library employees including librarians:

   Dakota County, Minn., 1981-82
   Fresno County, Calif., 1981-82
   Los Angeles County, Calif., 1981-83
   Queens Borough, N.Y., 1980-82
   Rapid City, S.D., 1980-81
   Seattle, Wash., 1978-81
   Torrance, Calif., 1980-81

Municipal employees including librarians:

   Boulder, Colo., 1982-83
   Bristol, Conn., 1981-82
   Burlington County, N.J., 1980-82
   Contra Costa County, Calif., 1981-83
   East Detroit, Mich., 1980-82
   Glendale, Calif., 1981-84
   Groton, Conn., 1979-82
   Huntington Beach, Calif., 1981-83
   Madison Heights, Mich., 1980-82
   Oakland, Calif., 1980-82
   Santa Ana, Calif., 1981-83
   San Jose, Calif., 1981-83

Schenectady, N.Y., 1981-82
Tampa, Fla., 1981-84
West Hartford, Conn., 1980-82
Warren, Mich., 1980-82

Public works, library, and office personnel including librarians:

Gladstone, Ore., 1981-82

Clerical and library employees including librarians:

Scituate, Mass., 1980-82

APPENDIX I:

Agreement Between City of Boston
and
Boston Public Library
Professional Staff Association

Effective: July 1, 1984
Expiring: June 30, 1987

Appendix I

TABLE OF CONTENTS

Article I	Persons Covered by this Agreement	p. 2
Article II	Non-Discrimination	p. 3
Article III	Payroll Deduction of Association Dues	p. 3
Article IV	Payroll Deduction of Agency Service Fee	p. 3
Article V	Management Rights	p. 4
Article VI	Discipline and Discharge	p. 5-6
	section 1. Probationary Employment	
Article VII	Grievance Procedure	p. 6-8
Article VIII	No-Strike Clause	p. 9
Article IX	Stability of Agreement	p. 10-12
	section 3-4. Layoff Procedure	
Article X	Hours of Work and Overtime	p. 12-13
Article XI	Vacancies	p. 14-16
	section 3. Seniority	
Article XII	Temporary Service in a Higher Position	p. 16-17
Article XIII	Holidays	p. 17
Article XIV	Annual Leave (Vacation)	p. 18-19
Article XV	Sick Leave	p. 20-25
	section 2A. Extended Sick Leave Fund	p. 21
	section 9. Sick Leave Buy-Back	p. 24
Article XVI	Other Leaves of Absence	p. 25-29
	section 2. Bereavement Leave	p. 27
	section 4. Jury Duty	p. 28
	section 6. Maternity Leave	p. 28-29
Article XVII	Leave Without Pay	p. 29
	section 3. Paternal Leave	p. 30
Article XVIII	Professional Staff-Management Committee	p. 30
Article XIX	Miscellaneous	p. 31-34
	section 6. Employee Personnel Files	p. 32
	section 13. Day After Thanksgiving	p. 33
	section 15. Residency	p. 34
Article XX	Safety and Health	
	section 2. Heat Relief	p. 34-35
Article XXI	Compensation	
	section 6. Longevity Payments	p. 35
	section 11. Compensation Grade Appeals	p. 36
	section 14. Tuition Reimbursement	p. 38
		p. 39
Article XXII	Duration of Agreement	p. 39-40

AGREEMENT

THIS AGREEMENT made under Chapter 150E, of the General Laws, by and between the City of Boston, hereinafter called "the City" or "the Municipal Employer", acting by and through its Mayor, and the Boston Public Library Professional Staff Association, hereinafter called "the Association".

WITNESSETH:

WHEREAS the above-cited statutory provisions grant to employees of political subdivisions of the Commonwealth the right to bargain collectively with their Municipal Employer; and

WHEREAS the parties to this Agreement desire to establish a state of amicable understanding, cooperation and harmony; and

WHEREAS the parties to this Agreement consider themselves mutually responsible to improve the public service through the creation of increased morale and efficiency;

NOW, THEREFORE, in consideration of the mutual promises and agreements herein contained, the parties mutually agree as follows:

ARTICLE I

PERSONS COVERED BY THIS AGREEMENT

The City recognizes the Association as the exclusive representative, for the purpose of collective bargaining relative to wages, hours and other conditions of employment, of all employees classified in the Pre-Professional Library Service, all Professional Library Service employees in grades P-1 through P-4, all employees in grades LA-10, M-10 and C-10, but excluding personnel officers and all other employees.

Appendix I

ARTICLE II

NON-DISCRIMINATION

The Municipal Employer and the Association agree not to discriminate in any way against employees covered by this Agreement on account of membership or non-membership in the Association, or on account of race, religion, creed, color, national origin, sex, age, physical handicap, marital status or sexual preference.

ARTICLE III

PAYROLL DEDUCTION OF ASSOCIATION DUES

In accordance with the provisions of Section 12A, Chapter 180, of the General Laws (Chapter 740 of the Acts of 1950), accepted by the City Council of the City of Boston on January 15, 1951, and approved by its Mayor on January 17, 1951, union dues shall be deducted weekly from the salary of each employee who executes and remits to the Municipal Employer a form of authorization for payroll deduction of union dues. Remittance of the aggregate amount of dues deducted shall be made to the Association's Treasurer within twenty-five (25) working days after the month in which dues are deducted.

ARTICLE IV

PAYROLL DEDUCTION AF AGENCY SERVICE FEE

Section 1. Pursuant to Chapter 335 of the Acts of 1969, to assure that employees covered by this Agreement shall be adequately represented by the Association in bargaining collectively on questions of wages, hours and other conditions of employment, the Collector-Treasurer of the City shall deduct from each payment of salary made to each such employee during the life of this collective bargaining agreement and pay over to the Association, the exclusive bargaining agent of such employee, as an agency service fee, an amount equal to the weekly union dues deduction from the salary of individual employees which amount is proportionately commensurate with the cost of collective bargaining and contract administration. The Association certifies that this collective bargaining agreement is formally executed pursuant to a vote of a majority of all employees in the bargaining unit.

Section 2. The Association agrees to indemnify the City for damages or other financial loss which the City may be required to pay or suffer by an administrative agency or court of competent jurisdiction as a result of the City's compliance with Section 1 of this Article.

ARTICLE V

MANAGEMENT RIGHTS

Section 1. The Municipal Employer shall not be deemed to be limited in any way by this Agreement in the performance of the regular and customary function of municipal management, and reserves and retains all powers, authority and prerogatives including, without limitation, the exclusive rights of the appointing authority to issue reasonable rules and regulations governing the conduct of his department, provided that such rules and regulations are not inconsistent with the express provisions of this Agreement.

Section 2. Subcontract Clause. The City reserves and retains the right to contract out work or subcontract out work. Pursuant to the exercise of such right, no employee shall be laid off if there

Appendix I

is available work in the same position or in a similar position which he is qualified to fill.

ARTICLE VI

DISCIPLINE AND DISCHARGE

Section 1. Probationary Employment. The first six months of employment shall be the normal period of probation for employees in the Pre-Professional and Professional Library Service and LA-10, C-10, and M-10 classifications. However, the period may be extended an additional six (6) months, provided a notice in writing setting forth the reasons therefor is furnished the employee and the Association prior to the completion of the normal probationary period. If the Library Department wants to extend the probationary period of any employee pursuant to this section, it must notify the employee and the association in writing no later than one month prior to the expiration date of the initial probationary period, if practicable.

Employees in the Pre-Professional Library Service are considered to be conditional employees until they graduate from library school.

Section 2. Permanent Employment. Employees in the Pre-Professional Library Service are considered to be conditional employees until they graduate from library school. Employees in the Pre-Professional Library Service shall be granted five (5) months to obtain a professional service position from the date of the employee's graduation from library school.

All employees in the Pre-Professional Library Service are eligible for application and selection to P1 positions pursuant to Article XI of this Agreement while in attendance during the last month of their last semester at library school. Applications for such positions must be accompanied or immediately followed by a letter form the graduate library school confirming when the degree requirements will be completed. Permanent appointment is contingent upon successful completion of the MLS requirement. The employee's seniority date in the P1 position shall be as of the date of acceptance into the position.

A permanent or conditional employee shall not be disciplined nor shall he have his employment terminated except for just cause. Any dispute concerning the discipline or discharge of a permanent or conditional employee shall be subject to the grievance and arbitration provisions of this Agreement. It is understood that just cause for terminating a conditional employee exists when there is no suitable vacancy upon the employee's graduation from library school.

ARTICLE VII

GRIEVANCE PROCEDURE

Section 1. Only matters involving the question whether the Municipal Employer is complying with the express provisions of this Agreement shall constitute grievances under this Article.

Section 2. Grievances shall be processed as follows:

> Step #1. The Association representative, with or without the aggrieved employee, shall present the grievance orally to the employee's immediate superior outside of the bargaining unit, who shall attempt to adjust the grievance informally, but shall in any event answer the grievance in writing within three (3) working days.
>
> Step #2. If the grievance is not settled at Step #1, it shall be presented in writing to the Appointing Authority or his delegate in the

Appendix I

department in which the aggrieved employee serves within ten (10) working days of the occurrence or failure of occurrence, whichever may be the case, of the incident upon which the grievance is based or it shall be deemed waived.

Step #3. If the grievance is not resolved at Step #2 within six (6) working days, the grievance may be submitted to the City's Office of Labor Relations which shall schedule a hearing within ten (10) working days after it receives the grievance. If the grievance is not presented at step #3 within ten (10) working days after receipt of the answer at Step #2, it shall be deemed waived.

Conducting the hearing shall be one or more of the staff of the Office of Labor Relations. In addition, the City's committee to hear grievances may include such other persons as the Office of Labor Relations may from time to time designate.

Section #4. If the grievance is not resolved at Step #3 within fifteen (15) working days, the Association, and only the Association, may submit the grievance to arbitration. If the grievance is not submitted to arbitration within thirty (30) working days after receipt of the Step #3 response, it shall be deemed waived. "Submission to arbitration" means a letter to the American Arbitration Association, postage prepaid, postmarked within the 30-working-day period, with a copy to the Office of Labor Relations.

The arbitrator shall be selected by the mutual agreement of the parties. If the parties fail to agree on a selection in the first instance, the American Arbitration Association shall be requested to provide a panel of arbitrators from which a selection shall be made. Expenses for the arbitrator's services shall be shared equally by the parties.

Section 3. Written submissions of grievances at Step #2 shall be in not less than triplicate, on forms to be agreed upon jointly, and shall be signed by the representative of the Association filing the grievances. If a grievance is allowed at any step of the grievance procedure, the adjustment shall be noted on the grievance form and shall be signed by the Municipal Employer's representative and the Association representative. At any step of the grievance procedure where the grievance is denied, the grievance form shall so indicate and shall include a written explanation denying the grievance, and shall be signed by both the Municipal Employer and the Association representatives, and referred to the next step of the grievance procedure as provided herein.

Section 4. Any incident which occurred or failed to occur prior to the effective date of this Agreement shall not be the subject of any grievance hereunder.

Section 5. The arbitrator hereunder shall be without power to alter, amend, add to, or detract from the language of this Agreement. The decision of the arbitrator shall be final and binding upon the parties. The arbitrator shall submit in writing his decision within thirty (30) days after the conclusion of testimony and argument, or as soon as practicable thereafter, unless extended by mutual consent. The arbitrator shall have no power to recommend any right or relief for any period of time prior to the effective date of this Agreement.

Section 6. Compliance. When an arbitration award is granted in favor of the Association, that award shall be complied with by the City within 30 calendar days of the date of the award was granted, unless the City, in a timely fashion, seeks to vacate the award.

If the City fails to comply with a monetary award within 45 days after the date of the award, 10% interest per year shall be added unless the award is ultimately vacated by a final court judgment.

Appendix I

ARTICLE VII
NO-STRIKE CLAUSE

Section 1. No employee covered by this Agreement shall engage in, induce or encourage any strike, work stoppage, slowdown, or withholding of services. The Association agrees that neither it nor any of its officers or agents will call, institute, authorize, participate in, sanction or ratify any such strike, workstoppage, slowdown, or withholding of services.

Section 2. Should any employee or group of employees covered by this Agreement engage in any strike, work stoppage, slowdown, or withholding of services, the Association shall forthwith disavow any such strike, work stoppage, slowdown, or withholding of services and shall refuse to recognize any picket line established in connection therewith. Furthermore, at the request of the Municipal Employer, the Association shall take all reasonable means to induce such employee or group of employees to terminate the strike, work stoppage, slowdown, or withholding of services and to return to work forthwith. Should any labor organization other than the Association establish a picket line at any facility wherein employees covered by this Agreement are employed, such employees shall be required to cross such pick line only if it is reasonable to do so.

Section 3. In consideration of the performance by the Association of its obligations under Section 1 and Section 2 of this Article, there shall be no liability on the part of the Association nor of its officers or agents for any damages resulting from the unauthorized breach of the agreement contained in this Article by the individual members of the Association.

ARTICLE IX
STABILITY OF AGREEMENT

Section 1. No agreement, understanding, alteration or variation of the agreements, terms or provisions herein contained shall bind the parties hereto unless made and executed in writing by the parties hereto.

Section 2. The failure of the Municipal Employer or the Association to insist, in any one or more incidents, upon performance of any of the terms or conditions of this Agreement shall not be considered as a waiver of relinquishment of the right of the Municipal Employer or of the Association to future performance of any such term or condition, and the obligations of the Association and the Municipal Employer to such future performance shall continue in full force and effect.

Section 3. If a layoff becomes necessary it shall occur as follows:

(a) The least senior employee shall be laid off first provided that a more senior employee has the qualifications and ability for the position.

(b) Seniority, for purposes of layoff shall be calculated by the length of service within the bargaining unit. Additionally, each two (2) years of service, in the Library Department outside of the bargaining unit shall count as one (1) year of bargaining unit service.

(c) The Library Department shall endeavor to provide one month's advance notice of layoff. If said notice is not provided, then the employee shall be entitled to one week's pay for each week he/she did not receive said notice up to a maximum of four (4) week

Appendix I

pay. This payment shall be in addition to any other compensation or benefits due to the employee.

(d) Any grievance relating to this section must be filed within five calendar days of notice of layoff, and if not resolved must be moved to expedited arbitration according to the rules of the American Arbitration Association within five calendar days after initial filing.

Section 4. Employees who have been laid off shall be returned to work in the inverse order in which they have been laid off provided that they are qualified and have the the ability to perform the work available. The right to be recalled and the right of laid off employees to accumulate seniority shall cease after two (2) years from the date of layoff. Seniority accumulated hereunder shall not count for purposes of longevity payments.

All laid off employees with seniority rights shall be given an opportunity to return to work if qualified and able to perform the work available before any employees are hired by the Library Department.

Section 5. In the event that employees are displaced from their positions due to Library restructuring, budget reductions, or job eliminations, and are not laid off pursuant to this Article, the following procedure shall apply:

A. The Library shall place these employees in different positions on an acting basis. The Library agrees to notify each affected employee of his/her impending transfer as soon as possible and to provide each employee with a reasonable opportunity, not more than 24 hours, to express his/her choice after due consideration for placement in the available positions. The Library agrees to honor the preference expressed by the employee insofar as possible, particularly for those employees in branches which are being converted into reading rooms.

B. Within three months of the date of the initial placement of the employees in an acting capacity, the employee will be selected for and placed in a vacancy in accord with Article XI. Said vacancy shall be posted and applicants selected pursuant to Article XI. All employees in the bargaining unit shall be eligible to apply for and be selected for these vacancies.

ARTICLE X
HOURS OF WORK AND OVERTIME

Section 1. The workweek shall normally consist of five (5) days of seven (7) hours each within a calendar week beginning Monday and ending Saturday. If so required by public service schedules, employees may be scheduled to work as few as four (4) and as many as eight (8) hours on a given day and two (2) evenings in a workweek.

Subject to the operating needs of the Library and the prior approval of the Division Head or delegate employees may rearrange their schedules in order to participate in Library related programs or activities, professional meetings, or school programs provided that the employee shall total seventy (70) hours within the two week payroll period.

It is understood that the workweek may include scheduled Sunday work at the rate of time-and-one-half the normal compensation rate on Sundays only during the period beginning with the first Sunday in October and extending through the last Sunday in May in Departments that are open to the public.

Appendix I

No employee shall be required to work more than seven (7) consecutive days (counting a scheduled Sunday for this limited purpose as a day or work).

No employee working part of a weekend shall be required to work any part of the following weekend unless the employee so requests.

The volunteer program shall be continued in effect for the term of this Agreement.

Section 2. Overtime may be paid or taken in compensatory time at the overtime rate, at the election of the employee, within a reasonable time after the date when the overtime was incurred. Overtime shall be paid with the approval of the Division Head; compensatory time shall be taken with the approval of either the Department Head or the Division Head.

Section 3. An employee shall not be denied overtime compensation for authorized overtime service by reason of authorized absence during the week in which such overtime service is performed. However, in the event of unauthorized absence in the week in which overtime service is performed, or in the event of absence without pay by reason of disciplinary action, such employee shall be compensated for such overtime service on a straight-time basis only.

Section 4. The City agrees to give the Association and affected employees reasonable notice of any proposed change in scheduled work shifts and an opportunity to discuss the proposed change. In the event of failure to agree on this proposed change, the City shall have the right to institute the change and the Union shall have the right to take the matter up as a grievance under the grievance procedure.

ARTICLE XI

VACANCIES

Section 1. Suitable notice of all vacancies within the bargaining unit and resulting promotional opportunities and lateral transfer opportunities will be given to staff and to the Association President, and sufficient time will be allowed for all employees to advance their candidacy. Notice will be effected by posting for five (5) consecutive workdays on suitable bulletin boards throughout the main and branch libraries. Such notice will include a description of the duties and location of the position in which the vacancy exists, together with its rank, title, pay grade, and the requisite qualifications.

On posting vacancies, the Library Department will consider previously and/or contemporaneously filed requests for lateral transfer to the branch library or unit in which the promotional vacancy exists. It is understood and agreed that the Library Department reserves and retains the right to assign employees to a particular branch library or unit or to transfer employees from one branch library or unit to another for the good of the service. However, no such transfer shall be made because of an employee's union activity.

New employees wishing to apply for positions in the grade in which they are employed shall not be deemed a lateral transfer until they have been employed in said grade for a period greater than one year.

Interviews of personnel who have applied for the announced vacancies shall begin within a reasonable time after the posting period for such vacancies has ended.

Appendix I   113

Section 2. Method of Selection. The selection of an employee for promotion or lateral transfer shall be made on the basis of qualifications and ability. Where qualifications and ability are relatively equal, seniority as defined in the following Section 3 shall be the determining factor except for the situation where an applicant for lateral transfer and an applicant for promotion are determined to have equal qualifications and ability, in which case the former shall be given preference regardless of seniority. In the event that the senior applicant for the position is not selected, the appointing authority shall, upon written request by the Association, submit reasons in writing why said senior employee was not selected to fill the position. The appointing authority shall be the sole judge of qualifications and ability, provided that such judgement shall not be exercised arbitrarily, capriciously, or unreasonably. Any dispute hereunder shall be subject to the grievance and arbitration procedure.

Section 3. Definitions. (a) Seniority, for purposes of promotion, shall be measured by the length of actual and continuous service in the Boston Public Library commencing with the date of employment in a position covered by this Agreement.

(b) Seniority, for purposes of lateral transfer, shall be measured by the length of actual and continuous service in the grade within which transfer is sought.

Any authorized leave of absence not exceeding one year shall not result in a break of continuous service for seniority purposes.

(c) Vacancy is defined as any opening in positions within the bargaining unit and shall also include the establishment of new classifications of comparable status and the reclassification of existing positions as provided in Section 400.05(b) of the Personnel Manual.

Section 4. Selection from among the eligible candidates shall be made within a reasonable time not to exceed one month after the close of the posting period. Notice of the selection made under this Article shall be sent by the Personnel Office directly to each applicant and the Association, and the Association shall also receive a list of all applicants within five (5) workdays after the close of the application period. Where no selection has been made, the Association shall be notified in writing five (5) working days after the close of the selection period.

If no candidate is selected for a certain vacancy and the position remains unfilled for a period of six months, then the Library shall repost the vacancy and proceed in accord with the provisions of this Article.

Section 5. Within 90 days of an employee's departure from a unit, the Library will inform the Association in writing as to its plans regarding the vacancy.

ARTICLE XII

TEMPORARY SERVICE IN A HIGHER POSITION

Section 1. An employee who is performing, pursuant to assignment, temporary service in a position classified in a grade higher than the grade of his regular position, other than for the purpose of vacation, shall, commencing with the sixth consecutive day of actual service in such higher position, be compensated at the rate of the higher position as if promoted to such position. Vacation, as used in this Section, shall mean annual leave but not

Appendix I

terminal leave. Selection of an employee to perform temporary service in such higher position shall be made in accordance with Article XI, Section 2.

Section 2. The Library shall have the right to make temporary assignments as long as these temporary assignments are not made for the purpose of avoiding permanent appointments to vacancies with the bargaining unit. The Library shall advise the Association of the reasons for such temporary assignments. Any question as to whether the appointing authority acted arbitrarily, capriciously, or unreasonably in making a temporary assignment to a vacancy within the bargaining unit shall be subject the grievance and arbitration procedure under this agreement.

ARTICLE XIII

HOLIDAYS

The following days shall be considered holidays for the purposes enumerated below:

New Year's Day

Martin Luther King, Jr.'s Birthday

Washington's Birthday

Evacuation Day

Patriots' Day

Good Friday (1/2) Day

Memorial Day

Bunker Hill Day

Independence Day

Labor Day

Columbus Day

Veteran's Day

Thanksgiving Day

Christmas Day

or the following Monday if any day aforesaid falls on Sunday.

ARTICLE XIV
ANNUAL LEAVE (VACATION)

Section 1. (a) Full-time employees earn annual leave from the first day of employment.

(b) Annual leave is earned at the rate of 0.4 days for each week of employment up to twenty (20) days annually. Employees with fifteen years or more of service will earn annual leave at the rate of 0.5 days for each week of employment up to twenty-five (25) days annually.

(c) Employees hired after June 30, 1978 shall be credited with one-half (1/2) of their annual leave upon completion of their first six months of employment, and may use this leave thereafter. On the July 1 or January 1 next following, they shall be credited with a pro rata amount of credit (equivalent to what they would have received if they resigned on that date), and they shall receive credit for one-half (1/2) of their annual leave on successive dates of July 1 and January 1 thereafter.

Employees hired prior to July 1, 1978 who pursuant to prior Agreements receive credit for their annual leave on January 1 and July 1 shall continue to do so. All other employees shall commence receiving credit for their annual leave on January 1 and July 1 as follows: Employees who pursuant to prior agreements would have

Appendix I   117

receive credit for one-half of their Annual Leave on a date from January 1, 1979 to June 30, 1979 shall receive said credit on said date; and shall receive on July 1, 1979 a pro rata amount of credit (equivalent to what they would have received if they resigned on July 1, 1979); the credit they would have received on a date from July 1, 1979 to December 30, 1979 shall not be so credited, but they shall receive credit for one-half of their annual leave on each January 1 and July 1 thereafter.

(d)(1) At any time an employee shall be allowed to carry his/her annual allotment of annual leave plus five (5) days. Permission to carry more than the above will be granted only with the express written permission of the Division Head, and failure to obtain such permission will result in the cancellation on January 1 of unused annual leave in excess of the above.

(e) Scheduling of annual leave, except for personal emergencies, is at the discretion of the Division Head. No employee may take annual leave without permission of the Division Head.

(f) Earned compensatory time or overtime may be taken as leave during the first six (6) months of employment, at the option of the new employee.

Section 2. Employees who leave the service of the library will be permitted to use all accrued annual leave prior to the last day of employment.

Section 3. Service with the Commonwealth of Massachusetts, the City of Boston, or County of Suffolk shall be included in computing length of service for the purpose of determining annual leave.

ARTICLE XV

SICK LEAVE

Section 1. (a) Effective January 1, 1981 and each July 1 thereafter, all employees shall receive 7 1/2 days of sick leave for use during the 6 month period except that new employees shall receive 1 day per month for each month of the year they are employed until the beginning of the next six month interval.

(b) On December 31 of each year, the unused portion of each employee's sick leave will be remanded to his/her personal sick leave bank.

(c) Any regular employee of the Library on the payroll as of December 31, 1962 who was allowed a "bank" of sick leave days on that date, shall not be allowed to renew the "bank " once it is exhausted.

(d) The Library will honor the unused sick leave balance of employees who transfer directly and without interruption of service from other City of Boston or Commonwealth of Massachusetts Departments. However, sick leave time accumulated elsewhere will not be counted toward the benefits of paragraph A and B of Section 8 of this Article.

Section 2. No employee shall be entitled to sick leave without loss of pay as provided in Section 1 of this Article unless:

(a) the employee has notified his immediate superior of his absence and the cause thereof before the expiration of the first hour of absence or soon thereafter as practicable;

(b) on, or within four weeks after the last day of each payroll week in which any such period of absence occurs, the employee or, in case of his incapacity evidenced by a physician's certificate

Appendix I   119

attached, or in case of his death, a person acting in his behalf, has in writing, on a form furnished by the Personnel Office, requested leave without loss of pay for such period of absence;

(c) except as provided in Section 7, the employee is unable to work due to illness, injury, or exposure to contagious disease, and medical and dental appointments;

(d) the appointing authority has approved such request. For periods of absence of five (5) consecutive working days or more, the appointing authority may require as a condition precedent to his approval of such request, evidence in the form of a physician's certificate for the necessity of such absence, or, if the cause of the absence is such as not to require the services of a physician, a written statement signed by the employee, setting forth the reason for the absence.

Section 2A. An extended sick leave fund (hereinafter the "Fund") shall be established according to the following terms and conditions.

(a) The Fund shall be administered by a committee designated by the Association.

(b) The purpose of the Fund shall be to permit employees who have exhausted their paid sick leave accumulation to continue on paid sick leave by withdrawing paid sick leave days from the Fund.

(c) The Fund shall be the accumulation of contributions by individual employees. Individual employees may contribute to the Fund two (2) days of paid sick leave each year from their personal accumulation. The Association shall notify the Library in writing on or before June 30 of each year the names of contributing employees and of the amounts contributed; said notification shall state that contributing employees irrevocably waive any personal rights to use or take advantage of the contributed days, and irrevocably waive any legal or equitable relief or recourse against the Library or against the Association relative to the Sick Leave Fund. Said notification shall be signed by contributing employees; upon said notification the Library shall reduce the accumulation of contributing employees accordingly; upon notification contributing employees may according to the terms of Section 9d) below, request withdrawals from the general fund.

(d) Only contributing employees who have exhausted their personal leave accumulation shall be allowed to withdraw from the Fund. Said withdrawals shall be requested by the employees, and must be approved by the Committee. (The Committee may approve withdrawal requests up to the balance remaining in the general Fund.) Expect with Library approval, which approval shall not be unreasonably withheld, the Committee shall not approve withdrawal requests for more than ten (10) days per contributing employees per calendar year.

(e) The Committee shall timely notify the Library in writing of approved withdrawals. The Library shall then adjust payroll and personnel records accordingly, except that, notwithstanding Committee approval, under no circumstances shall an employee who would not have been entitled to a paid sick leave benefit according to the terms of Section 2 of this Article be extended a paid sick leave benefit.

(f) Decision of the Committee shall be binding on contributing employees. The grievance provisions of this Agreement shall not apply regarding Fund decisions, except that the Association may

Appendix I

grieve the issue of whether the Library unreasonably withheld approval of Committee approval of withdrawal requests for more than ten (10) days. Decisions shall, in any event, be fair and equitable.

(g) The Committee may, after consultation with the Library, draft rules for administering Sick Leave Fund consistent with these provisions.

Section 3. Employees certified as able to work by their own physician cannot be refused work pending examination by a City physician. If the employee's physician and the City physician disagree in any case as to the employee's "fitness" to work, they will jointly designate a third physician, who, at the City's expense will examine the employee and render an advisory medical opinion, in writing as to the employee's "fitness" to work, copies of which will be sent to the City physician and the employee's personal physician. If they are unable to jointly agree on a third physician, a physician will be selected by them from a list established or suggested by the Commissioner of Public Health of the Commonwealth of Massachusetts. That physician, at the City's expense, will examine the employee and render an advisory medical opinion as stipulated above.

Section 4. An employee on leave because of an occupational disability may take such of the sick leave allowance to which he is entitled under this Article as, when added to the amount of any disability (Workmen's) compensation, will result in the payment to him of his full salary for any particular workweek.

Section 5. Up to five (5) days' sick leave credit will be restored to an employee's accumulated sick leave when such employee has used sick leave allowance between date of injury on the job and date disability (Workmen's) compensation is awarded, except that such sick leave shall be offset proportionately by a disability benefit that is awarded retroactively to date disability was incurred.

Section 6. An annual report of sick leave shall be made available upon request.

Section 7. Up to ten (10) days of existing sick leave annually is to be allowed for immediate family or household illness.

Section 8. Conversion of Sick Leave to Annual Leave.

A. (a) At the employee's option any accumulation of sick leave in excess of 150 days may be converted to annual leave at the rate one (1) annual leave day for each three (3) sick leave days.

B. In the last year before retirement, and if time permits, an employee may convert the first 150 days of unused sick leave time to annual leave at the rate of one (1) annual leave day for each four (4) sick leave days, and all days over 150 at one (1) for three (3).

C. Absence for illness in excess of accumulated balances will be charged to annual leave or, if none remains, to pay.

D. Whenever an employee is certified as too ill to work during five (5) or more consecutive working days during a vacation period, he may at his option, after returning to work, charge one half of those days to sick leave and have restored as vacation use one half of the time he was ill.

Section 9. Sick Leave Redemption. An employee who has used fewer than five (5) sick days in the twelve-month period ending December 31 of any year in which this Agreement is in effect may elect to redeem sick days in a lump sum cash payment in accordance

Appendix I   123

with the following schedule:

Sick Days Used	Cash Redemption
0	5 days' pay
1	4 days' pay
2	3 days' pay
3	2 days' pay
4	1 day's pay
5	0 day's pay

The per diem rate will be the employee's rate on December 31 of that year as specified in the Pay Schedule, inclusive, in force on December 31 of that year.

During January the City will notify each qualifying employee of his redemption options. An employee may elect or redeem all or part of his entitlement in full days. Unredeemed sick leave days will be accumulated in the normal manner.

ARTICLE XVI

OTHER LEAVES OF ABSENCE

Section 1. Subject to the operating needs of the Library, as determined by its Director (or his delegate), leave of absence without loss of pay will be permitted for the following reasons:

(a) Attendance by an employee who is a veteran as defined in Section 21, Chapter 31, of the General Laws as a pallbearer, escort, bugler, or member of a firing squad or color detail, at the funeral or memorial services of a veteran, as so defined, or of any person who dies under other than dishonorable circumstances while serving in the armed services of the United States in time of war or insurrection;

(b) Attendance by an employee who is a veteran as defined in Section 21, Chapter 31, of the General Laws as a delegate or alternate to state or national conventions of certain veterans' organizations as designated from time to time, during the life of this Agreement, by the Mayor;

(c) Prophylactic inoculation required by the Municipal Employer

(d) Red Cross donations;

(e) Medical examinations for retirement purposes;

(f) Attendance at hearings in Workmen's Compensation cases as the injured person or as a witness. Any witness fees received by such injured person or witness shall be remitted to the Municipal Employer:

(g) Voting time up to a maximum of two (2) hours for voting in a state, municipal, or other election, provided that the hour of opening and closing the polls in the city or town in which an employee is registered to vote would preclude him from voting outside regular working hours, taking into consideration travel time from the polls to his regular place of employment, or *vice versa*;

(h) Attendance at educational programs required or authorized by the Library; and

(i) Emergency medical treatment for employees injured during performance of assigned work. Employees who have returned to regular duty or to light duty after having been injured during performance of assigned work will be permitted reasonable time off without loss of pay for the purpose of attending follow-up physician's appointments which cannot be scheduled during off-duty hours.

Appendix I   125

(j) Attendance at monthly in-service training programs sponsored by the Library to foster professional development.

(k) Attendance at programs and conferences of appropriate professional library or library-oriented organizations. In the event that more than one member of a unit wishes to attend, preference will be given on the basis of these criteria in the following order:

1. Organization of or participation in the program or conference;

2. Date of membership in such organization;

3. Date of application to the Library for approval;

Approval to attend such events shall be rotated among the applicants to such program or conference in each unit of the Library.

The Library will make reasonable efforts to accommodate the employee's schedule if there is a conflict between the employee's scheduled hours of work and the conference.

(l) Attendance at court or administrative agency hearings by subpoena as a witness in matters involving the Library or related to the individual's employment with the City.

(m) In addition, upon written notification to the appropriate department head, to the members of the Executive Board of the Association to attend one (1) Executive Board meeting per month.

Section 2. <u>Bereavement Leave</u>. In the event of the death of a spouse, father, father-in-law, mother, mother-in-law, brother, sister, child, grandparent, or grandchild in the immediate family of an employee with six or more months of continuous active service and who is in active service at the time of such death, such employee shall be entitled to receive up to three (3) days' leave without loss of pay for the purpose of attending funeral services or arranging for burial. It is understood that these days must be days upon which the employee is regularly scheduled to work. Leave without loss of pay under this paragraph shall not be deducted from sick leave or vacation leave.

If an employee entitled to leave without loss of pay under this Section requires additional leave for such purposes, or in the event of a death in the immediate family of an employee not entitled to leave without loss of pay under this Section, leave for such purposes may be granted at the discretion of the Director of the Library or his delegate.

Section 3. Annual Military Training. Upon presentation of military orders, an employee will be granted two (2) weeks in a calendar year for the purpose of fulfilling his obligation as a member of the reserve of one of the United States Armed Forces or the National Guard. Additional days for travel will be granted for the duty at distant posts provided the authority which issued the orders verified the need for such travel time.

Section 4. Jury Duty. An employee required to serve on a jury will be paid his regular salary less the money received for his services as a juror.

Section 5. Reasonable time off with pay shall be allowed for the investigating and processing of grievances. Up to five (5) representatives of the Association may engage in the investigating and processing of grievances.

Section 6. Any employee shall be eligible to use accumulated sick leave for disability caused by pregnancy, childbirth or related conditions and recovery therefrom.

Appendix I

Any employee, upon request, shall be given a maternity leave of absence without pay; provided that an employee shall be eligible to use accumulated sick leave for such portion of the maternity leave of absence for which her physician certifies that she was disabled.

Except for the time period during which the employee uses her accumulated sick leave, as provided hereunder, the maternity leave shall be without pay and shall be for a period not to exceed one (1) year after the date of delivery.

Maternity leave without pay shall be given to employees for a period not to exceed one (1) year after the date of arrival of an adopted child.

When an employee becomes pregnant, she shall provide the personnel office with a statement from her physician indicating the expected delivery date. She may continue to work as long as her physician certifies that she is able to do so.

Prior to returning to work, an employee shall provide the personnel office with a statement from her physician indicating when she may resume her duties.

Upon returning to work from a maternity leave the employee shall regain her previous position without loss of seniority or longevity.

ARTICLE XVII

LEAVE WITHOUT PAY

Section 1. **Military Leave.** An employee who volunteers or is drafted for service in any of the armed forces of the United States shall be placed on leave without pay. He may return to the Library within two years following his discharge and be restored to a position and pay status not less than that obtaining at the time of his departure and without loss of seniority or longevity. Military leave is computed as time worked for retirement purposes.

Section 2. Other Reasons. While no employee has a right to leave without pay, a leave for any length of time for personal reasons, such as travel or study, or for professional reasons may be allowed. Application for such leave is at the discretion of the Division Head in accordance with the needs and requirements of the Library.

Section 3. Paternal Leave. An employee who wishes to care for his new born or adopted child shall be entitled to paternal leave without pay for a period of up to one week. Upon returning to work, the employees shall regain his previous position without loss of seniority or longevity.

ARTICLE XVIII

PROFESSIONAL STAFF - MANAGEMENT COMMITTEE

The Association and the Boston Public Library shall form a Professional Staff-Management Committee which shall meet bi-monthly for the purpose of discussing any matters pertaining to new or existing programs, policies, or physical facilities within the Library system, and problems with respect to administering this Agreement.

Each party shall designate five (5) members to the Committee. The Management members shall consist of the Director of the Library, the Associate Director, the Assistant Directors or their delegates. One Management member must be present at each meeting, and a total of three (3) members or delegates for each side shall constitute the necessary quorum for conducting a meeting.

Appendix I

The parties shall mutually agree on a meeting date during the first week of each month in which the Committee is to meet. Each party shall provide to the other party, at least one week in advance of the meeting, a written agenda of matters to be discussed. Where neither party has provided an agenda to the other party, the meeting shall be considered cancelled.

The Professional Staff-Management Committee shall discuss the determination of a formula whereby the work experience of the Pre-Professionals shall be credited toward progression into Professional status.

ARTICLE XIX
MISCELLANEOUS

Section 1. Bulletin board space will be provided for Association announcements in each library building. Such announcements shall not contain anything political, denunciatory, or inflammatory; nor anything derogatory of the Municipal Employer or any of its officers or employees. Any Association authorized violations of this Section shall entitle the Municipal Employer to disregard its obligations under this Section.

Section 2. All administrative notices shall be posted on library bulletin boards for inspection by employees. A file of all official notices and library publications pertaining to personnel shall be kept in the Personnel Office and shall be available for inspection by employees on request, at reasonable times, made to the Assistant Director for Personnel or his delegate.

Section 3. The Association shall furnish the Director of the Library with a list of its officers and authorized representatives and shall promptly notify the Director in writing of any changes therein.

Section 4. The Association Negotiating Committee shall be excused from duty without loss of pay for the purpose of time spent in contract negotiations.

Section 5. Personnel changes within the bargaining unit, including grade change, location change, transfers, and new employees and employees who have left library service, shall be provided to the Association on a monthly basis in order that the Association may keep its seniority listing current.

Section 6. Employee Files. (a) No material derogatory to an employee's conduct, service, character or personality shall be place in the personnel files unless the employee has had an opportunity to read the material. The employee shall acknowledge that he has read such material by affixing his signature on the actual copy to be filed. Such signature does not necessarily indicate agreement with its contents, but merely signifies that the employee has read the material to be filed.

(b) The employee, within thirty (30) calendar days after notice of the action taken under Section 6(a), shall have the right to answer any material filed, and such answer shall be attached to the file copy.

(c) Any employee shall have the right, on request at reasonable times, to examine all material in his personnel file in the presence of an officer in the Personnel Office. A copy of any such material shall be furnished the employee at his request.

Section 7. Those sections of the Personnel Manual not inconsistent with the provisions of this agreement are hereby

Appendix I   131

incorporated into the Agreement.

Section 8. Each Division Head and Branch Librarian shall have a copy of the Personnel Manual available for inspection by the employees.

Section 9. Should any provision of this Agreement be held unlawful by a court or administrative agency of competent jurisdiction, all other provisions of this Agreement shall remain in force for the duration of the Agreement.

Section 10. The rights and benefits of employees provided in this Agreement are in addition to those provided by the City, State and Federal law, rule and regulation, including, without limitation, all applicable pension laws and regulations.

Section 11. An employee may file a PAR through normal supervisory channels requesting a revision of his/her assigned job description. The Personnel Office will review all such requests and shall allow the employee to participate in such review.

Section 12. The letter of April 24, 1970, signed by Philip J. McNiff, regarding the P-5 positions is hereby rescinded. The Boston Public Library agrees herein to inform the Association and post vacancies (including a brief summary of the job duties and responsibilities) in new and existing positions in the P-5 pay grade and will accept applications from staff members to fill such vacancies for a period of ten (10) working days after the notice. The failure of the Boston Public Library to choose a bargaining unit member and anything related to the P-5 position, are not grievable under the collective bargaining agreement.

Section 13. The day after Thanksgiving shall be a skeleton day.

Section 14. The City and the Association believe in a meaningful and active Affirmative Action program and to this end agree to initiate an Affirmative Action Committee with representatives of the Association on the Committee.

Section 15. All members of the bargaining unit hired after the execution of the Agreement shall be subject to the terms of the City of Boston residence ordinance enacted July 6, 1976 (Ord. 1976 c.9).

ARTICLE XX

SAFETY AND HEALTH

Section 1. Both parties to this Agreement shall cooperate in the enforcement of safety rules and regulations. Complaints with respect to unsafe or unhealthy working conditions shall be brought immediately to the attention of the employee's superior and shall be a subject of grievance hereunder.

The Municipal Employer and the Association shall establish a joint safety committee consisting of representatives of each party in each department for the purpose of promoting sound safety practices and rules.

Section 2. When the THI indicator reads 82.2 the Library Department will grant heat relief provided that the temperature is 88° or higher and that the humidity is 50% or greater.

Hear relief shall be granted within three hours after the THI-humidity index has reached the level indicated above.

When heat relief is granted, the Library Department will either close the building or shall have a skeleton staff remain on duty. Skeleton staff remaining on duty shall receive compensatory time at a later time. The Library may assign employees granted heat relief

Appendix I   133

to air conditioned units provided that the employees services are necessary to the operation of the air conditioned unit and provided that there are at least three hours remaining in the work day. If employees are assigned hereunder, the Library Department agrees to make the assignments as soon as possible after the granting of heat relief.

ARTICLE XXI

COMPENSATION

Section 1. Effective January 1, 1985, increase all rates by 2%.

Effective July 1, 1985, increase all rates by 2%.

Effective January 1, 1986, increase all rates by 4%.

Effective July 1, 1986, increase all rates by 3%.

~~Effective January 1, 1987, increase all rates by 3%.~~ See attached salary Scale.

A $450.00 bonus is to be paid upon execution of this Agreement to all employees employed as of the date of execution of this Agreement and to all former employees with five or more years of continuous service in the Boston Public Library employed as of July 1, 1984 who retired or resigned prior to the execution of this Agreement.

The City agrees to implement the new base salary rates within thirty (30) days after notice of ratification by the Association of this written Agreement, or else interest will accrue at the rate of eight percent (8%) per annum on all amounts due. The City further agrees to pay the retroactive monies due employees under this Section within sixty (60) days after notice of ratification by the Association of this written Agreement, or else interest will accrue at the rate of eight percent (8%) per annum on all amounts due.

Section 2. All employees who have earned an additional Masters degree in a subject area in addition to their Masters in Library Science shall receive annual additional compensation of $500. Degrees earned after the execution of the Agreement must be job-related.

Section 3. Every permanent employee whose position is classified in a pay grade with a prefix "P" shall, upon completion of one year, two years, three year, four years, five years, and six years of service in the position, be advanced to the rate specified for the grade of the position in the next numerically numbered column, if any, for said grade.

Section 4. Employees classified in the pay grade with the prefix "PP shall, upon completion of the qualifications set forth in Section 305.05 of the Personnel Manual, be advanced to appropriate rate specified for the position.

Section 5. Salaries shall be computed on a weekly basis at the rate of 1/52.2 of the annual salary. Except as otherwise provided for Pre-Professionals, pay steps will be based upon length of service in grade and will be received automatically in the first full payroll of the month of the employee's appointment in each year

Section 6. At the end of eleven (11) years', and again at the end of sixteen (16) years' service in the library, an employee in the Professional Library Service will be paid a four-hundred-and-fifty dollars ($450) longevity payment.

Effective July 1, 1983, the eleven year longevity payment shall be increased by an additional $50 to raise the eleven year longevity payment to $500.

Appendix I

Section 7. (a) On the promotion of an employee within the Professional Library Service to a higher pay grade, said employee's pay increase shall be at least equal to two (2) steps in the new pay grade. Except for the addition of longevity increments, as provided in Section 6 of this Article, the new salary shall not exceed the maximum of the new grade.

(b) Where an employee within the Professional Library Service is receiving a longevity increment(s) and is promoted, after his/her pay increase has been determined on his/her base pay as in paragraph (a) above, the longevity increment(s) shall be added thereto. An employee receiving longevity increments on promotion in this manner, but who has not reached the maximum salary for the grade to which he/she is promoted, shall receive the annual step increase to maximum with the longevity increment(s) added each step.

Section 8. Compensation due deceased employees shall be paid to the designated beneficiary, then to the estate of the employee in accordance with Massachusetts General Laws, Chapter 41, Section 111I.

Section 9. Any employee who is permanently separated from employment shall receive the accrued compensation unpaid to the date of separation.

Section 10. Employees who resign and subsequently are re-employed within six (6) months shall be placed in the salary step which they held at the time of resignation, and shall be credited with all service-related benefits other than sick leave which they held at the time of resignation and which are not in contradiction of law or executive order.

Section 11. The Association shall have the right to appeal in writing to the Director of the Library relative to the propriety of the compensation grade assigned to any existing position on the effective date of this Agreement.

Within ten (10) working days of the filing of such appeal, the Director of the Library and/or whomever else he may designate, shall conduct a hearing on the appeal and shall answer the appeal in writing within ten (10) working days after the hearing is held.

If the compensation grade appeal is denied, or if no written answer is given within twenty (20) working days after the filing of such appeal, the Association, and only the Association, may submit the appeal to final and binding arbitration. Such submission shall be made within thirty (30) days after the expiration of the twenty working days referred to herein, and in all other respects must conform to the requirements set forth in Step #4 of the grievance and arbitration procedure.

The Association agrees that any position for which an appeal is made was properly graded on the effective date of this Agreement. In any arbitration case arising from any such appeal, the arbitrator shall not examine changes in job content which occurred prior to the effective date of this Agreement in the position for which the appeal is claimed, but shall restrict himself to the sole issue whether, after the effective date of this Agreement, there was a change in the job content of such position which should have the effect of changing its compensation grade.

Section 12. The City's contribution to group hospitalization insurance premiums shall be 75% of total premium, including Master Medical.

Appendix I

Section 13. No monies shall be paid under this Agreement unless and until the funds necessary to implement this Agreement has been appropriated.

Section 14. Employees in the bargaining unit shall, subject to funding, be eligible to participate in the City-wide tuition reimbursement program to the same extent and with the same limitations as other Library employees.

Section 15. The provisions of Section 18 of Chapter 190, Acts of 1982, are incorporated into this Agreement.

ARTICLE XXII
DURATION OF AGREEMENT

Except as otherwise provided herein this Agreement shall take effect as of July 1, 1984, and shall continue in force to and including midnight on June 30, 1987, but in no event thereafter. On or after March 15, 1987, the Association or the City may notify the other of the terms and provisions it desires in a successor Agreement. The parties shall proceed forthwith to negotiate with respect thereto. Notification under this Section shall be accomplished by the Association delivering a copy of its proposals to the Office of Labor relations, or vice versa.

* * *

The parties also agree to attempt to establish a mutually acceptable evaluation system by a six person committee, three members selected by the Library and three selected by the Association. Said committee shall meet regularly during the year following the execution of this Agreement in an attempt to establish an evaluation system mutually acceptable to the Association membership and the Library. The Association understands that the City intends to propose an evaluation system during the negotiations for the collective bargaining agreement commencing July 1, 1987 if no mutually agreeable system is established by the committee.

(This provision shall not be placed in the collective bargaining agreement.)

Appendix I

ARTICLE II

COMPENSATION

1. Amend Article XXI, Compensation by adding a new section 1A.:

"Section 1A. Effective first Wednesday following the ratification of this Memorandum of Agreement the employees covered by this Agreement shall be compensated in accordance with the following salary schedule:

PAY GRADE	STEP 1	STEP 2	STEP 3	STEP 4	STEP 5	STEP 6	STEP 7
PP	15,870	16,795	17,725	18,650	19,575	20,505	21,430
	304.02	321.74	339.56	357.28	375.00	392.82	410.54
P 1	21,430	22,680	23,930	25,180	26,430	27,680	28,930
	410.54	434.48	458.43	482.38	506.32	530.27	554.21
P 2	23,620	25,000	26,375	27,755	29,135	30,510	31,890
	452.49	478.93	505.27	531.70	558.14	584.48	610.92
P 3	26,040	27,560	29.080	30,595	32,115	33,635	35,150
	498.85	527.97	557.09	586.11	615.23	644.35	637.37
P 4	28,700	30,375	32,050	33,725	35,400	37,075	38,750
	549.81	581.90	613.98	646.07	678.16	710.25	742.34

2. All employees shall be placed on the salary schedule contained above pursuant to the grade and step they hold on the effective date of implementation.

3. The salary schedule contained above is not subject to, and is in lieu of, the three percent (3% increase effective January 1, 1987, contained in Section 1 herein.

CITY OF BOSTON

By *[signature]*
Raymond L. Flynn, Mayor

Dated: 1-16-86

In the presence of:

[signature]
Anna McKeon
Assistant Corporation
Counsel, Office of Labor
Relations

[signature]
Raymond Dooley
Director of Administrative
Services

[signature]
Kevin Moloney, President
Trustees of the Public
Library of the City of
Boston

BOSTON PUBLIC LIBRARY
PROFESSIONAL STAFF
ASSOCIATION

[signature]
Edna Cardillo, President

APPROVED AS TO FORM:

[signature]
Joseph I. Mulligan
Corporation Counsel

APPENDIX II:

University of California
and
University Federation of Librarians
University Council--A.F.T.
Agreement

Professional Librarians Unit
July 1, 1985--June 30, 1988

Appendix II

Table of Contents

Article	Name	Page
	Agreement	1
I	Recognition	1
II	Nondiscrimination	2
III	Professional Activities and Development	2
IV	Process for Promotion and Advancement	4
V	Personnel Files	5
VI	Transfer and Reassignment	7
VII	Layoff	7
VIII	Health and Safety	10
IX	UFL Rights	10
X	Release Time	12
XI	Dues Deduction	12
XII	Salary	14
XIII	University Benefits	14
XIV	Fee Waiver	14
XV	Per Diem	15
XVI	Management Rights	15
XVII	Temporary Appointees	16
XVIII	Leaves of Absence	16
XIX	Special Leaves of Absence	17
XX	Sick Leave	20
XXI	Vacation	21
XXII	Holidays	22
XXIII	Indemnity	24
XXIV	Corrective Action, Dismissal, Release	24
XXV	Grievance Procedure	27
XXVI	Arbitration	32
XXVII	Concerted Activities	34
XXVIII	Severability	35
XXIX	Waiver	35
XXX	Duration of Agreement	37
Appendix A	Salary Scale	39

Appendix II

AGREEMENT

This memorandum of understanding, hereinafter referred to as the "Agreement" is entered into by and between The Regents of the University of California, a corporation, hereinafter referred to as the "University" and the University Federation of Librarians, University Council - American Federation of Teachers, hereinafter referred to as the "UFL".

I. **RECOGNITION**

   A. The University recognizes the UFL as the exclusive bargaining agent for matters in the scope of representation for all librarians in the PERB-certified unit (SF-HR-17) at the University of California Berkeley, Davis, Irvine, Los Angeles, Riverside, San Diego, San Francisco, Santa Barbara, and Santa Cruz campuses, excluding employees designated as managerial, supervisory, and confidential and excluding all University of California student employees whose employment is contingent upon their status as students.

   B. The recognized unit may be modified by agreement of the parties pursuant to the rules and regulations of the Public Employment Relations Board. Any approved modification automatically becomes part of this Agreement.

   C. The terms "librarian" or "librarians" in this Agreement, whether specifically stated or not when used, shall refer to librarians who are in the bargaining unit covered by this Agreement.

   D. Any new librarian title shall be subject to meeting and conferring to determine bargaining unit status. If the University proposes to move an individual in the Librarian Series in or out of the bargaining unit, it shall give notice of such action to the UFL and, upon request, will meet and confer concerning the impact of the action. If the University proposes to create a new position in the bargaining unit, it shall give notice of such action to the UFL and, upon request, will meet and confer concerning the impact of the action. If the University proposes to create a new position in the Librarian Series outside the bargaining unit, it shall give notice to the UFL. If the parties are unable to agree, either party may pursue PERB procedures.

The unit shall INCLUDE:

Title Code	Job Title
3612	Librarian - Career Status
3613	Librarian - Potential Career Status
3614	Librarian - Temporary Status
3616	Associate Librarian - Career Status
3617	Associate Librarian - Potential Career Stat
3618	Associate Librarian - Temporary Status
3620	Assistant Librarian - Career Status
3621	Assistant Librarian - Potential Career Stat
3622	Assistant Librarian - Temporary Status
3635	Law Librarian
3637	Assistant Law Librarian

The unit shall EXCLUDE:

All management, supervisory, and confidential employees as defined by the Higher Education Employer-Employee Relation Act, and all UC student employees whose employment is contingent upon their status as students.

II. **NONDISCRIMINATION**

The provisions of this Agreement shall be applied to all member of the unit within the limits imposed by law or University regulations without regard to race; color; religious belief or non-belief; marital status; national origin; sex; sexual orientation; physical or mental handicap; medical condition (according to the California Fair Employment and Housing Act); political affiliation; union activity; or status as a Vietnam-e veteran or disabled veteran, or, because of age or citizenship. Complaints alleging unlawful discrimination are reviewable as grievances only if they allege a violation of a section of this Agreement which is subject to the grievance procedure and only the extent that that section is reviewable.

III. **PROFESSIONAL ACTIVITIES AND DEVELOPMENT**

A. Librarians in the unit are required to devote their time a energies to service on behalf of the University. Certain commitments established by the University will involve specific schedules and obligations that shall be met by th unit member. Choice of other activities such as study, writing, research, public service, and requests to attend workshops, institutes, and conferences, as well as the cho of professional organizations in which to be active, are l to the discretion of the individual librarian in the unit. There shall be reasonable flexibility and reasonable

Appendix II

individual discretion for librarians in the unit in the use of University time so that they may function as academic appointees of the University of California.

B. The University shall provide funding and opportunities for research and other professional development activities. Other professional development activities include creative activities, professional meetings, conferences, seminars, and workshops. Such funding and opportunities shall be allocated and distributed on a competitive basis at the campus level in accordance with the established procedures. The mix of funding between research and other professional development activities may fluctuate from year to year according to individual campus needs.

C. The University of California has allocated $116,800 per year in various campus amounts for members of the unit to use for research, creative activities, professional meetings, conferences, seminars, and workshops. These funds shall be a minimum amount and shall not preclude the allocation of additional funds at the discretion of the University. Such additional funds shall be distributed through the same procedures as the funds agreed to in this paragraph.

The campus allocations are:

Berkeley	$28,000
Davis	11,700
Irvine	8,100
Los Angeles	38,100
Riverside	5,700
San Diego	6,300
San Francisco	4,800
Santa Barbara	8,700
Santa Cruz	5,400

D. A special University-wide research fund of up to $21,810 shall be allocated by the Office of the President and distributed in accordance with the established procedures. This fund may be used to support research involving more than one campus, joint support with one or more campuses of a research project, and other similar research ventures such as individual research projects which cannot be funded at the campus level.

E. Any encumbered balances in the campus funds or the University-wide research fund will be carried over into the next fiscal year. For the purpose of this Article encumbered funds are funds for which a commitment has been made to an individual.

F. Should the number of unit members increase because of ongoing discussions between the parties regarding the unit status of librarians, the amounts in the campus funds and the University-wide research fund will be adjusted accordingly.

G. Nothing in this Article shall preclude librarians in the unit from applying for and receiving funding from other sources. Such awards shall not affect their eligibility for awards from the funds established in this Article.

H. In the event of a grievance under this Article culminating in arbitration, to the extent that the University's action is based upon academic judgment, the arbitrator shall have no authority or jurisdiction to substitute his/her judgment for that of the University and its agents.

IV. PROCESS FOR PROMOTION AND ADVANCEMENT

A. Local campus procedures for peer review must include the following provisions:

1. The Call for Recommendations for Academic Merit Increases, Promotions, Fourth (4th) Year Reviews, and Career Status Actions and the Calendar of Due Dates for the Appraisal and Review Process shall be issued and distributed every year to each librarian no later than thirty (30) calendar days prior to the first required action following the issuance of the Call. The Calendar shall be adhered to by all parties, except that provisions for reasonable extensions shall be developed.

2. Each year, librarians shall be notified in writing of their status for review.

3. A librarian has the right to request a review.

4. A deferred review may be requested only when there is insufficient evidence to evaluate performance due to prolonged absence since the last personnel review.

5. The final non-confidential contents of the review packet and, upon request, a summary of the confidential letters solicited for this review shall be given to the individual librarian for examination before the packet is forwarded to the Peer Review Committee. The librarian shall have the opportunity to make copies of any non-confidential part of his/her review packet.

6. There shall be a Certification Statement signed by the individual librarian certifying that prescribed procedures have been followed and a Documentation Checklist listing the forms and documentation included in the review packet.

7. If the review committee finds that it needs additional documentation to complete its work, such documentation may be added to the review packet after the librarian under review has been given copies of any non-confidential material added or, upon request, a summary of the confidential material in the file. No further documentation, other than the recommendation(s) of the Peer Review Committee(s) may be added to the review packet without the annotation of the Certification Statement.

8. Review committees shall be established on each campus according to procedures developed to accommodate local campus needs.

9. A librarian may request, for reasons set forth, that a person who, in the view of the librarian, might not objectively evaluate the librarian's qualifications or performance, not serve on his/her review committee.

10. A summary of the confidential material in the review file may be requested by the librarian in writing at the conclusion of the review. The University shall comply with such a written request.

B. Application of the Grievance and Arbitration procedures to this Article is limited solely to the failure to include the above provisions in local campus procedures. The only remedy available is thus limited to an order that such provisions be added to local campus procedures.

V. PERSONNEL FILES

A. <u>Access</u>. An accessible personnel file is the official personnel file for employment and personnel actions which do not involve review, evaluation, and assessment activities. Librarians in the unit shall have the right of access to all non-confidential reports, documents, correspondence, and other material in their personnel file(s). Librarians in the unit shall be entitled to comprehensive summaries of confidential material, if any, in their personnel file(s).

B. <u>Right to Inspect</u>. The University shall designate an office in which the personnel file shall be maintained. The University shall also designate an office with overall responsibility for personnel files. The office so designated will be the office to which a librarian in the unit would make a request to inspect his or her file(s). Librarians shall have the right to have a person of their choice accompany them to inspect their file(s) so long as the person chosen is not a supervisor, manager or confidential employee. Upon reasonable notice, the librarian in the unit, with or without a representative, may examine non-confidential material in the librarian's personnel file(s). Librarians may give written authorization to a representative to review their file(s) in their absence. The written authorization shall be valid for thirty (30) calendar days from the date of the signature of the authorization or within a written time limit specified by the librarian, whichever is shorter. The representative shall be entitled to examine all non-confidential material except that only the librarian may receive any comprehensive summary of confidential material if there is such a summary in the file. Records protected by recognized legal privilege and records exempted from disclosure by law may be withheld from the librarian and the librarian's representative. Subject to these exceptions, unsolicited documents shall not be confidential.

C. <u>Right to Copy Material</u>. Under normal circumstances, within ten (10) working days of a written request, a librarian shall be given a complete copy of the requested non-confidential items in the personnel file and a listing of the types of confidential material within the file. If a written request for a summary of confidential material in a personnel file is received by the University, the request shall be fulfilled within thirty (30) working days, under normal circumstances. The University will provide the first copy of such material at no cost to the librarian in the unit. Subsequent copies will be provided at a cost of ten cents ($.10) per page.

D. Any non-confidential item placed in a personnel file shall be clearly identified as to its source or originator and its date of receipt by the University.

E. A librarian in the unit may request, in writing, corrections or deletions of materials in his or her personnel file if the librarian believes the material is not accurate, relevant, timely, or complete. The request to the appropriate University official shall include the reason(s) for the correction or deletion. This statement shall become part of the librarian's file. Within thirty (30) calendar days, the University shall determine whether the request will be honored and so inform the librarian in writing. If the request is denied, the reasons shall be included in the written notice.

F. Only authorized personnel shall have access to a unit member's personnel file. Such access shall be solely for official University business.

G. Confidential material, legal privilege, and records exempted by law from disclosure shall be as defined in the California Evidence Code or by other statutes and relevant case law and shall not be subject to the Grievance and Arbitration procedures of this Agreement.

Appendix II

VI. TRANSFER AND REASSIGNMENTS

A. <u>Transfers</u>. When a librarian in the unit is appointed in the Librarian Series at another campus of the University of California, the unit member shall retain career status, seniority for purposes of merit review and promotion, accrued sick leave, vacation, and retirement credits.

B. <u>Reassignment</u>

1. Reassignment is defined as a change in working title or department of a unit member in the Librarian Series on the same campus.

2. A written description of the new assignment, including its duration if not indefinite, shall be given to the affected unit member.

3. When an involuntary reassignment is anticipated, the University will offer to meet with the unit member to discuss the proposed change.

4. Reassignment is not a form of corrective action and does not affect the rank, step, and career status of the librarian in the unit.

VII. LAYOFF

A. <u>Responsibility and Notice</u>

1. The University shall determine when layoffs are necessary.

2. Ninety (90) calendar days before a proposed layoff is to be implemented, the University will notify the UFL of the intention to lay off librarians in the unit.

3. Within ten (10) calendar days after notification, the University will provide the UFL with relevant financial or other information related to the proposed layoffs on the affected campus(es).

4. Upon request, the University will meet with the UFL to discuss the proposed layoff(s).

5. A librarian in the unit shall be given written notice of the effective date, the type, and duration where appropriate, of a pending layoff at least sixty (60) calendar days in advance of the date of the layoff, except in case of an emergency layoff.

B. Definitions

1. A layoff is a separation from employment because of budgetary reasons or lack of work. Layoffs may be temporary, indefinite, or emergency.

2. A temporary layoff is a layoff in which the University specifies a date for recall to work, but in no case shall the layoff be greater than six (6) months in duration.

3. An indefinite layoff is a layoff for which no date for recall to work is specified.

4. An emergency layoff is a layoff the need for which is unforeseen or sudden due to crisis or catastrophic act. An emergency layoff can be either a temporary or an indefinite layoff.

C. Order of Layoff

1. If, in the judgment of the University, academic program, budgetary, or operational considerations make it desirable to curtail operations and/or to reduce the hours of the workforce, staffing levels will be reduced in accordance with this Article. Before laying off a librarian in the unit, the University shall attempt to avoid layoffs through attrition. If layoffs are still necessary, the University shall ask librarians in the unit who are willing to reduce voluntarily their percent of time on pay status what percentage of reduction is acceptable. If librarians in the unit voluntarily apply for leaves of absence without pay, early retirement, or transfers to vacant positions on campus, and the University is able to accommodate those requests programmatically, then the need to lay off librarians in the unit may be unnecessary. The selection of the function and title code(s) on a particular campus within which the staffing levels are to be reduced shall be at the discretion of the University.

2. The order of layoff for appointees in the librarian title codes shall be on the basis of special skill, knowledge, or ability that is essential to the operation of a library as determined by the University. When there is no substantial difference in the possession of special skill essential for a particular purpose, seniority shall be taken into account as a factor in determining the order of layoff, with preference for retention accorded to Career Status Librarians.

Appendix II

3. If, in the sole discretion of the University, application of seniority would impair the University's ability to achieve or maintain affirmative action goals, objectives, or responsibilities, seniority need not be followed.

4. The University will endeavor to notify other campuses within the University of pending layoffs in an effort to find employment for a librarian who is faced with a layoff.

D. Seniority

1. Seniority is based upon the number of months of continuous service for the University at fifty percent (50%) or more of full time on pay status and is prorated accordingly. Employment at the University prior to a break in service shall not be counted.

2. Reemployment in a bargaining unit position within the period of right to reemployment, or return after an approved leave of absence provides continuity of service and continuation of previous seniority.

E. Reemployment

1. Whenever the University decides to fill a vacancy at the same or lower rank and step within the unit at the campus from which a unit member has been laid off, the unit member on layoff shall be reemployed provided:

    a. the librarian on layoff is within one (1) year of being placed on layoff; and

    b. the librarian on layoff is qualified for the position and available to begin work. If more than one qualified person is on layoff from the same campus, the order of reemployment shall be in inverse order of layoff, except that the librarian who possesses special skills may be reemployed regardless of order of layoff.

2. The University shall keep a roster of any librarians in the unit who have been laid off during the preceding twelve (12) month period. This list shall be updated monthly.

3. The right to reemployment terminates if a librarian in the unit:

    a. refuses to respond affirmatively to University inquiries concerning the desire of the librarian to return to work; or

b. refuses an offer of reemployment; or

c. accepts an appointment in the Librarian Series in the University.

F. <u>Temporary</u> <u>Librarians</u>. Temporary librarians who are laid off shall have reemployment rights to positions in the same title codes coterminus with the original expiration date of their temporary appointment. No temporary librarian shall be reemployed while a career or potential career librarian with equal professional skills and knowledge for the maintenance of library services is involuntarily laid off.

G. In the event of a grievance under this Article culminating in arbitration, to the extent that the University's action is based upon academic judgment, the arbitrator shall have no authority or jurisdiction to substitute his/her judgment for that of the University and its agents.

VIII. HEALTH AND SAFETY

A. The UFL and the University agree that the safety of each librarian in the unit is a concern of the employer and the union.

B. The University agrees that it has the responsibility and will make reasonable efforts to provide, maintain, and supervise working conditions and equipment at all times and will comply with appropriate and applicable federal, state, and local statutes and regulations regarding health and safety conditions.

C. It is also agreed that librarians in the unit are responsible for cooperating with all aspects of the safety and health program, including compliance with all rules and regulations for continuously practicing safety while performing their duties. Each librarian in the unit has the additional responsibility of reporting unsafe conditions or equipment to the appropriate University official.

IX. UFL RIGHTS

A. <u>Meetings</u>. The UFL and the University designee(s), at the request of either party, shall meet to discuss problems of mutual concern. Up to three (3) UFL representatives shall receive a reasonable amount of time, without loss of compensation, for meetings with Office of Labor Relations representatives. Whenever practicable, meetings concerning a local campus problem will be held on the affected campus.

Appendix II

B. __Master Employee Lists__. Within thirty (30) calendar days after the execution of this Agreement, the University will provide the UFL with a list of all bargaining unit librarians, showing names, title codes, dates of hire, campus work address, and home addresses provided the librarians have agreed to release their home addresses. Where the home address has been shielded by the librarian, the University will supply a work address.

C. __Master List Updates__. On or before the tenth (10th) of each month subsequent to the establishment of the Master List, the University will provide the UFL notice of any changes to the information, the names of librarians who have resigned, retired, or have been terminated, as well as information on new hires.

D. __Copies of this Agreement__. Copies of this Agreement shall be prepared for printing by the University. As soon as practicable after a review of the material by the UFL, the University shall print the document. A copy of this Agreement shall be given by the University to each librarian in the unit, including any librarians in the unit who are hired after the effective date of this Agreement. Copies shall be made available to the UFL for purchase.

E. __Use of Facilities__. Subject to the campus time, place, and manner rules for employee organizations, the UFL shall be able to use general classrooms and meeting rooms when not in use for University purposes. Information tables may be used in accordance with the campus time, place, and manner rules for employee organizations. The UFL shall have the right to post union notices on bulletin boards in accordance with campus time, place, and manner rules. Such notices shall be no larger than 8.5 x 14 inches, shall contain the name or letterhead of the UFL and shall be dated. Such material may be removed after thirty (30) calendar days. No literature or other materials may be affixed to furniture, walls, floors, ceilings, elevators, stairways, light fixtures, doors, window coverings, or similar objects or fixtures. Distribution of materials shall be subject to the time, place, and manner rules of the campus and shall be made by librarians in the unit outside of their work time and during meal times.

F. __Membership Solicitation__. The UFL and its members shall not attempt to solicit or sign up members during work time.

G. __U. S. Mail Delivery__. United States mail which is received by the University bearing a name and specific campus address will be distributed to the librarian in the unit in the normal manner.

H. __Use of Mailboxes__. In locations where employee mailboxes exist, the UFL may reasonably use such boxes in accordance with existing campus procedures.

I. **Regents Material.** The UFL shall be provided with agendas a supporting documentation for the meetings of the Board of Regents in accordance with current practice.

J. **Information Requests.** The University will provide the UFL with copies of the Academic Personnel Manual, local campus manuals or regulations related to academic employees, and updates and changes as they are distributed. UFL requests for personnel and budgetary information and reports relating to employment conditions of librarians in the unit shall be fulfilled to the extent required by law. One copy of the Academic Personnel Manual and the local campus manual or regulations related to academic employees will be provided without cost. The UFL will bear all appropriate costs associated with additional copies or other information requests.

K. **UFL Leave.** Subject to ten (10) working days' notice and the University's ability to accommodate such requests based upon operational needs, the University shall grant up to three (. working days of leave without pay each year to UFL officers for UFL business. The six (6) UFL officers eligible for the leave are the Chair, Northern Coordinator, Southern Coordinator, Secretary, Treasurer, and Chief Negotiator.

X. RELEASE TIME

In accordance with ground rules for negotiations agreed to by bo parties for this Agreement, four (4) members of the UFL bargainir team will be provided paid release time from work assignments to attend scheduled bargaining sessions for the purpose of negotiating reopeners and a successor agreement. The number of persons on release time may be subject to change under new ground rules adopted for negotiating a successor agreement.

XI. DUES DEDUCTION

A. Upon receipt of a written authorization by a librarian in th unit using a form provided by the University, the University shall deduct and remit to the UFL the standard initiation fee, periodic dues, and general assessments of the UFL until such time as the librarian submits written notification to the University to discontinue the employee's assignments. The University shall calculate the amount to be deducted, based upon a percentage of the librarian's monthly gross salary. The University shall recalculate the dues deductior when changes in salary occur. The University shall recalculate the dues deduction when notified by the UFL that its dues formula has changed provided that the formula changes no more than once per fiscal year. The University shall also remit an alphabetical list showing the names of payees and the amounts deducted and remitted. The Universit

Appendix II

shall process the librarian's dues deduction authorization or dues deduction withdrawal expeditiously. The transaction shall be completed no later than the second pay check after the receipt of the information by the University. The payroll deadline dates for each campus will be provided to the UFL.

B. It is specifically agreed that the University assumes no obligation other than that specified in Paragraph 1, or liability, financial or otherwise, arising out of the provisions of this Article. Further, the UFL hereby agrees that it will reimburse the University for any costs ($10 per check charge and $.07 per transaction charge) and indemnify and hold the University harmless from any claims, actions, or proceedings by any person or entity, arising from deductions made by the University hereunder.

C. If a librarian in the unit fails to fill out a dues deduction form correctly, the University shall assume no responsibility to correct such omission or error retroactively. The University shall return any incorrect dues deduction forms to the UFL as soon as the errors are detected. Once the funds are remitted to the designated representative of the UFL, their disposition thereafter shall be the sole and exclusive responsibility of the UFL. It is expressly understood and agreed that the UFL shall refund to the librarian any deductions erroneously withheld from an employee's wages by the University and paid to the UFL. In the event the UFL fails to refund such deductions within a reasonable period of time following notification of the error, the University will make such refund and deduct the amount from the amount due to the UFL.

XII. **SALARY**

Provided a timely agreement is reached at the bargaining table and the University is notified of ratification, the University agrees to increase the current rate of pay of librarians in the unit by the same range adjustment percentages as are funded for academic employees generally, by the 1985-86 Budget Act for the University of California. Once these range adjustment percentages become known, the University agrees to publish and distribute Appendix A setting forth the salary ranges for unit members.

XIII. **UNIVERSITY BENEFITS**

A. Librarians in the unit who are eligible to participate in a number of retirement, health, dental, and other benefit programs participate to the same extent as other eligible non-Senate academic employees of the University.

B. For the life of this Agreement, the University's maximum monthly rates of contribution for librarians in the unit who are eligible for and elect to take the health care plan and/or the dental plan shall be the same as the contribution rates for such plans for other academic employees. Costs in excess of the University's contributions are to be paid by the librarian in the unit, normally through payroll deduction. The coverage(s) and the carrier(s) of the health and dental plans shall be the same as for other academic employees at the same location.

C. The parties agree to meet during September of each year to discuss the fringe benefit plans, coverages, benefits schedules, carriers, providers, premium rates, eligibility criteria, and employer/employee contributions, if any. The UFL understands and agrees that, except as provided below, the University may alter the coverage, rate of contribution or the carrier of these plans during the term of this Agreement and that, if the University does so, such changes will apply to librarians in the unit eligible for benefits the same extent as they apply to other eligible non-Senate academic employees at the same campus. The sole exception the above shall be any alterations proposed by the University which affect only librarians in the unit, in which case the University agrees to meet and confer with respect to the proposed change.

XIV. **FEE WAIVER**

A. Career and potential-career librarians in the unit appointed at **fifty percent (50%)** or more of full time, who are **residents** of the State of California, and who meet the **admission** requirements of the University, are eligible for **two-thirds (2/3)** reduction of both the University

Appendix II

registration fee and the University educational fee, for up to nine (9) units or three (3) regular session University courses per quarter, or up to six (6) units or two (2) regular session University courses per semester, whichever is greater. University extension courses are not included.

B. Eligibility for partial fee reductions for other University courses is at the sole discretion of the University.

C. Disputes arising from this Article regarding admission and residence requirements shall not be subject to the Grievance and Arbitration procedures of this Agreement.

XV. PER DIEM

For required travel on official University business, the University shall reimburse members of the unit for per diem. Mileage expenses shall be reimbursed whenever the librarian uses his or her personal car for such travel. Reimbursement rates shall be those provided to academic employees. The per diem rates are to be used for subsistence expenses unless actual, itemized expenses are approved by the University.

XVI. MANAGEMENT RIGHTS

A. The management of the University is vested exclusively in the University to establish, plan, direct, and control the University's missions, programs, objectives, activities, resources, and priorities including Affirmative Action plans and goals; to establish and administer procedures, rules and regulations, and direct and control University operations; to alter, extend, curtail, or discontinue existing methods, equipment, facilities and location of operations; to subcontract all or any portion of any operations; to determine or modify the number, scheduling, and assignment of librarians; to establish or modify standards, duties, and responsibilities and maintain quality of performance; to establish and require librarians in the unit to observe the then current University rules and regulations and reasonable standards of conduct; to maintain order, and to impose corrective action or dismiss librarians in the unit; and to establish, maintain, modify, and enforce safety standards and programs. The foregoing enumeration of management rights is not inclusive and does not exclude other management rights not specified, nor shall the exercise or non-exercise of rights retained by the University be construed to mean that any right is waived. Except to the extent limited by the express and specific terms of the provisions of this Agreement, the University has the right to make and implement decisions relating to areas including but not limited to those enumerated above.

B. The University may continue any current policies and practices which do not conflict with the express written provisions of this Agreement.

C. No management right shall be subject to the Grievance and Arbitration procedures of this Agreement.

XVII. TEMPORARY APPOINTEES

Temporary Librarian Series appointees may apply for professional development funds, except that such funds may not be awarded to them for activities with a time duration longer than the terms of their appointments.

XVIII. LEAVES OF ABSENCE

A. <u>Military Leaves</u>

1. Compensation - A librarian in the unit shall be entitled to receive salary or compensation for a maximum of thirty (30) calendar days during one fiscal year while engaged in the performance of military duty provided the appointee has been in the service of the University for a full year prior to the commencement of the military leave.

2. Reserve Training Duty - Military leave of absence for the length of time of duty shall be granted to a librarian in the unit who is ordered to military reserve training duty. Paid leave is not granted for regular meetings or drills required to maintain reserve status; however, unpaid leave may be granted for such meetings or drills. Such military leaves shall not reduce accumulated vacation time.

3. Extended Military Leave - Extended military leave of absence without pay shall be granted to a librarian in the unit who enters the Armed Forces of the United States under the Selective Service Act (or a corresponding law) in accordance with applicable state and federal laws. Compensation, if any, and the right to return to employment shall be in accordance with applicable state and federal laws and the then current University policy. Whenever feasible, a person replacing an appointee who has been granted a military leave of absence for military service or defense work shall be appointed on a temporary basis to facilitate reappointment of the person on leave.

B. <u>Jury Duty</u> - A librarian in the unit shall be eligible for a leave of absence with pay to serve on jury duty. Upon receipt of initial notification for jury duty the librarian shall promptly notify the appropriate library administrator. Verification of actual service for jury duty shall be provided by the librarian to the appropriate University officer upon request.

C. <u>Emergency</u> Leave - An emergency leave with pay may be granted to a librarian in the unit by the University in the event of a natural catastrophe or emergency situation that places the health and safety of the librarian, or members of his/her immediate family or property in jeopardy. Such leaves shall normally be of short duration.

D. <u>Witness Leave</u> - When a librarian in the unit is attending administrative or legal proceedings on behalf of the University or is subpoenaed to appear as a witness in an administrative or legal proceeding, leave with pay will be granted for the actual time spent in proceedings and in related travel not to exceed the librarian's normal work day and work week. Leave with pay will not be granted when a librarian is a plaintiff or defendant in a proceeding unrelated to University employment, is called or subpoenaed as a paid expert witness not on behalf of the University, or is called or subpoenaed because of duties for another employer.

XIX. SPECIAL LEAVES OF ABSENCE

A. <u>Governmental Agencies</u>

1. A leave of absence without pay may be granted by the University to a librarian in the unit for service with a governmental agency. Full pay may be granted for leaves of absence of thirty (30) calendar days or less when the University determines that such leaves are appropriate and meaningful. Partial pay may be granted for leaves of more than thirty (30) calendar days in exceptional cases when considerations of value to the University are involved.

2. Governmental agencies as used in this Article refers to an agency of the Federal government, the State of California, a county or city within California; or any part, section, subsidiary, or agency thereof.

3. No leave of absence with full pay will be granted by the University unless other librarians in the unit are able and willing without extra compensation to carry on the duties which the recipient of the leave is unable to perform while on leave.

4. A librarian in the unit may apply for a leave of absence by providing information dealing with the disposition of work during the proposed leave, the nature of the

services to be rendered to the governmental agency, the amount of compensation to be received from the agency, the length of the leave, and the amount of compensation, if any, sought from the University.

B. Leaves of Absence Without Pay

1. Special Two-Month Leave

    a. A unit member may apply to the appropriate University administrator for a two-month (2) leave without pay. The request shall be submitted at least six (6) months prior to the proposed leave with sufficient information to allow the University to make a decision. Only one such leave shall be taken within any twelve-month (12) period.

    b. The unit member's application shall identify which two (2) months s/he wishes to be on leave. The two (2) months on leave need not be consecutive and shall be scheduled at a time mutually agreeable to the librarian in the unit and the University.

    c. The unit member shall be advised of the decision in writing in a timely manner. If the request is denied, the reason(s) for denial shall not be arbitrary, capricious, or unreasonable.

    d. A two (2) month leave shall not constitute a break in service for purposes of computing seniority for layoff. Such leave shall also not affect consideration of the librarian for merit and promotion.

    e. University-provided life insurance, University-sponsored health plans, and University-sponsored dental coverage continue during the special two-month (2) leave to the same extent and under the same conditions that would cover the librarian in the unit if s/he were not on leave. If possible, and if requested, arrangements will be made to allow a librarian granted such leave without pay to receive salary payments during the period of leave without pay.

    f. If the librarian is on special leave without pay for more than half a calendar month, sick leave, vacation, seniority credit, and retirement credit do not accrue.

    g. Special two-month leaves shall not be taken in conjunction with other leaves without pay.

2. Other Leaves Without Pay

   a. A unit member may apply to the appropriate University administrator for other leaves of absence without pay, which may be granted at the discretion of the University. Such leaves shall not exceed one (1) year. In exceptional circumstances, such leaves may be extended at the discretion of the University.

   b. A librarian in the unit who wishes to apply for leave shall submit a timely request with sufficient information to allow the University to make a decision. The unit member's application shall identify the period during which s/he wishes to be on leave. The unit member shall be advised of the decision in writing in a timely manner. If the request is denied, the reason(s) for denial shall not be arbitrary, capricious, or unreasonable.

   c. A librarian in the unit on approved leave of absence without pay may elect to continue University-sponsored life insurance, health plans and dental coverage for the period of the leave. A librarian in the unit who so elects must make arrangements with the University prior to commencement of the leave to pay the entire premium amount herself/himself.

   d. If the librarian is on leave without pay more than half a calendar month, sick leave, vacation, seniority credit and retirement credit do not accrue.

C. Leaves With Pay

   1. Leave With Pay to Attend Professional Meeting. A librarian in the unit may be granted a leave with pay to attend a professional meeting. Request for such leave shall be made by the librarian in the unit who will provide the University with sufficient specific information so that a decision can be made. Request for such leave shall be made early enough to allow time for a reasoned decision.

   2. Other Leaves With Pay. Other leaves of absence with pay may be granted to a librarian in the unit for good cause. Librarians who wish a leave of absence with pay shall submit a timely request for such leave with sufficient specific information to allow the University to make a decision.

D. This Article does not establish a right of a unit member to receive leave under this Article.

E. In the event of a grievance under this Article culminating in arbitration, to the extent that the University's action is based upon academic judgment, the arbitrator shall have no authority or jurisdiction to substitute his/her judgment for that of the University and its agents.

XX. SICK LEAVE

A. Eligibility. Librarians in the unit on pay status for at least fifty percent (50%) or more of full time are eligible to accumulate sick leave credit based on the percentage of time on pay status up to a maximum of one (1) working day per month for full time service. Sick leave may be accumulated without limit. Sick leave is earned during leave with pay. Sick leave is credited at the end of the month it is earned.

B. Use of Accumulated Sick Leave

1. Librarians are expected to use sick leave in keeping with normally approved purposes--personal illness, disability, medical appointment, attendance to the illness of a family member, or bereavement. Accumulated sick leave may be used for temporary disability related to pregnancy, childbirth, and recovery therefrom.

2. A librarian in the unit may be required to submit satisfactory proof of illness or disability.

3. Sick leave shall not be used prior to the time it is credited nor shall sick leave be used beyond a predetermined separation date.

4. Regularly scheduled days off and University administrative holidays shall not be charged against sick leave.

5. While receiving injury or health compensation under the Worker's Compensation Act, an absent librarian in the unit may also receive sick leave benefits provided the total of the sick leave pay and worker's compensation does not exceed the employee's regular salary for the period.

C. Reporting. Once a month, each librarian in the unit shall report sick leave used to the appropriate office. Once a month, the University shall report to each librarian in the unit on the accumulation and use of sick leave.

D. Sick Leave Retirement Credit. Upon retirement, accumulated sick leave shall be converted to retirement service credit at the rate of .004 of a year (2,080 work hours in a year divided into 8 equals .00384 which is then rounded off) for each day of unused accumulated sick leave.

Appendix II

XXI. **VACATION**

   A. Accumulation

      1. Vacation accumulates at the rate of two (2) working days a month for full time service for members of the unit appointed for six (6) months or more. For part time librarians in the unit appointed at fifty percent (50%) or more of full time, vacation accumulates at a proportionate rate of full time credit. For part time librarians in the unit appointed less than fifty percent (50%) of full time, there is no vacation allowance.

      2. Vacation allowance shall not accumulate during a leave of absence without pay. Vacation credit shall be accumulated by a librarian in the unit on a leave of absence with pay.

      3. Vacation credit may accumulate to a maximum of forty-eight (48) working days.

   B. Use of Accumulated Vacation

      1. Accumulated vacation shall be used at a time or times in keeping with the program of work being conducted by the librarian in the unit, and approved by the designated University official. When a librarian is not able to use accumulated vacation because of the programmatic needs of the campus and the librarian's accumulation reaches the forty-eight (48) working day maximum, a one-time exception will be granted to allow the librarian to accumulate six (6) additional vacation days. Upon request of the librarian in the unit, the reason for denial of a vacation request shall be provided in writing.

      2. Regularly scheduled days off and University administrative holidays shall not be charged against vacation time.

      3. Except when a campus allows the use of anticipated vacation in times of holiday closures, a librarian in the unit may not anticipate vacation, that is, vacation is limited to the vacation time actually accumulated by the date set for the librarian's vacation.

      4. During holiday closures librarians in the unit who are not required to work may use vacation, take leave without pay, or request alternative arrangements. The University's decision regarding alternative arrangements shall not be capricious or unreasonable and shall not be subject to the Arbitration procedures of this Agreement.

C. Terminal Vacation Pay

  1. A librarian in the unit who is resigning or otherwise leaving University service and who has been unable to use accumulated vacation time, shall be paid for vacation in an amount equal to the salary which would have been received for the vacation period if the librarian in the unit had continued in University service subject to the following restrictions:

     a. terminal vacation pay may not exceed forty-eight (48) working days' salary;

     b. a librarian in the unit who resigns within six (6) months after initial appointment is entitled to terminal vacation pay;

     c. the last day of work shall be the effective date of termination except that a librarian in the unit who is retiring may use vacation up to the effective date of retirement.

  2. A librarian in the unit who dies shall have his or her accumulated vacation credit paid to his/her designated beneficiary.

D. Usage. A librarian in the unit with accumulated vacation credit who is granted extended military leave shall be paid for vacation credit through his/her last day of work.

E. Reporting. Once a month, each librarian in the unit shall report vacation used to the appropriate office. Once a month, the University shall report to each librarian in the unit on the accumulation and use of vacation leave.

XXII. HOLIDAYS

A. Observance

  1. The University observes the following days as administrative holidays:

New Year's Day	Thanksgiving Day
Third Monday in January	Friday following Thanksgiving Day
Third Monday in February (or announced equivalent)	(or announced equivalent)
	December 24 (or announced equivalent)
Last Monday in May	Christmas Day
Fourth of July	December 31 (or announced equivalent)

Appendix II

        Labor Day   one administrative holiday to be selected by the University.

Unless alternate days are designated by the University, when a holiday falls on a Sunday, the following Monday is observed; and when a holiday falls on a Saturday, the preceding Friday is observed.

2. A librarian in the unit required to work on a holiday listed in paragraph 1 of this section shall be paid regular pay for the day. In addition, s/he shall receive time off equivalent to the time worked.

3. A librarian in the unit whose regular day off falls on a holiday listed in paragraph 1 of this section shall receive one (1) day off.

4. A librarian in the unit may observe a special or religious holiday by charging time off to accumulated vacation or leave without pay.

B. Eligibility

1. To be eligible for holiday pay a librarian in the unit must have been on pay status or on approved leave with pay on his/her last scheduled work day before the holiday and first scheduled work day after the holiday. New and rehired full-time librarians in the unit shall receive pay for any holiday immediately preceding their first day of work if the holiday is the first working day(s) of the month. A terminating full-time librarian in the unit shall receive holiday pay for any holiday immediately following his/her last day of work provided the holiday is last working day(s) of the month. Librarians in the unit appointed at fifty percent (50%) or more of full time shall receive pro rata holiday pay.

2. This policy may be waived by the University at times of campus holiday closures.

3. Periods of academic recess are not regarded as holidays.

C. Usage

All time off with pay, mentioned in the above paragraphs, shall be scheduled at times mutually convenient to the librarian in the unit and the University.

XXIII. **INDEMNITY**

The University shall provide the defense and indemnification for a librarian in the unit sued on account of acts or omissions in the course and scope of his or her employment where required by the provisions of California Government Code section 995, et seq. (State Tort Claims Act). Disputes arising under this Article shall be subject to the Grievance but not the Arbitration procedures in this Agreement.

XXIV. **CORRECTIVE ACTION, DISMISSAL, RELEASE**

A. Definitions

1. Corrective action is a written censure or suspension.

2. Dismissal is the termination of the employment of a potential career or career status librarian in the unit initiated by the University for just cause.

3. Release is the termination of the employment of a temporary librarian in the unit prior to the completion of her/his appointment.

B. Grounds

1. Librarians in the unit may be subject to corrective action or dismissal for just cause. Corrective action or dismissal for just cause in this Article shall not be based upon academic judgments.

2. Release. Temporary librarians in the unit who are released prior to the conclusion of their period of appointment shall be given written notice and a right to an informal hearing under Section F-1 of this Article.

C. Written censure is a formal reprimand which must be delivered confidentially to the recipient. It is to be distinguished from an informal spoken warning, which is not an official corrective action. If a copy of the written censure is to be placed in the unit member's personnel file, the University shall provide at least five (5) calendar days' prior notice of the pending action in order that the librarian in the unit may request a conference with the initiator of the written censure. The purpose of the meeting is to discuss the reasons for the written censure and seek alternative resolution of the causes of the proposed action. If a copy of the written censure is placed in the librarian's personnel file, it shall be done according to procedures listed in Article V (Personnel Files) of this Agreement. If there is no recurrence for a period of one (1) year of the reasons

Appendix II

which caused placement of the written censure in the librarian's file, the censure shall be returned to the librarian at the completion of the then current review cycle.

D. Interim suspension with full pay is a precautionary action, not a form of corrective action, which may be imposed when the librarian's continued assignment to regular duties will be immediately and seriously harmful to the continued and efficient operation of the library. The University will immediately provide written reasons for the interim suspension to the librarian affected. In any circumstance the University shall either reinstate the librarian or initiate corrective action procedures within fifteen (15) working days of the notification of interim suspension.

E. Notice

1. When required. The University may take corrective action without prior notice by imposing suspension without pay for five (5) working days or less. The University shall provide written notice, as described in Section E-2 below, of intent to discipline by suspension without pay for more than five (5) working days, or by dismissal.

2. Issuance and Content.

    a. Issuance. Written notice of intent shall be given to the affected librarian in the unit, either by delivery of the notice to the librarian in the unit in person, or by placing the Notice of Intent in the United States Mail, certified, postage-paid, in an envelope addressed to the librarian's last known home address. Such personal delivery or mailing shall be conclusively presumed to provide actual notice of the intended action to the affected librarian. The University shall simultaneously send a copy of the notice to the UFL. It shall be the responsibility of each librarian in the unit to inform the University in writing of his/her current home address and of any change in such address, and the information so provided shall constitute "the librarian's last known home address." Whether delivery is made in person or by mail, the Notice of Intent shall contain a "statement of delivery or mailing" indicating the date on which the Notice of Intent was personally delivered or deposited in the United States Mail. Such date of delivery or mailing shall be the "date of issuance" of a Notice of Intent.

b. Content. The notice shall:

  1) inform the librarian in the unit of the intended corrective action and the effective date of the intended action;

  2) provide the reason(s) for the intended action, including, where available, materials upon which the intended action is based;

  3) inform the librarian of the right to respond, the right of his/her representation by the UFL or a person of his/her choice, the person to whom any response must be directed, and the fact that the librarian is entitled to an informal hearing to discuss the proposed corrective action; and

  4) indicate that the University must receive (a) a written response within ten (10) calendar days, or (b) a written request for an informal hearing within ten (10) calendar days from the date of the mailing of the Notice of Intent and/or date of delivery in person.

F. Response to Notice

The librarian may have a review of the University's proposed corrective action by responding to the Notice of Intent either: (a) at an informal hearing; or (b) directly to the University in writing.

  1. If an informal hearing occurs, it shall be conducted by the initiator of corrective action and/or an appropriate University official. The librarian in the unit is entitled to representation by the UFL or a representative of his/her choosing. The purpose of this informal hearing is to seek a resolution outside the formal grievance procedure. At the conclusion of the informal hearing or no later than five (5) working days thereafter, the University will provide the librarian in the unit with a written response stating its decision. If no resolution is forthcoming from the informal hearing, a Potential Career Status or Career Status librarian may seek further redress through the formal Grievance procedure.

  2. If the librarian responds in writing to the University in a timely manner, the University, in turn, will respond in writing to the librarian prior to the imposition of the corrective action. The University response will give reasons for any corrective action

Appendix II

which is to be taken. Such action may not be more severe than that described in the Notice of Intent, but it may be less severe.

G. Appeal

1. A librarian in the unit may appeal a decision of the University to impose corrective action.

2. Within ten (10) calendar days of the issuance of the written response by the University in F above, the librarian may file a written notice of appeal in accordance with Step 3 Formal Review of the Grievance Procedure, Article XXV.

H. Time Limits. Time limits for filing an appeal under the Grievance Procedure for corrective action shall commence when the University issues the Notice of Intent unless the librarian (a) requests an informal hearing, or (b) responds in writing. In these cases, the time limit begins when the University responds to the librarian with the University's decision as outlined in Section F.

XXV. GRIEVANCE PROCEDURE

A. Definition, Standing, Consolidation and Representation

1. Definition. A grievance is a claim that during the term of this Agreement the University has violated, misapplied, or misinterpreted certain Articles of this Agreement.

2. Standing. Except as otherwise provided in this Agreement, a grievance may be brought to the attention of the University through this procedure by a librarian in the unit or by the UFL. A grievance may not be brought through this procedure by the University.

3. Consolidation. Grievances brought by, or related to, two (2) or more librarians in the unit, and multiple grievances by or related to the same unit member, which concern the same incident, issue or course of conduct, may be consolidated for the purposes of this procedure; provided that the time limits described in this Article shall not be shortened for any grievance because of the consolidation of that grievance with other grievances. Consolidated grievances may be severed. Consolidation or severance of a grievance shall occur by agreement between the librarian in the unit or the librarian's representative and the University.

4. Representation. A librarian in the unit grieving pursuant to this Article may be represented by him/herself or by any one person of the librarian's choice so long as that representative's duties at the University are not managerial, supervisory, or confidential within the meaning of the Higher Education Employer-Employee Relations Act. When a unit member is represented by the UFL, that representative may be assisted in meetings by other unit members or AFT staff. Whenever a representative other than an official of the UFL is to provide representation, the librarian in the unit shall provide written notice of such representation to the University. The University shall notify the UFL of any formal grievances filed where a UFL official is not chosen as the representative of the grievant.

B. Step 1. Informal Discussion. As soon as practicable, the librarian in the unit shall discuss the grievance with his or her immediate supervisor. Informal resolutions, although final, shall not be precedential under this Agreement. Settlement offers made in the informal process shall be inadmissible in subsequent steps. An oral response may be given in the course of the informal discussion. If not, an oral response shall be given within five (5) working days following the informal discussion. If the complaint is not resolved through this informal discussion, the librarian may seek review as set forth below. Attempts at informal discussion do not extend the time limit to file for a formal review unless an extension of the time limit has been agreed to by the librarian in the unit or the librarian's representative and the University grievance officer, in writing, prior to the filing of the grievance.

C. Step 2. Informal Review. Following completion of Step 1, the grievant may seek a review with a designated University official of the discussions held at Step 1 with a view to resolving the grievance. The same conditions stated in Step 1 shall apply to Step 2. The informal review shall take place within five (5) working days of the request. Attempts at informal review do not extend the time limit to file for a formal review unless an extension of the time limit has been agreed to by the librarian in the unit or the librarian's representative and the University grievance officer, in writing, prior to the filing of the grievance.

D. Step 3. Formal Review

1. Filing. A grievant who has completed Step 1 of this procedure may file a formal grievance as set forth in a-d below.

   a. The grievance must be filed in writing on a grievance form agreed to by the parties provided by the University, and agreed to at a later time by

Appendix II

the parties. This form provided by the University shall identify by name, title, and campus address the designated University official with whom the grievance must be filed (hereinafter, the "grievance officer").

b. The grievance officer must receive the written grievance within thirty (30) calendar days after the date on which the librarian in the unit or the UFL knew or could be expected to know of the event or action which gave rise to the grievance or within fifteen (15) calendar days after the date of the librarian's separation from University employment, whichever occurs first.

c. Any grievance which is filed out of compliance with these time limits is waived by the grievant and the UFL. Attempts at informal resolution do not extend the time limit to file for a formal review unless an extension of the time limit has been agreed to by the librarian in the unit or the librarian's representative and the University grievance officer, in writing, prior to the filing of the grievance.

d. The written grievance must contain the following information:

   1) the specific section or subsection of the Agreement alleged to have been violated, misapplied, or misinterpreted;

   2) the action grieved and how it violated the above-described part of the Agreement;

   3) how the librarian was adversely affected; and

   4) the remedy requested.

2. <u>Campus Review.</u> Within fifteen (15) working days of the receipt of the formal grievance, the grievance officer or his or her designee shall complete a review to determine the merits of the grievance. If either the grievant or the grievance officer requests a meeting, one shall be conducted as soon as reasonably possible to discuss the grievance. If a meeting occurs, the grievant and/or the grievant's representative may be present. Also, the grievant or the grievant's representative shall be able to bring people to the meeting to present information about the grievance. The grievant is encouraged to present known evidence and contentions relevant to the grievance at this campus

review. Contentions not made known by the parties at this time are inadmissible in subsequent stages of Step 3 Formal Review.

3. Initial Decision. The University shall render a written decision within fifteen (15) working days of the completion of the campus review. Notice to the grievant of the University's decision will be as set forth in a. and b. below.

   a. For grievances where the UFL represents the grievant, the decision of the University shall become final within twenty (20) calendar days of the mailing of the decision to the grievant and the grievant's representative by the University, unless within that time, the grievant has appealed the decision to a designated University official.

   b. For grievances where the UFL does not represent the grievant, the University will mail to the UFL a copy of the grievance and the proposed resolution. The decision of the University shall become final so long as the adjustment is not inconsistent with the terms of this Agreement and provided that the UFL has been given ten (10) calendar days to file a response. The University will then mail its decision to the grievant or the grievant's representative, if any. The decision shall become final within twenty (20) calendar days of the mailing of the decision to the grievant or the grievant's representative, if any, by the University, unless within that time, the grievant has appealed the decision to a designated University official.

E. Step 4 Final University Decision

1. The appeal shall be considered by the designated University official, who shall render a final decision as soon as practicable, but not later than thirty (30) working days after the receipt of the appeal.

2. Copies of all final determinations shall be mailed to the grievant or the grievant's representative and the UFL. The University's determination shall become final twenty (20) calendar days after its mailing unless the UFL appeals to arbitration in a timely fashion.

3. Except by agreement between the grievant and/or the grievant's representative and the University, documents and communications related to the process of a grievance that are filed with the University shall be kept separate from the grievant's personnel files.

Appendix II

F. **Time Limits.** Any time limit herein may be extended by mutual agreement of the parties in writing in advance of the expiration of that time limit. If a University official fails to heed a deadline, the grievant may move the grievance to the next step in the process. Deadlines which fall on days which are not business days at the campus at which the grievance is filed will be automatically extended to the next business day.

G. **Pay Status**

   1. Whenever a grievant or a grievant's representative who is a University employee attends a meeting to consider a grievance, and that meeting takes place at the University's request during the scheduled worktime of the librarian or the representative, then reasonable released time shall be granted to the grievant and/or the grievant's representative, provided that each such employee has arranged his/her absence in advance and the work needs of the library do not require the librarian's presence during the time in question.

   2. One (1) UFL representative per campus may use up to four (4) hours per week on released time to process grievances provided that each such employee has arranged his/her absence in advance and the work needs of the library do not require the librarian's presence during the time in question.

   3. Any other time spent by grievants or their representatives in meetings relating to grievances, and all other time spent in investigation and preparation of a grievance, shall not be on pay status.

H. **Sexual Harassment Complaint Resolution Procedure**

   The UFL agrees that a librarian in the unit covered by this Agreement may elect to substitute a University Sexual Harassment Complaint Resolution Procedure for the **Step 1 Informal Discussion** described in this Article, provided that at the grievant's request a UFL representative may be present at the meeting on behalf of the grievant.

I. The procedures described in this Article shall be the sole and exclusive means of resolving grievances related to this Agreement submitted by a librarian in the unit or the UFL with the exception of Sexual Harassment Complaint Resolution Procedure (H. above) and the Appeal procedure in Article XXIV, Corrective Action, Dismissal, Release. This does not preclude a librarian in the unit from seeking redress in an agency or court of competent jurisdiction for grievances which are not subject to the Arbitration Procedure in Article XXVI. Should a librarian institute any action before an agency or court of competent jurisdiction involving an issue which is being processed in the grievance procedure of this Agreement, the filing of the action outside the grievance procedure shall constitute an automatic withdrawal of the grievance.

XXVI. **ARBITRATION**

   A. An appeal to arbitration may be made only by the UFL and only after the timely exhaustion of Article XXV of this Agreement. The appeal to arbitration must be received by the designee of the Office of the President within twenty (20) calendar days of the mailing of the final University decision to the UFL (Article XXV E. Step 4). Proof of service must accompany the appeal to arbitration. In the appeal, the UFL must set forth the issues and remedies remaining unresolved. Absent resolution during this period, the designee of the Office of the President shall forward the grievance to arbitration within twenty (20) calendar days of the mailing of the appeal.

   B. Panel of Arbitrators

   1. The parties shall select a panel of arbitrators at a later date.

   2. In the event of a vacancy in the panel of arbitrators, such vacancy shall be filled by the parties within fifteen (15) calendar days if the parties agree that a replacement is necessary.

   3. The parties shall alternately strike one name each from the above list(s), the first strike being determined by a flip of a coin, and the last name remaining shall be the arbitrator.

   C. Prior to arbitration, the UFL and the University shall attempt to stipulate as to the issue(s) to be arbitrated and to as many facts as possible. When possible, the parties shall inform each other who shall be witnesses at least five (5) calendar days prior to the hearing.

   D. Expedited Arbitration. The parties may agree to use an expedited form of arbitration. When the parties agree to use an expedited form of arbitration, the case shall be heard by the arbitrator at his/her earliest date. There shall be no transcript of the proceedings. Post-hearing briefs will be waived and the arbitrator will issue a written decision within ten (10) working days following the close of the hearing record. In all other procedures the arbitrator shall be guided by the American Arbitration Association Expedited Arbitration Rules where applicable.

Appendix II

E. Arbitration

1. The arbitration proceeding shall provide an opportunity for the UFL and the University to examine and cross-examine witnesses under oath and to submit relevant evidence. The parties shall not seek to introduce new issues and allegations at the arbitration hearing which were not introduced during Step 3 Formal Review of the Grievance Procedure, Article XXV, unless they were unknown at that time and could not have been discovered with reasonable diligence. Settlement offers made during the Grievance Procedure shall not be introduced as evidence in arbitration.

2. The arbitration hearing shall be closed unless the parties otherwise agree in writing.

3. The arbitrator shall consider the evidence presented and render a written decision within thirty (30) calendar days of the close of the record of the hearing. The arbitrator's decision will set forth the arbitrator's findings of fact, reasoning, and conclusions on the issues submitted by the parties. The arbitrator's authority shall be limited to determining whether the University has violated the provision(s) of this Agreement. The arbitrator shall not have jurisdiction or authority to add to, amend, modify, nullify, or ignore in any way the provisions of this Agreement nor shall the arbitrator review any academic judgment. To the extent that the University's action is based upon academic judgment, the arbitrator shall have no authority or jurisdiction to substitute his/her judgment for that of the University and its agents.

4. If the grievance is sustained in whole or in part, the remedy shall not exceed restoring to the librarian the pay, benefits, or rights lost as a result of a violation of the Agreement, less any compensation from any source recognized by law as appropriate to offset such a remedy. The decision and award of the arbitrator, within the limits described herein, shall be final and binding upon the parties to this Agreement and the librarians in the unit.

5. The arbitrator's fees shall be borne equally by the parties. Concerning transcripts, the cost shall be equally borne by the parties, if a transcript is requested by the arbitrator or both parties. If a copy of the transcript is requested by only one party, that party shall incur the expense.

F. Extension of Time Limits. Time limits may be extended by mutual agreement of the parties in writing in advance of the expiration of the time limit.

G. Pay Status. Upon advance request, the grievant, the grievant's representative, and witnesses called by the parties who are University employees shall be granted leave with pay to attend arbitration hearings and meetings convened by the University to consider grievances if such hearings and meetings occur during their regularly scheduled hours of work. Such leave with pay will be considered time worked. Time spent in arbitration hearings and meetings outside of a librarian's regularly scheduled hours of work is without pay.

H. Except as otherwise specifically provided, the University will not be liable on a grievance claiming back wages or other monetary reimbursement for:

1. any period of time during which an extension of time limits has been granted at the request of the UFL;

2. any period of time between the first date the arbitrator is available for an arbitration hearing and the date of the hearing, when the first date is rejected by the UFL; and

3. any period of time greater than thirty (30) calendar days prior to the date of the Informal Review, Step 2 under Article XXV, except for mathematical, calculation, recording, or accounting errors.

XXVII. CONCERTED ACTIVITIES

A. During the term of this Agreement, or any written extension thereof, the University agrees that there will be no lockout by the University.

B. During the term of this Agreement, or any written extension thereof, the UFL, on behalf of its officers, agents and unit members, agrees that there shall be no concerted activities which would interfere with the operations of the University nor any strikes.

C. During the term of this Agreement, or any written extension thereof, the UFL, its officers, agents, and unit members agree that they shall not in any way participate in, or lend support to, any strikes or concerted activities of any kind in violation of this Article.

D. Any librarian in the unit who violates this Article may be subject to corrective action up to and including termination of employment. The UFL shall have the right to appeal any action constituting corrective action administered to a librarian in the unit by the University under this Article.

Appendix II

- E. Should any activities in violation of this Article occur, the UFL shall immediately take whatever affirmative action is necessary to prevent and/or bring about the termination of such action or interference with the operations of the libraries. Such affirmative action shall consist of sending an immediate written notice to all unit members at their work and home addresses stating that they must cease their violation of this Agreement, and that they may be subject to corrective action up to and including dismissal.
- F. Nothing herein constitutes a waiver of the University's right to seek appropriate legal relief in the event of a violation of this Article.

XXVIII. **SEVERABILITY**

- A. In the event that any provision of this Agreement is declared invalid or void by statute or judicial decision, or when an appropriate administrative agency has issued a final decision, such action shall not invalidate the entire Agreement. It is the express intention of the parties that all other provisions not declared invalid or void shall remain in full force and effect. In the event that any provision of this Agreement is declared invalid or void, the parties agree to meet within thirty (30) calendar days upon request of either party in an attempt to reach an agreement on a substitute provision.
- B. In the event of a final judicial determination requiring the University to provide access to confidential material and/or to its internal campus mail system, the parties agree to meet within thirty (30) calendar days upon request of either party in an attempt to reach an agreement on a substitute provision for the appropriate Article(s) of this Agreement.

XXIX. **WAIVER**

- A. The University and the UFL acknowledge that during the negotiations which resulted in this Agreement, each party had the right and opportunity to make demands and proposals with respect to any subject or matter not removed by law from the area of collective bargaining, and that this Agreement constitutes the entire contract arrived at by the parties after the exercise of that right and opportunity.
- B. Although the memorandum of understanding constitutes the entire Agreement between the parties, the University and the UFL agree that certain specific policies and procedures related to:

1. Recruitment;
2. The Librarian Code of Professional Conduct;
3. The Librarian Series;
4. The application of the Academic Personnel Manual;
5. The Librarians Association of the University of California (LAUC);
6. Peer Review;
7. Professional Activities and Development;
8. Programs, Service and Technological Change; and
9. Review Packet Inspection

are not part of this Agreement. Upon the ratification and concurrence of this Agreement by the parties these policies and procedures shall become effective immediately as provisions of the Academic Personnel Manual (APM). The content of these policies and procedures shall be attached to and circulated with this Agreement. These policies and procedures shall remain in full force and effect unless or until modified by the University and LAUC. The UFL waives its right to meet and confer on these professional concerns for the duration of the Agreement; however, the UFL reserves its right to meet and discuss these matters with the University. In recognition of this the UFL further agrees that these matters are not subject to the Grievance and Arbitration Procedures in this Agreement, but the issue of compliance with the distribution of the contents and the inclusion in the APM are grievable and arbitrable. The processes for addressing these professional concerns are expressly understood by the parties to be outside this Agreement and are not intended to bear on or modify the terms of this Agreement in any way.

C. Except as otherwise provided for in this Agreement, or upon mutual consent of the parties to seek written amendment thereto, the University and the UFL, for the term of this Agreement, each voluntarily and unqualifiedly waive the right, and each agrees that the other shall not be obligated to bargain collectively with respect to any subject or matter whether or not raised during negotiations or specifically referred to or covered in this Agreement, even though such subject or matter may not have been within the knowledge or contemplation of the parties at the time they negotiated or signed this Agreement.

Appendix II

XXX. DURATION OF AGREEMENT

A. The terms and conditions of this Agreement shall remain in full force and effect until June 30, 1988.

B. Each party shall have the opportunity to reopen the Agreement for each of the fiscal years 1986-1987 and 1987-1988 subject to the public notice provision of HEERA. The University and the UFL shall each have the right to reopen the Agreement in each of these fiscal years for the purpose of negotiating amendments to the provisions of the Salary Article and the University Benefits Article and not more than three (3) other Articles of this Agreement. Each party shall have the right to make proposals related to the Article(s) designated for amendment by the other party. In addition, each party shall have the opportunity to introduce one (1) new article at each reopener period.

C. The requirements for the University and/or the UFL to reopen this Agreement are as follows:

   1. Fiscal Year 1986-1987:

      a. For the fiscal year 1986-1987 the UFL shall, no later than one hundred and twenty (120) calendar days prior to July 1, 1986, serve in writing upon the Assistant Vice President, Labor Relations of the University notice of its intent to reopen this Agreement. Included in such notice shall be the designation and identification by heading of the Articles which the UFL intends to amend.

      b. The University shall, no later than ninety (90) calendar days prior to July 1, 1986, serve in writing upon the UFL notice of its intent to reopen this Agreement. Included in such notice shall be the designation and identification by heading of the Articles which the University intends to amend.

   2. Fiscal Year 1987-1988

      a. For the fiscal year 1987-1988 the UFL shall, no later than one hundred and twenty (120) calendar days prior to July 1, 1987, serve in writing upon the Assistant Vice President, Labor Relations of the University notice of its intent to reopen this Agreement. Included in such notice shall be the designation and identification by heading of the Articles which the UFL intends to amend.

      b. The University shall, no later than ninety (90) calendar days prior to July 1, 1987, serve upon the UFL in writing notice of its intent to reopen this Agreement. Included in such notice shall be the designation and identification by heading of the Articles which the University intends to amend.

   3. Timely notice as indicated in 1. and 2. above given by either or both parties to this Agreement shall impose the duty to engage in meeting and conferring for the purposes of negotiating amendments to the Articles so specified.

   4. Neither party shall have any obligation or requirement to negotiate on any provision of any Article not timely designated.

   5. During the period of negotiations on Articles properly designated as reopeners, the terms and conditions of this Agreement, including those Articles designated for amendment, shall remain in full force and effect.

   6. In the event that neither the University nor the UFL accomplishes timely notice of intent to reopen, the terms and conditions of this Agreement shall remain in full force and effect until the expiration of this Agreement in 1988.

D. Proposals for a successor Agreement shall be presented to the University by the UFL no later than February 1, 1988.

APPENDIX A

Rank	Step	Normal Period at Salary	7/1/85 Annual	Scales Monthly
Assistant Librarian	I	one year	$22,224	$1,852
3620 Career	II	one year	23,208	1,934
3621 Potential Career	III	one year	24,456	2,038
3622 Temporary	IV	one year	25,728	2,144
	V	one year	27,156	2,263
	VI	one year	28,428	2,369
Associate Librarian	I	one year	27,156	2,263
3616 Career	II	one year	28,428	2,369
3617 Potential Career	III	two years	29,820	2,485
3618 Temporary	IV	two years	31,872	2,656
	V	two years	34,080	2,840
	VI	two years	36,504	3,042
	VII	two years (or--)	39,108	3,259
Librarian	I	two years	36,504	3,042
3612 Career	II	two years	39,108	3,259
3613 Potential Career	III	three years	41,712	3,476
3614 Temporary	IV	three years (or--)	45,936	3,828
	V	- -	50,604	4,217

Rank	Step	Normal Period at Salary	1/1/86 Annual	Scales Monthly
Assistant Librarian	I	one year	$22,872	$1,906
3620 Career	II	one year	23,892	1,991
3621 Potential Career	III	one year	25,176	2,098
3622 Temporary	IV	one year	26,472	2,206
	V	one year	27,948	2,329
	VI	one year	29,256	2,438
Associate Librarian	I	one year	27,948	2,329
3616 Career	II	one year	29,256	2,438
3617 Potential Career	III	two years	30,696	2,558
3618 Temporary	IV	two years	32,808	2,734
	V	two years	35,076	2,923
	VI	two years	37,572	3,131
	VII	two years(or--)	40,248	3,354
Librarian	I	two years	37,572	3,131
3612 Career	II	two years	40,248	3,354
3613 Potential Career	III	three years	42,936	3,578
3614 Temporary	IV	three years (or--)	47,292	3,941
	V	- -	52,092	4,341

Librarians' Agreements

FOR THE UNIVERSITY OF CALIFORNIA

Sarah Jo Gilpin-Bishop
Sarah Jo Gilpin-Bishop
Chief Negotiator

Sharon Hayden
Sharon Hayden
Asst. Negotiator/Chronologer

Barbara Davia
Barbara Davia, UCI

Allan Dyson
Allan Dyson, UCSC

Jeffery Frumkin
Jeffery Frumkin
Office of the President

Virginia George
Virginia George
Office of the General Counsel

Debra Harrington
Debra Harrington, UCB

Karl J. Hittelman
Karl J. Hittelman, UCSF

Katherine F. Mawdsley
Katherine F. Mawdsley, UCD

Myron Okada
Myron Okada
Office of the President

Sandra Rich
Sandra Rich, UCLA

John Tanno
John Tanno, UCR

FOR THE UNIVERISTY
FEDERATION OF LIBRARIANS
UNIVERSITY COUNCIL - AFT

Miki Goral
Miki Goral, UCLA
Chief Negotiator

Robert E. Fessenden
Robert E. Fessenden, UCSC

Justine Roberts
Justine Roberts, UCSF

William L. Whitson
William L. Whitson, UCB

Appendix II

UNIVERSITY FEDERATION OF LIBRARIANS
UNIVERSITY COUNCIL - AMERICAN FEDERATION OF TEACHERS

By: _____   _____7/3/85_____
    Nancy Elnor, President   Date

THE REGENTS OF THE UNIVERSITY OF CALIFORNIA

By: _____   _____7/3/85_____
    Richard M. Catalano   Date
    Assistant Vice President
    Labor Relations

Approved as to Form:

By: _____   _____June 7, 1985_____
    James N. Odle   Date
    Managing Associate Counsel of the Regents
    of the University of California

Appendix II

INDEX

Article

Arbitration	XXVI
Campus Closures, Use of Vacation	XXI
Concerted Activities	XXVII
Contract Distribution	IX
Corrective Action	XXIV
Dental Program	XIII
Discrimination	II
Dismissal	XXIV
Dues Deduction	XI
Duration	XXX
Emergency Leave	XVIII
Fee Waiver	XIV
Government Leaves	XIX
Grievance Procedure	XXV
Health and Safety	VIII
Health Plans	XIII
Holidays	XXII
Indemnity	XXIII
Jury Duty Leave	XVIII
Layoff	VII
Leaves of Absence	XVIII
Lockouts	XXVII

Article

Management Rights	XVI
Military Leave	XVIII
Non-Discrimination	II
Payroll Deductions	XI
Per Diem	XV
Personnel Files	V
Process for Promotion and Advancement	IV
Professional Activities	III
Professional Development	III
Promotion Procedures	IV
Reassignment	VI
Recognition	I
Release Time	X
Research Funds	III
Salary	XII
Salary Scale	Appendix A
Severability	XXVIII
Sick Leave	XX
Special Leave With Pay	XIX
Special Leave Without Pay	XIX
Special Two-Month Leave	XIX
Strikes	XXVII
Temporary Appointments	XVII
Time, use of	III
Transfer	VI

Appendix II

Article

Two-Month Leaves..XIX
UFL Rights..IX
Union Rights..IX
University Benefits.......................................XIII
Vacation..XXI
Waiver..XXIX
Witness Leave...XVIII

NOTA BENE

The attached information concerning professional and governance concerns is being circulated with the Agreement between the University of California and the University Federation of Librarians. This material is not a part of the Agreement. This material became a part of the Academic Personnel Manual (APM) of the University of California in accordance with the understandings reached by the parties as stated in the Waiver Article of the Agreement. This distribution is for informational purposes to provide individuals with the textual changes in the APM until such time as revisions to the APM can be completed.

Appendix II

PROFESSIONAL and GOVERNANCE CONCERNS

Introduction

It is widely acknowledged that the University of California is a distinguished institution, one of the world's outstanding centers of learning. The libraries have contributed significantly to its excellence. In a very real sense, this reflects the quality of the librarians who develop and maintain the libraries' collections and services. Peer review, along with several other aspects of academic and professional activities, is at the heart of the University's ability to identify, reward, and nurture excellence in its midst. It is in the spirit of strengthening these traditional, proven foundations of excellence that the parties proposed various other professional governance mechanisms and academic practices be addressed separately from the Agreement.

The Legislature has recognized that joint decision making and consultation between the University administration and academic employees are long-accepted traditions of governance in institutions of higher learning and are important to the performance of the educational missions of such institutions. A stated purpose of the Higher Education Employer-Employee Relations Act is to preserve and encourage that process. The principle of peer review is specifically mentioned as a principle that shall be preserved. Further, in defining "employee organization," the Act states that an academic senate or other similar academic body shall not be considered an employee organization for the purposes of HEERA. Peer review, shared governance, and the activity of the Librarians Association of the University of California are important to the parties and recognized by the statute as being unique to academic employees.

In this first set of negotiations between the University of California and the University Federation of Librarians, the parties have an opportunity to increase creative involvement and dynamic problem solving of critical issues important to the parties. The document that follows represents the first attempt to codify certain procedures and principles for all. It embodies procedures that will evolve as the needs of the University and the librarians change. Success will depend upon the sense of trust and mutual dependency the parties have been able to develop in their brief bargaining history, the commitment of the University of California administration to implement these codified solutions, and the role LAUC assumes in the evolution of these processes.

LIBRARIAN SERIES

A. Potential Career appointees in the Librarian Series are eligible for career status, merit increases and promotion through the ranks from Assistant Librarian to Librarian.

B. A librarian need not assume administrative responsibilities in order to reach the highest rank.

C. All librarians at a given rank and step shall be paid identical salaries, in accordance with the published salary scales for the Librarian Series, regardless of the presence or absence of administrative responsibilities.

D. Temporary Appointees in the Librarian Series are expected to perform their duties with the same proficiency as the Career Status and Potential Career Status appointees in accordance with the terms of their appointment letters.

ACADEMIC PERSONNEL MANUAL

Those sections of the then current Academic Personnel Manual (APM) which apply to librarians will continue in full force and effect unless modified by these revisions of the APM.

LIBRARIANS ASSOCIATION OF THE UNIVERSITY OF CALIFORNIA

A. The Librarians Association of the University of California (LAUC) shall continue to advise the University, the campus, and the library administration on the operations and policies of the libraries. One copy of each report filed by the LAUC President with the University will be forwarded by the University to the UFL.

B. LAUC will not advise the University, the campus, and the library administration with respect to matters which are covered by the memorandum of understanding between the University and the UFL.

PROGRAM, SERVICE, AND TECHNOLOGICAL CHANGES

The Librarians Association of the University of California shall advise the University, the campus, and the library administration in the planning, evaluation, and implementation of any major program, services, or technological changes in the libraries of the University of California.

RECRUITMENT

The University, in accordance with campus procedures developed in consultation with the Librarians Association of the University of California, shall continue to recruit the most qualified librarians to fill professional positions on its staff. Open recruitment, which is essential to the selection of qualified librarians, shall occur for Career Status and Potential Career Status positions whenever the University determines that such positions are open for outside recruitment. Librarians currently employed by the University who appl for a vacancy shall be considered with all other applicants in keeping

Appendix II

with the recruitment process as developed by the campus where the vacancy exists. Review Committee(s) will continue to participate in the appointment process.

PEER REVIEW

A. Criteria for Promotion and Merit shall be those found in the Academic Personnel Manual sections 360-10 (b)(c)(d) and 210-4(e).

B. Campus review procedures should ensure that all decisions and recommendations shall be based solely upon material within the review packet.

C. The University shall invite LAUC to study the peer review process at the campus and University level and make recommendations, where appropriate, for improvement and refinement.

REVIEW PACKET INSPECTION

A. A review packet shall be created for each librarian who is being considered for an academic merit increase, promotion, or career status action.

B. Access

The University shall designate officials on each campus who shall have overall responsibility for the review packet for librarians. Librarians who wish to inspect their packets would make a request through the office of the officials so designated. Such inspections shall take place before the start of the Peer Review Process or after the University's decision in the Peer Review Process.

CODE OF PROFESSIONAL CONDUCT

The Librarian Code of Conduct will be set forth in the Academic Personnel Manual after its development under the direction of the Librarians Association of the University of California. The "Administration of Academic Discipline", predicated upon the Code and including procedural safeguards designed to assure fairness in the academic process for written censure, suspension, and dismissal, will be set forth in the Academic Personnel Manual after its development under the direction of the Librarians Association of the University of California.

PROFESSIONAL ACTIVITIES AND DEVELOPMENT

A. The University of California recognizes professional development of librarians as beneficial to the individual, the libraries, and the University. Professional development

opportunities contribute to the professional growth of the
librarian, enabling greater effectiveness as academic
appointees and thus enhancing her/his service to the
University.

B. The Librarians Association of the University of California
shall recommend procedures for the allocation of funds for
research and creative activity, and procedures for the
allocation of funds for attendance at professional meetings,
conferences, seminars, and workshops.

Appendix II

1986 Agreement

III. PROFESSIONAL ACTIVITIES AND DEVELOPMENT

C. The University of California has allocated $127,000 per year in various campus amounts for members of the unit to use for research, creative activities, professional meetings, conferences, seminars, and workshops. These funds shall be a minimum amount and shall not preclude the allocation of additional funds at the discretion of the University. Such additional funds shall be distributed through the same procedures as the funds agreed to in this paragraph.

The campus allocations are:

Berkeley	$31,300
Davis	11,700
Irvine	10,200
Los Angeles	38,100
Riverside	5,700
San Diego	9,900
San Francisco	4,800
Santa Barbara	9,900
Santa Cruz	5,400

1986 Agreement

XII. SALARY

Provided a timely agreement is reached at the bargaining table and t
University is notified of ratification, the University agrees to
increase the current rate of pay of librarians in the unit by the sa
range adjustment percentage(s) as is funded for academic employees
generally, by the 1986-87 Budget Act for the University of Californi
Once the range adjustment percentage(s) becomes known, the Universit
agrees to publish and distribute a revised Appendix A setting forth
new salary ranges for unit members.

Appendix II

1986 Agreement

XIII. UNIVERSITY BENEFITS

A. Librarians in the unit who are eligible to participate in a number of retirement, health, dental, and other benefit programs participate to the same extent as other eligible non-Senate academic employees of the University.

B. For the life of this Agreement, the University's maximum monthly rates of contribution for librarians in the unit who are eligible for and elect to take the health care plan and/or the dental plan shall be the same as the contribution rates for such plans for other academic employees. Costs in excess of the University's contributions are to be paid by the librarians in the unit, normally through payroll deduction. The coverage(s) and the carrier(s) of the health and dental plans shall be the same as for other academic employees at the same location.

C. Upon request the University will meet once each year to discuss the fringe benefit plans, coverages, benefits schedules, carriers, providers, premium rates, eligibility criteria, and employer/employee contributions, if any. The UFL understands and agrees that, except as provided below, the University may alter the coverage, rate of contribution, or the carrier of these plans during the term of this Agreement and that, if the University does so, such changes will apply to librarians in the unit eligible for benefits to the same extent as they apply to other eligible non-Senate academic employees at the same campus. The sole exception to the above shall be any alterations proposed by the University which affect only librarians in the unit, in which case the University agrees to meet and confer with respect to the proposed change.

1986 Agreement

ARTICLE XXXI. MEDICAL SEPARATION

A. Medical separation is a separation from employment when a librarian in the unit is unable to perform essential assigned functions satisfactorily, as determined by the University, because of any handicap or medical (including psychological) condition. A librarian in the unit who is medically separated is eligible for special reemployment procedures as set forth in Section H. below. Except by mutual consent, a librarian in the unit shall not be medically separated under this Article while on any authorized leave.

B. Except as provided in C below, a medical separation shall be based on:

   1. a statement describing the essential functions the librarian in the unit is not performing satisfactorily; and,

   2. any medical, psychiatric or other pertinent information presented by the librarian in the unit, the medical examiner of the librarian in the unit, or the University.

C. A medical separation may be based on the receipt of long term disability payments from a retirement system to which the University contributes, such as UCRS or PERS.

D. The University shall pay the reasonable costs of any medical and/or psychiatric examinations requested by the University. Where feasible, the University will present the librarian in the unit with a list of authorized medical practitioners from which the librarian in the unit shall make a selection, unless the parties mutually agree to use a medical practitioner not on the list.

E. When the University intends to medically separate a librarian in the unit, the librarian in the unit shall be given written notice of the intent to separate for medical reasons. The notice shall

   1. be given to the librarian in the unit either by delivery of the notice to the librarian in the unit in person, or by mail with proof of service;

   2. state the reason for the medical separation;

   3. include copies of pertinent material considered, except that excluded by medical privilege or applicable statute;

   4. state that the librarian in the unit or representative has the right to respond, and to whom, within ten (10) calendar days from the date of issuance of such notice of intent, either orally or in writing, regarding the medical separation; and

1986 Agreement

5. state the proposed effective date of the action, which shall be no earlier than thirty (30) calendar days from the date of this notice.

F. Upon written request of the librarian in the unit, the University will request that copies of medical records from the University appointed medical examiner be forwarded to the physician of record or choice of the librarian in the unit.

G. If the University determines that a medical separation is appropriate and that no reasonable accommodation can be made, the librarian in the unit will be given written notice of the medical separation. The notice shall:

1. specify the effective date of the medical separation;

2. state the reasons for the medical separation;

3. provide a description of any reasonable accommodations considered and why these have not enabled the librarian in the unit to perform essential assigned functions satisfactorily; and

4. state the right of the librarian in the unit to grieve the action under Articles XXV Grievance Procedure and XXVI Arbitration of this Agreement.

H. For a period of one year following the date of a medical separation, a medically separated librarian may be selected for a position within the unit without the requirement that the position be publicized. In order to be eligible for rehire under this Article, the medically separated librarian must provide a medical certification from a University approved medical physician describing in detail the medically separated librarian's ability to return to work. However, if the medically separated librarian is receiving disability benefits from a retirement system to which the University contributes, the eligibility period shall be three (3) years from the date the disability benefits commenced. If a librarian separated under this Article is reemployed in the unit within the allowed period, neither a break in service nor loss of career status shall occur.

I. Only the procedural aspects of this Article are grievable and arbitrable.

1986 Agreement

APPENDIX A
LIBRARIAN SERIES
Fiscal Year

Rank	Step	Normal Period at Sal.	Scale 7-1-86 Annual	Monthly
ASSISTANT	I	1 yr.	24,012	2,001.00
LIBRARIAN	II	1 yr.	25,092	2,091.00
3620-Career	III	1 yr.	26,436	2,203.00
3621-Potential	IV	1 yr.	27,792	2,316.00
Career	V	1 yr.	29,340	2,445.00
3622-Temporary	VI	1 yr.	30,720	2,560.00
ASSOCIATE	I	1 yr.	29,340	2,445.00
LIBRARIAN	II	1 yr.	30,720	2,560.00
3616-Career	III	2 yrs.	32,232	2,686.00
3617-Potential	IV	2 yrs.	34.452	2,871.00
Career	V	2 yrs.	36,828	3,069.00
3618-Temporary	VI	2 yrs.	39,456	3,288.00
	VII	2 yrs. or ---	42,264	3,522.00
LIBRARIAN	I	2 yrs.	39,456	3,288.00
3612-Career	II	2 yrs.	42,264	3,522.00
3613-Potential	III	3 yrs.	45,084	3,757.00
Career	IV	or ---	49,656	4,138.00
3614-Temporary	V	---	54,696	4,558.00

Appendix II

Signature Sheet for UC/UFL 1986 Reopener Negotiations

FOR THE UNIVERSITY OF CALIFORNIA

[signed] 5/13/86
Sarah Jo Gilpin-Bishop
Chief Negotiator

[signed]
Joseph Boisse

[signed]
Calvin Boyer

[signed]
Allan Dyson

[signed]
Debra Harrington

[signed]
Sharon Hayden

[signed]
Karl J. Hittelman

[signed]
Jane Marshall

[signed]
Myron Okada

[signed]
Sandra Rich

[signed]
John Tanno

[signed]
Susan M. Thomas

FOR THE UNIVERISTY FEDERATION OF LIBRARIANS

[signed]
Miki Goral
Chief Negotiator

[signed]
Robert E. Fessenden

[signed]
Susana Hinojosa

[signed]
Phil Hoehn

UNIVERSITY FEDERATION OF LIBRARIANS
UNIVERSITY COUNSEL - AMERICAN FEDERATION OF TEACHERS

By: *Thomas Dublin*　　　　　　　　6/26/86
　　　Thomas Dublin, President　　　　　Date

THE REGENTS OF THE UNIVERSITY OF CALIFORNIA

By: *Richard M. Catalano*　　　　　　5/30/86
　　　Richard M. Catalano　　　　　　　Date
　　　Associate Vice President
　　　Labor Relations

Approved as to Form:

By: *James N. Odle*　　　　　　　　May 30, 1986
　　　James N. Odle　　　　　　　　　Date
　　　Managing University Counsel of
　　　The Regents of the University
　　　of California

APPENDIX III:

Agreement Between Board of Regents
State University System of Florida
and
United Faculty of Florida

1985-1988

Appendix III

TABLE OF CONTENTS

	PAGE
Table of Contents	
Preamble	1

Article
1. Recognition 2
2. Consultation 3
   - 2.1 Consultation with Chancellor 3
   - 2.2 Consultation with Presidents 3
   - 2.3 Affirmative Action Reports 4
3. UFF Privileges 4
   - 3.1 Use of Facilities and Services 4
   - 3.2 Bulletin Boards 4
   - 3.3 Leave of Absence 4
   - 3.4 Course Reduction 5
4. Reserved Rights 7
5. Academic Freedom 8
6. Nondiscrimination 8
7. Minutes, Rules and Budgets 9
8. Appointment 9
9. Assignment of Responsibilities 14
10. Annual Employee Performance Evaluation 18
11. Personnel Evaluation File 21
12. Reappointment 22
13. Layoff and Recall 23
14. Promotion Procedure 24
15. Tenure 25
16. Termination and Other Action 27
17. Leaves 28
    - Compensated Leaves 28
    - 17.1 Accrual During Leave with Pay 28
    - 17.2 Holidays 29
    - 17.3 Sick Leave 29
    - 17.4 Job-Related Disability Leave 32
    - 17.5 Annual Leave 32
    - 17.6 Jury Duty and Court Appearances 35
    - 17.7 Military Leave 35
    - 17.8 Leave Pending Investigation 36
    - 17.9 Personal Leave Days 36
    - 17.10 Uncompensated Leave 36
    - 17.11 Compulsory Disability Leave 36
    - 17.12 Child Care Leave 37
    - 17.13 Emergency Condition Leave 37
18. Copyrights and Patents 38
19. Conflict of Interest/Outside Activity 39

20	Grievance Procedure and Arbitration	41
21	Other Employee Rights	47
	21.1 Professional Meetings	47
	21.2 Office Space	47
	21.3 Safe Conditions	48
	21.4 Tuition-free Courses	48
	21.5 Limitation on Personal Liability	48
	21.6 Travel Advances	48
	21.7 Working Papers	48
22	Professional Development Program and Sabbaticals	49
23	Salaries	53
24	Fringe Benefits	63
25	Insurance Deduction	68
26	Payroll Deduction	68
27	Maintenance of Benefits	69
28	Miscellaneous Provisions	69
29	Severability	70
30	Amendment and Duration	71
31	Totality of Agreement	71
32	Definitions	72
Signature Page		73

Appendix A: Class Titles in Bargaining Unit
Appendix B: Dues Check-off Authorization Form
Appendix C: Grievance Form
Appendix D: Request for Review of Step 1 Decision
Appendix E: Notice of Arbitration
Appendix F: Salary Increases
Appendix G: Salary Increase Notification
Appendix H: Memorandum of Understanding, Board of Regents and United Faculty of Florida Exclusive Assignment Dispute Resolution Procedure

Appendix III

PREAMBLE

The intent of the parties hereto in carrying out their responsibilities to negotiate the terms and conditions of employment of members of the bargaining unit is to promote the quality and effectiveness of education in the State University System and to maintain high standards of academic excellence in all phases of instruction, research, and service. The parties concur that these objectives are facilitated by amicable adjustment of matters of mutual interest. It is recognized by the parties that mutual benefits are to be derived from continual improvement in the State University System, and that participation of faculty and professional employees in the formulation of policies under which they provide their services is educationally sound.

While the United Faculty of Florida (hereinafter UFF), as the elected bargaining agent, retains the exclusive right to negotiate and reach agreement on terms and conditions of employment for the members of the bargaining unit, and the Board of Regents (hereinafter the Board) retains its rights, under law, to manage and direct the State University System, the parties recognize the desirability of a collegial governance system for faculty and professional employees in areas of academic concern. It is desirable that the collegial system of shared governance be maintained and strengthened throughout the State University System so that employees will have a mechanism and procedure, independent of the collective bargaining process, for making recommendations to appropriate administrative officials.

Collegiality in academic governance on each campus of the State University System can best be accomplished through Senates selected by representatives of the appropriate campus constituencies in accordance with each institution's constitution and tradition. Appropriate matters of concern should be brought before the Senate by its members or steering committee, or by the President of the university or representatives. Among matters which may be of concern to Senates include: (a) curriculum policy and curricular structure, (b) requirements for degrees and granting of degrees, (c) policies for recruitment, admission and retention of students, (d) the development, curtailment, discontinuance, or reorganization of academic programs, (e) grading policies, and (f) other matters of traditional concern.

In such a collegial system, departments or other traditional governance structures should play an active and responsible role in academic matters, including significant involvement in the recruitment of new faculty and professional employees, the development of high quality programs, participation in the development of tenure, promotion, and merit salary increase criteria, participation in the selection of instructional and library materials, and other matters of professional concern. The collegial relationship is most effective when peers work critically together to carry out their duties in the most professional manner possible.

In recognition of the importance of the collegial system of governance described herein, the Presidents or their representatives shall confer regularly with representatives from university Senates or equivalent bodies.

This Preamble is a statement of intent and policy and is, therefore, not subject to Article 20, Grievance Procedure.

ARTICLE 1
RECOGNITION

1.1 Pursuant to the Verification of Election Results of the Florida Public Employees Relations Commission, dated November 21, 1984, wherein the Commission ordered that Certification number 218, previously issued to United Faculty of Florida on April 2, 1976, remain in effect, and Commission Order number 84-E-112, dated June 14, 1984, wherein the Commission adopted the bargaining unit agreed to by the Board of Regents and United Faculty of Florida, as amended, the Board has recognized UFF as the exclusive representative, solely for the purpose of collective bargaining with respect to wages, hours, and other terms and conditions of employment as specifically set forth in this Agreement, for all employees in the bargaining unit described in the certification as amended by the above Order. Attached as Appendix "A", for information purposes only and not made a part of the Agreement, is the listing of titles included in that certification as amended.

1.2 (a) The Board shall supply the UFF with a copy of the Board's rules and each university shall supply the local chapter of UFF with a copy of its rules. If there is an inconsistency or conflict between an existing university rule or policy or Board policy and an express provision of this Agreement, the rule or policy shall be promptly amended to remove the inconsistency or conflict or the rule or policy shall be repealed. In the case of a Board rule, the Board shall promptly seek to have its rule amended to remove the inconsistency or conflict or to have the rule repealed.

(b) No new or amended Board or University rule, policy, or resolution shall apply to employees if it conflicts with an express term of the Agreement.

(c) The Board and the universities shall provide to UFF or the local UFF chapter, respectively, an advance copy of any proposed rule or policy changing a term or condition of employment contained in this Agreement. The Board or the university, as the case may be, shall provide the advance copy of a proposed rule no later than the date of publication under the provisions of the Administrative Procedure Act. The advance copy of a policy shall be provided to the UFF or its local chapter, as appropriate, at least two weeks in advance of its effective date so as to permit the UFF or its chapter to seek consultation with respect to it. With respect to a rule adopted pursuant to the emergency provisions of the Administrative Procedure Act, an advance copy shall be provided as far in advance of its effective date as is feasible under the circumstances.

Appendix III

- (d) If the Board or a committee of the Board has scheduled public hearings on any Board action that would conflict with an express term of this Agreement, the UFF shall not be denied the opportunity to address the matter.

- (e) If any proposed rule, policy, or resolution would modify an express term of this Agreement, the Board or its designee shall engage in collective bargaining with respect to the change upon UFF request.

1.3 (a) The Board shall furnish to UFF a copy of the agenda of each Board meeting or Board committee meeting at the time those agenda are made available to members of the Board, and a copy of the minutes of Board meetings at the time they are made available to the general public.

(b) UFF shall be granted a place on the agenda at each public Board meeting for the purpose of addressing any item on the Board's agenda that affects the wages, hours, or other terms and conditions of employment of employees.

1.4 Nothing contained in this Agreement shall be construed to prevent the Board or its representatives from meeting with any individual or organization to hear views on any matter; provided however, that as to any such matter which is a proper subject of collective bargaining and covered by a term of this Agreement, any changes or modification shall be made only through negotiation and agreement with UFF.

ARTICLE 2
CONSULTATION

2.1 Meetings between the Chancellor and/or designated representatives and up to ten representatives of UFF, or such other number as the parties may agree, shall from time to time be held, upon the advance request of either party, to discuss matters pertinent to the implementation or administration of this Agreement or any other mutually agreeable matters. Actions by the Board or its representatives affecting any other terms and conditions of employment of employees may also be raised in consultation with the Chancellor and/or designated representatives. The meetings shall be held on a mutually convenient date in Tallahassee unless the parties agree to another location and shall be scheduled once each 90 days or more frequently as the parties may agree. The parties shall submit to each other a written list of agenda items no less than one week in advance of the meeting. The parties understand and agree that such meetings shall not constitute or be used for the purpose of negotiations.

2.2 The Presidents or their representatives on each campus shall meet locally with UFF Chapter representatives to discuss matters pertinent to the implementation or administration of this Agreement, university actions affecting terms and conditions of employment unique to the university, or any other mutually agreeable matters according to the procedure described in 2.1, above, at least once each 90 days.

2.3 The UFF chapter, through its President, shall be provided without cost a copy of all university affirmative action programs and university, college, and departmental affirmative actions reports.

ARTICLE 3
UFF PRIVILEGES

3.1 Use of Facilities and Services. Subject to the rules of the Board and its representatives, UFF shall have the right to use university facilities at each university for meetings and all other services on the same basis as they are generally available to other university-related organizations which are defined as follows:

> "University-Related Groups and Organizations. These groups and organizations may or may not receive budgetary support. Examples of such groups include: student organizations, honor societies, fraternities, sororities, alumni associations, faculty committees, career service staff council, direct support organizations, the United Faculty of Florida, etc."

3.2 Bulletin Boards. UFF may post bulletins and notices relevant to its position as the collective bargaining agent on a reasonable number of existing bulletin boards but on at least one bulletin board per building where a substantial number of employees have offices. Specific locations shall be mutually selected by the university and the UFF university chapter in the course of consultation pursuant to Article 2, Consultation. All materials placed on the designated bulletin boards shall bear the date of posting and may be removed by the President or representatives after having been posted for a period of 30 days. In addition, such bulletin boards may not be used for election campaigns for public office or exclusive collective bargaining representation.

3.3 (a) At the written request of UFF, provided no later than May 15th of the year prior to the beginning of the academic year when such leave is to become effective, a full-time or part-time leave of absence for the academic year shall be granted to up to 18 employees designated by UFF for the purpose of carrying out UFF's obligations in representing employees and administering this Agreement, including lobbying and other political representation. Such leave may also be granted to up to nine employees for the entire summer term, upon written request by UFF provided no later than March 15th of the preceding academic year. Upon the failure of UFF to provide the Board or its representatives with a list of designees by the specified deadlines, the Board or its representatives may refuse to honor any of the requests which were submitted late.

Appendix III

- (b) No more than three employees from any university, nor more than one employee per 15 employees per department or comparable academic or administrative unit, need be granted such leave at any one time.

- (c) UFF shall reimburse the university for the employee's salary, fringe benefits, and retirement.

- (d) Employees on full-time leave under this paragraph shall be eligible to receive salary increases in accordance with the provisions of Article 17.10. Employees on less than full-time leave under this paragraph shall be eligible to receive salary increases on the same basis as other employees.

- (e) Beginning with the 1985-86 academic year, an employee who has been granted leave under this Article for two consecutive academic years shall not again be eligible for such leave until two consecutive academic years have elapsed following the end of the leave. Four employees, designated by UFF, shall be exempt from the provisions of this subsection. Other exceptions may be granted at the discretion of the Board or its representatives, upon prior written request by UFF.

- (f) The university or the Board shall not be liable for the acts or omissions of said employees during the leave and UFF shall hold the university and Board harmless for any such acts or omissions, including the cost of defending against such claims.

- (g) An employee on such leave shall not be evaluated for this activity nor shall such activity be considered by the university in making personnel decisions.

3.4 (a) The Board agrees to provide a total of 34 units of released time per semester of the academic year to employees designated by UFF for the purpose of carrying out UFF's obligations in representing employees and administering this Agreement. UFF may designate employees to receive released time during the academic year, subject to the following conditions:

  (1) A maximum of eight released time units per semester may be granted to employees at any one university, provided however, that no more than a total of five employees per university shall be granted released time per semester.

  (2) No more than one employee per 15 employees per department or comparable administrative or academic unit may be granted released time at any one time, nor may any employee be granted more than a two unit reduction in a single semester.

  UFF shall provide the Board or its representatives with a list of requested designees for the academic year no later than May 15th of the preceding academic year. Upon approval of the designees by the Board or its representatives, the designees shall serve for one full academic year (fall and spring semesters). Substitutions for the spring semester may be made upon written notification submitted by UFF to the Board or its representatives no later than October 15th.

(b) A "unit" of released time shall consist of a reduction in teaching load of one course per semester for instructional employees or, for nonteaching employees, a reduction in workload of ten hours per week. Two units shall consist of a reduction in teaching load of two courses per semester for instructional employees or, for nonteaching employees, a reduction in workload of 20 hours per week.

(c) Released time shall not be used for purposes of lobbying or other political representation. Leave for such purposes may be purchased by UFF pursuant to Article 3.3.

(d) Employees who are on leave of any kind, other than leave pursuant to Article 3.3, shall not be eligible to receive released time.

(e) Upon the failure of UFF to provide a list of designees by the specified deadlines, the Board or its representatives may refuse to honor any of the released time requests which were submitted late. Substitutions submitted after the October 15th deadline shall be allowed in the discretion of the Board or its representatives.

(f) Beginning with the 1985-86 academic year, an employee who has been granted released time for two consecutive academic years shall not again be eligible for released time until two academic years have elapsed following the end of such released time. Nine employees, designated by UFF, shall be exempt from the provisions of this subsection. Other exceptions may be granted at the discretion of the Board or its representatives, upon prior written request by UFF.

(g) Employees on released time shall be eligible for salary increases on the same basis as other employees, but their released time activities shall not be evaluated nor taken into consideration by the universities in making personnel decisions. Salary increases for 1985-86 for employees on released time during the 1984-85 academic year shall be awarded according to the terms of the Memorandum of Understanding between the Board and UFF, dated May 17, 1985.

(h) Employees on released time shall retain all rights and responsibilities as employees but shall not be considered representatives of the university or Board for any activities undertaken on behalf of UFF. UFF agrees to hold the university and Board harmless for any claims arising from such

Appendix III

activities, including the cost of defending against such claims.

(i) UFF may designate a total of nine employees systemwide to receive one unit, and a total of two employees systemwide to receive two units, of released time during the entire summer term. UFF shall provide the Board or its representatives with a list of requested designees no later than April 7th of the academic year preceding the summer term. Summer released time shall be subject to the following conditions:

   (1) No more than two employees per university may be granted summer released time, nor may more than one employee per university be granted two units of released time during the summer.

   (2) No more than one employee per 15 employees per department or comparable academic or administrative unit may be granted summer released time, nor may any employee be granted more than than two units of released time.

   (3) All other provisions contained in Article 3.4, except 3.4(a), shall apply to summer released time.

   Released time for summer term 1985, including eligibility for salary increases, shall be provided in accordance with the Settlement Agreement between the Board and UFF, dated April 23, 1982.

(j) This provision shall take effect upon the ratification of this Agreement. The Board or its representatives will grant released time for the 1985-86 academic year, according to the provisions of this Article, to those employees whom UFF recommends, in writing, no later than June 15, 1985.

ARTICLE 4
RESERVED RIGHTS

The Board retains and reserves to itself the rights, powers, and authority vested in it, including the right to plan, manage, and control the State University System and in all respects carry out the ordinary and customary functions of management.

All such rights, powers, and authority are retained by the Board, subject to those limitations imposed by this Agreement. Only violations of such limitations shall be subject to Article 20, Grievance Procedure.

ARTICLE 5
ACADEMIC FREEDOM

Academic freedom and responsibility are essential to the full development of a true university and apply to teaching, research, and creative activities. In the development of knowledge, research endeavors, and creative activities, an employee to whom such activities are assigned must be free to cultivate a spirit of inquiry and scholarly criticism and to examine ideas in an atmosphere of freedom and confidence.

A similar atmosphere is required for university teaching. Consistent with the exercise of academic responsibility, employees to whom such teaching is assigned must have freedom in the classroom to discuss their own academic subject, and to select instructional materials and determine grades in accordance with university and Board policies. Objective and skillful exposition of such subject matter, including the acknowledgement of a variety of scholarly opinions, is the duty of every such employee.

It is the policy of the Board and UFF to maintain and encourage full academic freedom. In the exercise of this freedom, employees shall be free to present their own subjects frankly and forthrightly, without fear of censorship, and to engage in scholarly and creative activity and publish the results in a manner consistent with their professional obligations. Academic freedom is accompanied by the corresponding responsibility to indicate when appropriate that one is not an institutional representative unless specifically authorized as such.

ARTICLE 6
NONDISCRIMINATION

6.1 The parties, in negotiating this Agreement, and separately in documents such as affirmative action plans, have recognized the obligations imposed upon them by the Civil Rights Act of 1964, Section 110.112(5) of the Florida Statutes (1983), and by other federal and State laws, rules, and regulations prohibiting discrimination, including those prohibiting sexual harassment, and have made clear their support for the concepts of affirmative action and equal employment opportunity. They desire to assure equal employment opportunities within the SUS and recognize that the purpose of affirmative action is to provide equal opportunity to women, minorities, and other affected groups to achieve equality in the SUS. The implementation of affirmative action programs will require positive actions that will affect terms and conditions of employment and to this end the parties have, in this Agreement and elsewhere, undertaken programs to ensure equitable opportunities for employees to receive salary adjustments, tenure, promotion, sabbaticals, and other benefits. This statement of intent is not intended to be subject to Article 20, Grievance Procedure.

6.2 Neither the Board nor UFF shall discriminate against any employee based upon race, color, sex, religious creed, national origin, age, veteran status, handicap, political affiliation, or marital status, nor shall the Board or UFF abridge any rights of employees granted under Chapter 447, Florida Statutes (1983). Claims of such discrimination by

Appendix III

the Board or its representatives may be presented as grievances pursuant to Article 20, Grievance Procedure. It is the intent of the parties that matters which may be presented as grievances under Article 20, Grievance Procedure, be so presented and resolved thereunder instead of using other procedures. The UFF agrees not to process cases arising under this Article when alternate procedures to Article 20 are initiated by the grievant.

6.3 No employee shall be refused a request to inspect and copy documents relating to the employee's claim of discrimination, except the evaluative documents described in Article 11.8.

6.4 As part of the consultation process described in Article 2, the Board or its representatives, and the universities or their representatives, shall discuss efforts made to retain women and minority employees.

ARTICLE 7
MINUTES, RULES AND BUDGETS

The Board shall regularly place a copy of the following documents in a single, easily accessible location in the main library of each of the nine universities of the State University System: a) the minutes of the meetings of the Council of Presidents, b) the minutes of the meetings of the Board, c) Board rules published under the Administrative Procedure Act, d) a copy of the current BOR/UFF Agreement and all supplements to the Agreement, e) that university's operating budget, and f) that university's rules published under the Administrative Procedure Act.

ARTICLE 8
APPOINTMENT

8.1 The Board shall exercise its authority to determine the standards, qualifications, and criteria so as to fill appointment vacancies in the bargaining unit with the best possible candidates. In furtherance of this aim, the Board shall, through the universities, (a) advertise such appointment vacancies, receive applications and screen candidates therefor, and make such appointments as it deems appropriate under such standards, qualifications and criteria, and (b) commit to an effort to identify and seek qualified women and minority candidates for vacancies and new positions.

8.2 Bargaining unit vacancies shall be advertised throughout the State University System as specified in the position vacancy announcement system. Copies of the position vacancy announcements shall be posted in a public place in each building where employees have offices. Specific locations may be designated pursuant to Article 2, Consultation. The advertisement shall include the qualifications for the positions. Employees of lower or equivalent ranks, employees who are spouses of employees, and employees who are local residents shall not, in the hiring process, be disadvantaged for that reason. All employees who are candidates for new and vacant positions shall be advised of the salaries of employees in the department or equivalent unit, or of salaries of university employees in the same job classification, as appropriate, prior to the negotiation of the candidate's initial salary. Prior to making the decision to hire a candidate to fill a bargaining unit vacancy, the appropriate administrator should consider recommendations which may have been made through the collegial system of shared governance.

8.3 All appointments shall be made on a standard SUS employment contract and signed by the university President or representative and the employee. The university may enclose informational addenda, except that such addenda may not abridge the employee's rights or benefits provided in this Agreement. All academic year and calendar year appointments for employees at a university shall begin on the same date. The SUS standard employment contract shall contain the following elements.

(a) Date;

(b) Professional Classification System title, class code, rank, and appointment status;

(c) Employment unit (e.g., department, college, institute, area, center, etc.);

(d) The length of the appointment;

(e) Special conditions of employment;

(f) A statement that the position is (1) tenured, (2) non-tenure earning, or (3) tenure-earning (specifying prior service in another institution to be credited toward tenure);

(g) A statement that the employee's signature on the standard employ-ment contract shall not be deemed a waiver of the right to process a grievance with respect thereto in compliance with Article 20;

(h) The following statement, if the appointment is not subject to the notice provisions of Article 12.1: "Your employment hereunder will cease on the date indicated. No further notice of cessation of employment is required.";

(i) A statement that the appointment is subject to the Constitution and laws of the State of Florida and the United States, the rules and regulations of the Board, and this Agreement;

(j) Percent of full-time effort (FTE) assigned;

(k) Salary rate;

(l) The minimum salary, if any, for the rank or job classification;

Appendix III

(m) The statement: "The BOR-UFF Collective Bargaining Agreement (Article 6) prohibits discrimination against any employee based upon race, color, sex, religious creed, national origin, age, veteran status, handicap, political affiliation, marital status, or employee rights related to union activity as granted under Chapter 447, Florida Statutes. Claims of such discrimination by the Board or its representatives may be presented as grievances pursuant to Article 20, Grievance Procedure"; and

(n) An optional statement informing the employee of the obligation to report outside activity under the provisions of Article 19 of the Agreement.

8.4 Employees currently serving on twelve-month (calendar year) appointments may request to be assigned to nine-month (academic year) appointments, or to annual leave accruing appointments of less than 12 months but more than nine months. In considering such requests, the President or representative shall take into account the needs of the university, the recommendation of the supervisor, the circumstances of the employee, and other relevant factors. Upon approval by the university President or representative of a change from a calendar year to an academic year appointment, and assuming that the assigned responsibilities remain substantially the same, the employee's salary shall be adjusted to 81.8 percent of the calendar year base salary or, for an employee whose appointment was previously changed from academic year to calendar year at a salary adjustment other than 122.2 percent, to the percent which is the reciprocal of the percent previously used.

Upon approval of a change from a calendar year appointment to an annual leave accruing appointment of less than 12 months but more than nine months, the employee's salary shall be adjusted to a percent of the calendar year base salary which is mathematically proportionate.[1]

A different salary adjustment percent may be used upon the agreement of the employee and the President or representative.

8.5 Employees currently serving on academic year appointments may request to be assigned to calendar year appointments. Upon approval of such change by the university President or representative, and assuming that the assigned responsibilities remain substantially the same, the employee's salary shall be adjusted to 122.2 percent of the academic year base salary or, for an employee whose appointment was previously changed from calendar to academic year at a salary adjustment other than 81.8 percent, to the percent which is the reciprocal of the percent previously used. A different salary adjustment percent may be

---

[1] For example, a faculty member whose calendar year salary is $30,000 shall, upon a change to a ten-month appointment, receive a salary of 10/12 of $30,000, i.e., $25,000.

used upon the agreement of the employee and the President or representative.

8.6 Academic Year Appointments.

Employees on academic year appointments shall normally be appointed for an academic year consisting of a fall and spring semester totaling 39 contiguous weeks, unless the employee and the university agree to an alternative 39 weeks appointment. The period for instruction shall not exceed an average of 75 days per semester and the period for testing, advisement, and other scheduled assignments shall not exceed an average of ten days per semester. Within each semester, activities referred to above shall be scheduled during contiguous weeks with the exception of the spring break, if any.

8.7 Supplemental Appointments.

Available supplemental appointments shall be offered equitably and as appropriate to qualified employees, not later than five weeks prior to the beginning of the appointment, if practicable, in accordance with written criteria which may exist, or that shall be developed and specified by the Board or its representatives by February 1, 1986. The criteria shall be posted in each department or equivalent unit.

An employee shall receive approximately the same total salary for teaching a course during a supplemental appointment as the employee received for teaching the same course, or a course similar in length and content, during the academic year, regardless of the length of the supplemental appointment. The instructional assignment shall include the normal activities related to such an assignment as defined by the department and the nature of the course, such as examinations, advisement and counseling, course preparation, minor curriculum development, and minor committee activities. Where the instructional portion of a supplemental assignment immediately follows the academic year appointment, the employee may be asked to perform reasonable and necessary noninstructional duties related to the supplemental assignment prior to the conclusion of the academic year appointment.

Research or service duties assigned for a supplemental appointment need not be allocated according to the same FTE equivalent as during the academic year, provided that any reduction in FTE corresponds to an appropriate reduction in assigned duties. During a supplemental appointment, an employee's assignment shall not exceed 1.0 FTE.

All supplemental appointments shall be made in accordance with §240.243, F.S. (the "twelve hour law").

Salary for a supplemental appointment shall be computed in accordance with the following formulae:

Appendix III

(a) $$\text{FTE for Supplemental Appointment} = \text{FTE for Semester Instructional Assignment}^2 \times \frac{\text{No. of Weeks (19.5) in Semester Appointment}}{\text{Number of week in Supplemental Appointment}} + \text{FTE for Research and Service Assigned During Supplemental Appointment}$$

(b) $$\text{Salary for Supplemental Appointment} = \text{Biweekly Salary rate During Semester Appointment} \times \text{FTE for Supplemental Appointment} \times \text{Number of Pay Periods In Supplemental Appointment}$$

---

2   The instructional FTE refers to the percentage assignment for the same course or courses similar in length and content taught during a regular semester in the preceding academic year. If the instructional assignment in the supplemental appointment is for instructional duties different from those existing during a semester, an appropriate FTE, as determined by the University, will be assigned to such duties.

Examples (based on a $24,000 AY salary or $12,000 per semester):

Weeks in Salary Appt.	Sample FTE for Assigned Instruc. Duty	Biweekly Salary Rate	Number of Pay Periods	Total for Instruction
19.5	.333	$1231	9.75	$3997
13.0	.500	1231	6.50	4001
10.0	.650	1231	5.00	4001
8.0	.812	1231	4.00	3998
6.5	1.000	1231	3.25	4001
19.5	.300	$1231	9.75	$3601
13.0	.450	1231	6.50	3601
10.0	.585	1231	5.00	3601
8.0	.731	1231	4.00	3599
6.5	.900	1231	3.25	3601
19.5	.250	$1231	9.75	$3001
13.0	.375	1231	6.50	3001
10.0	.488	1231	5.00	3004
8.0	.609	1231	4.00	2999
6.5	.750	1231	3.25	3001
5.0	.975	1231	2.50	3001

8.8 The year of service for employees in developmental research schools shall be 190-196 days of service.

8.9 Overload shall be defined as any instructional duties in an extension or continuing education activity in excess of a full appointment. Available overload appointments shall be offered equitably and as appropriate to qualified employees in sufficient time to allow voluntary acceptance or rejection.

8.10 Visiting appointments shall extend for no more than three years, except that such appointments may be extended due to special circumstances as determined by the university.

8.11 The use of adjuncts at a university shall, upon the request of UFF chapter representatives, be a subject of consultation under the provisions of Article 2.1 and 2.2.

ARTICLE 9
ASSIGNMENT OF RESPONSIBILITIES

9.1 The professional obligation is comprised of both scheduled and non-scheduled activities. The parties recognize that it is a part of

Appendix III

the professional responsibility of employees to carry out their duties in an appropriate manner and place. For example, while instructional activities, office hours, and other duties and responsibilities may be required to be performed at a specific time and place, other non-scheduled activities are more appropriately performed in a manner and place determined by the employee. Employees shall not be penalized for making such appropriate determinations, in consultation with their supervisors.

9.2 Long Term Expectations. When first employed, each employee shall be apprised of what is expected, generally, in terms of teaching, research and other creative activities, and service, and specifically, if there are specific requirements and/or other duties involved. If and when these expectations change during the period of service of the employee, that employee shall be apprised of the change.

9.3 Annual Assignment.

(a) Employees shall be apprised in writing, at the beginning of their employment and at the beginning of each year of employment thereafter, of the duties and responsibilities in teaching, research and other creative activities, service, and of any other specific duties and responsibilities assigned for that year.

(b) Each employee earning eligibility for tenure or promotion shall be given assignments which provide equitable opportunities, in relation to other employees in the same department, to meet the required criteria for promotion and tenure.

(1) For the purpose of applying this principle to promotion, assignments shall be considered over the entire period since the original appointment or since the last promotion, not solely over the period of a single annual assignment. In no event shall the period under consideration be less than four years. The rights contained in this paragraph shall not apply to assignments made for the 1978-79 academic year or earlier.

(2) For the purpose of applying this principle to tenure, assignments shall be considered over the entire probationary period and not solely over the period of a single annual assignment.

(3) Prior service credit shall not be counted in computing the periods described in 9.3(b)(1) and (2).

(4) If an arbitrator determines that the employee was not provided an "equitable opportunity" as described in this section, the arbitrator may award additional employment requiring the university to provide the "equitable opportunity" as described herein. The arbitrator also may retain jurisdiction for purposes of determining

whether the ensuing assignment provides such "equitable opportunity".

9.4 Except for an assignment made at the beginning of an employee's employment, the person responsible for making an assignment shall contact the employee prior to making the final written assignment. The assignment should be communicated to employees no later than six weeks in advance of its starting date, if practicable. Such contact shall also take place prior to changes which become necessary in an assignment, and such changes shall be specified in writing. The employee shall be granted, upon request, a conference with the person responsible for making the assignment to express concerns regarding:

(a) the employee's qualifications, including professional training, and preferences;

(b) the character of the assignment, including but not limited to the number of hours of instruction, the preparation required, whether the employee has taught the course in the past, the average number of students enrolled in the course in past semesters and the time required by the course, whether travel to another location is required, the number of preparations required, the employee's assignments in other semesters, and the availability and adequacy of materials and equipment, secretarial services, student assistants, and other support services needed to perform the assignments; and

(c) the opportunity to fulfill applicable criteria for tenure, promotion, and merit salary increases.

9.5 The Board and UFF recognize that, while the Legislature has described the minimum full academic assignment in terms of 12 contact hours or equivalent research and service, the professional obligation undertaken by a faculty member may properly be broader than that minimum. In like manner, the professional obligation of other professional employees is not easily susceptible of quantification. The Board, acting through its representatives, has the right, in making assignments, to determine the types of duties and responsibilities which comprise the professional obligation and to determine the mix or relative proportion of effort an employee may be required to expend on the various components of the obligation.

Furthermore, the Board or representative properly has the obligation constantly to monitor and review the size and number of classes and other activities, to consolidate inappropriately small offerings, and to reduce inappropriately large classes.

No employee's assignment shall be imposed arbitrarily or unreasonably. If an employee believes that the assignment has been so imposed, the employee should proceed to address the matter through the procedures in Appendix "H" of this Agreement, which shall be the exclusive method for resolving such disputes.

9.6 Each employee shall be assigned one principal place of employment. Where possible, an employee shall be given at least 90 days notice of assignment to a second instructional location more than 15 miles from the employee's principal place of employment. If the assignment to a second location is made within a regular full-time appointment, the supervisor is encouraged to make an appropriate adjustment in the assignment in recognition of time spent traveling to a second instructional location. Travel expenses, including overnight lodging and meals, if necessary, for all assignments not at the employee's principal place of employment shall be paid at the State rate and in accordance with the applicable provisions of State law and rules and regulations having the force and effect of law.

9.7 It is desirable that teaching schedules be established so that the time between the beginning of the first assignment and the end of the last for any one day does not exceed eight hours.

9.8 When special equipment is required for classes, it is desirable that there be sufficient equipment to accommodate the students assigned thereto. The Board and UFF are committed to seek funding to provide for the replacement of obsolete equipment, recognizing the necessity for maintaining an adequate inventory of technologically current equipment.

9.9 Scheduled hours for all employees shall not normally exceed 40 hours per week. Time shall be allowed within the normal working day for research, teaching, or other activities required of the employee, when a part of the assigned duties. Supervisors are encouraged to make appropriate reductions or adjustments in the number of hours scheduled in recognition of evening, night, and weekend assignments, and for periods when an employee is on call. Evenings, nights, and weekends when an employee is on call shall be considered in making other assignments. See Article 17.2 regarding schedule adjustment for holiday assignment.

9.10 The parties agree that a joint BOR/UFF committee be established to study employment issues relating to the use of instructional media such as videotaped lectures, teaching machines, computer-assisted instructional programs, etc. The committee shall make recommendations and proposals no later than November 30, 1985.

9.11 Staffing for SUS Libraries is based on the "new Washington Formula." The Board, like the State of Washington, is committed to funding a percentage of the staffing needs as defined by the formula. The Board or its representative shall, through the consultation process provided in Article 2.1, provide UFF with a report of the progress made toward the achievement of the stated goals of the Washington formula once each year.

ARTICLE 10
ANNUAL EMPLOYEE PERFORMANCE EVALUATION

10.1 The performance of employees, other than those who have received notice of nonreappointment under Article 12.1 or those not entitled to receive notice of nonreappointment under Article 12.1, shall be evaluated at least once annually and they shall be advised of the academic term during which such annual evaluation will be made. Personnel decisions shall take such annual evaluations into account, provided that personnel decisions need not be based solely on written employee performance evaluations.

10.2 The employee, if assigned teaching duties, shall be notified at least two weeks in advance of the date, time, and place of any direct classroom observation or visitation made in connection with the employee's annual evaluation.

10.3 The evaluation shall be in writing and the employee shall be offered the opportunity to discuss the evaluation with the evaluator prior to it being placed in the employee's evaluation file. The evaluation shall be signed by the person performing the evaluation, and by the person being evaluated, who may attach a concise comment to the evaluation. A copy of the evaluation shall be made available to the employee.

10.4 Those persons responsible for supervising and evaluating an employee shall endeavor to assist the employee in correcting any performance deficiencies reflected in the employee's annual evaluation.

10.5 The annual performance evaluation shall be based upon assigned duties, and shall take into account the nature of the assignments, in terms, where applicable, of:

   (a) Teaching effectiveness, including effectiveness in presenting knowledge, information, and ideas by means or methods such as lecture, discussion, assignment and recitation, demonstration, laboratory exercise, practical experience, and direct consultation with students. The evaluation shall include consideration of effectiveness in imparting knowledge and skills, and effectiveness in stimulating students' critical thinking and/or creative abilities, and adherence to accepted standards of professional behavior in meeting responsibilities to students.

   (b) Contribution to the discovery of new knowledge, development of new educational techniques, and other forms of creative activity. Evidence of research and other creative activity shall include, but not be limited to, published books; articles and papers in professional journals; musical compositions, paintings, sculpture; works of performing art; papers presented at meetings of professional societies; and research and creative activity that has not yet resulted in publication, display, or performance. The evaluation shall include consideration of the employee's productivity,

Appendix III   225

including the quality and quantity of what has been done during the year, and of the employee's research and other creative programs and contributions; and recognition by the academic or professional community of what is done.

(c) Service that is related to and furthers the mission of the university, including service on departmental, college, and university committees, councils, and senates; service in appropriate professional organizations; participation in professional meetings, symposia, conferences, workshops; service on local, State, and national governmental boards, agencies and commissions; and service to public schools. Evaluation of service shall include consideration of contribution to:

   (1) the orderly and effective functioning of the employee's academic unit (program, department, school, college) and/or the total university;

   (2) the university community;

   (3) the local, State, regional, and national communities, and scholarly and professional associations; and

   (4) the development or revision of curriculum, course structure, or other elements of the professional obligation, as a result of changes in calendar.

(d) Other assigned university duties, such as advising, counseling, and supervision of interns, or as described in a Position Description, if any, of the position held by the employee.

(e) Such other responsibilities as may be appropriate to the assignment.

10.6   No employee shall be evaluated as deficient in oral English language skills unless proved deficient in accordance with the appropriate procedures and examinations established by Section 240.246, Florida Statutes, and Board of Regents rule 6C-5.120, for testing such deficiency.

(a) Faculty involved in classroom instruction, other than in courses conducted primarily in a foreign language, found by their supervisor, as part of the annual evaluation, to be potentially deficient in English oral language skills, shall be tested in accordance with appropriate procedures and examinations established by statute and rule cited above for testing such skills. No reference to an alleged deficiency shall appear in the annual evaluation or in the personnel file of a faculty member who achieves a satisfactory examination score determining proficiency in oral English as specified in the rule (currently "220" or above on the Test of

Spoken English, or "3" or above on the Foreign Service Institute Language Proficiency Interview.)

(b) Faculty who score within a specified range on an examination established by statute and rule cited above for testing oral English language skills ("190-210" on the Test of Spoken English or "2+" on the Foreign Service Institute Proficiency Interview), may continue to be involved in classroom instruction up to one semester while enrolled in appropriate English language instruction, as described in paragraph (d) below, provided the appropriate administrator determines that the quality of instruction will not suffer. Only such faculty members who demonstrate, on the basis of examinations established by statute and rule, that they are no longer deficient in oral English language skills may be involved in classroom instruction beyond one semester.

(c) Faculty who score below a minimum score on an examination established by statute and rule for determining proficiency in oral English (currently "190" on the Test of Spoken English or "2+" on the Foreign Service Institute Language Proficiency Interview) shall be assigned appropriate non-classroom duties for the period of oral English language instruction provided by the university under paragraph (d) below, unless during the period of instruction the faculty member is found, on the basis of an examination specified above, to be no longer deficient in oral English language skills. In that instance, the faculty member will again be eligible for assignment to classroom instructional duties and shall not be disadvantaged by the fact of having been determined to be deficient in oral English language skills.

(d) It is the responsibility of each faculty member who is found, as part of the annual evaluation, to be deficient in oral English language skills by virtue of scoring below the satisfactory score on an examination established by statute and rule for determining such proficiency (see paragraph (a)), to take appropriate actions to correct these deficiencies. To assist the faculty member in this endeavor, the university shall provide appropriate oral English language instruction without cost to such faculty members for a period consistent with their length of appointment and not to exceed two consecutive semesters. The time the faculty member spends in such instruction shall not be considered part of the individual assignment or time worked, nor shall the faculty member be disadvantaged by the fact of participation in such instruction.

(e) If a university determines, as part of the annual evaluation, that one or more administrations of a test to determine proficiency in oral English language skills is necessary, in accordance with statute and rule and this section, the

Appendix III

university shall pay the expenses for up to two administrations of the test. The faculty member shall pay for additional testing that may be necessary.

ARTICLE 11
PERSONNEL EVALUATION FILE

11.1 There shall be one file in which all written materials used in the evaluation process are maintained. When evaluations and personnel decisions are made, the only documents which may be used are those contained in that file. Employees shall be notified, upon request, of the location of the personnel evaluation file and the identity of the custodian. A notice specifying the location of the official evaluation file shall be posted in each department or comparable unit.

11.2 An employee may examine the evaluation file, upon reasonable advance notice, during the regular business hours of the office in which the file is kept, normally within the same business day as the employee requests to see it, and under such conditions as are necessary to insure its integrity and safekeeping. Upon request, an employee may paginate with successive whole numbers the materials in the file, and may attach a concise statement in response to any item therein. Upon request, an employee is entitled to one free copy, during the life of this Agreement, of any material in the evaluation file. Additional copies may be obtained by the employee upon the payment of a reasonable fee for photocopying. A person designated by the employee may examine that employee's evaluation file with the written authorization of the employee concerned, and subject to the same limitations on access that are applicable to the employee.

11.3 UFF agrees to indemnify and hold the Board, its officials, agents, and representatives harmless from and against any and all liability for any improper, illegal, or unauthorized use by UFF of information contained in such evaluation files.

11.4 In the event a grievance proceeds to arbitration, the Board, UFF, the arbitrator, and the grievant shall have the right to use copies of materials from the grievant's evaluation file relevant thereto in the arbitration proceeding.

11.5 No anonymous material shall be placed in an evaluation file, except for student evaluations which are part of a regular evaluation procedure of classroom instruction.

11.6 Evaluative materials, or summaries thereof, prepared by peer committees as part of a regular evaluation system may be placed in an evaluation file when signed by a representative of the committee.

11.7 Materials shown to be contrary to fact shall be removed from the file. This section shall not authorize the removal of materials from the evaluation file when there is a dispute concerning a matter of judgment or opinion rather than fact. Materials may also be removed pursuant to the resolution of a grievance.

11.8 Except as noted above, only the employee and the employee's representative, and university and Board officials responsible for the supervision or evaluation of the employee, may inspect information reflecting evaluation of employee performance contained in the employee's file, except upon order of a court of competent jurisdiction.

ARTICLE 12
REAPPOINTMENT

12.1 All employees except: (a) those holding visiting appointments; (b) those who are appointed for less than one academic year; or (c) those with less than five years continuous service who are on "soft money", e.g., contracts and grants, sponsored research funds, and grants and donations trust funds, are entitled to written notice that they will not be offered further appointment as follows:

(a) for employees in their first two years of university service, one full semester;

(b) for employees with two or more years of continuous university service, one full year.

In the event of a break in service for more than one semester in one full year or more than two semesters in two full years, only service following such break shall be counted for purposes of determining length of service. Paid or unpaid leaves shall not be considered a break in service.

Employees not entitled to written notice of non-reappointment shall have the following statement included in their employment contracts:

"Your employment hereunder will cease on the date indicated. No further notice of cessation of employment is required."

12.2 An employee, other than one specified in 12.1 as not entitled to written notice of non-reappointment, who receives a written notice that the employee will not be offered further appointment shall be entitled, upon request, to a written statement of the basis for the decision not to reappoint within 25 days following such notice. Thereafter, the President or representative shall provide such statement within 25 days of such request. Such employee may not contest the decision under Article 20, Grievance Procedure, unless a grievance is filed within 25 days after the receipt of the statement and it is claimed that such action (a) violated the employee's constitutional rights or (b) violated a specific term of this Agreement. If such decision not to reappoint was based solely upon reasons which would form the basis for a layoff, then such employee shall have the rights of recall under Articles 13.2 and 13.4, Layoff and Recall, and shall be so informed.

12.3 No appointment shall create any right, interest, or expectancy in any other appointment beyond its specific terms, except as provided in Articles 13 and 15.1.

Appendix III

12.4 An employee who wishes to resign has the professional obligation, when possible, to provide the university with at least one full semester's notice. Upon resignation, all consideration for tenure and reappointment shall cease.

12.5 Notice of appointment and non-reappointment shall not be contained in the same document.

ARTICLE 13
LAYOFF AND RECALL

13.1 The following principles will govern the selection of employees to be laid off:

(a) Tenure-earning position: No tenured employee shall be laid off if there are untenured employees in the layoff unit.

(b) Others: No employee in a non-tenure earning position with more than five years of continuous service shall be laid off if there are any such employees with less than five years service in the layoff unit.

(c) The provisions of (a) and (b) will apply unless the Board determines that an Affirmative Action employment program will be adversely affected.

(d) Where employees are equally qualified under (a) or (b) above, those employees will be retained who, in the judgment of the Board or its representatives, will best contribute to the mission and purpose of the institution and the State University System. In making such judgment, the Board or its representative shall take into account appropriate factors, including but not limited to performance evaluation by students, peers, and supervisors, and the employee's academic training, professional reputation, compatibility with colleagues, teaching effectiveness, research record or quality of the creative activity in which the employee may be engaged, service to the community and public, and length of service.

(e) No tenured employee shall be laid off solely for the purpose of creating a vacancy to be filled by an administrator entering the bargaining unit.

13.2 The university and Board shall make a reasonable effort to locate appropriate alternate or equivalent employment for laid-off employees, first within the university and second within the State University System, and to make known the results of the effort to the person affected.

13.3 Employees should be informed as soon as practicable, recognizing that it is desirable, where circumstances permit, to provide at least one year's notice to employees with three or more years of service and at least six-months notice to other employees. Employees who have received notice of layoff shall be afforded the recall rights granted under Articles 13.2 and 13.4.

13.4 For a period of two years following layoff, an employee who has been laid off and who is not otherwise employed in an equivalent full-time position shall be offered reemployment in the same or similar position at the university at which previously employed at the time of layoff, should an opportunity for such reemployment arise. All persons on the recall list shall regularly be sent the SUS position vacancy announcements. For this purpose, it shall be the employee's responsibility to keep the university advised of the employee's current address. Should a vacancy occur at another university within the State University System, the employee may apply for the position and shall be considered therefor in accordance with the normal hiring procedures of that university. Any offer of reemployment pursuant to this section must be accepted within 15 days after the date of the offer, such acceptance to take effect not later than the beginning of the semester immediately following the date the offer was made. In the event such offer of reemployment is not accepted, the employee shall receive no further consideration pursuant to this Article. An employee who held a tenured appointment on the date of termination by reason of layoff shall resume the tenured appointment upon recall. The employee shall receive the same credit for years of service for purposes of layoff as held on the date of layoff.

The laid off employee shall also be eligible for consideration for retraining, under the provisions of Article 22.4, for a period of two years following layoff.

13.5 The provisions of this article shall not apply to employees holding visiting appointments, to those appointed for less than one academic year, or to those appointed for less than five years continuous service who are appointed to positions funded from "soft money", e.g., contracts and grants, sponsored research trust funds, and grants and donations trust funds.

ARTICLE 14
PROMOTION PROCEDURE

14.1 Promotion decisions shall be based upon criteria specified by the Board or its representatives. All affected employees shall be given a copy of the criteria. The Board or its representatives may modify these criteria so long as the UFF Chapter President (in the case of Board criteria, UFF) has been notified of the proposed changes and offered an opportunity to discuss such changes in consultation with the university President or representative (in the case of Board criteria, the Board or its representative). Changes in criteria shall not become effective until one full year following adoption of the changes, unless mutually agreed to in writing by the UFF Chapter President and the university President (in the case of Board criteria, the Board or its representative). In the event the criteria are developed or modified after the effective date of this Agreement, copies of such criteria shall be available for discussion by the members of the affected departments or equivalent units.

14.2 Promotion decisions are not merely a totaling of an employee's annual performance evaluations. Rather, the university, through its faculty, professional employees, and administrators, assesses the employee's potential for growth and scholarly contribution as well as past performance. Upon written request no more than every other year, beginning with the second full year of employment, employees eligible for consideration for promotion shall be apprised of their progress toward promotion. The purpose of the appraisal is to provide assistance and counseling to candidates to help them to qualify themselves for promotion. The appraisals are not binding upon the university.

14.3 Recommendations for promotion shall begin with the employee's supervisor and shall be submitted to the appropriate officials for review. Prior to the consideration of the employee's promotion, the employee shall have the right to review the contents of the promotion file and may attach a brief and concise response to any material therein. It shall be the responsibility of the employee to see that the file is complete. If any material is added to the file after the commencement of consideration, a copy shall be sent to the employee, who may attach within five days thereafter a brief and concise response thereto.

Recommendations for promotion shall include a copy of applicable promotion criteria and, if the employee chooses, the employee's promotion appraisal(s). The reviewers at any stage in the review may request to view the appraisal(s).

14.4 If any employee is denied promotion, the employee shall be notified by the appropriate administrative official within ten days, or as soon as possible thereafter, of that decision. The notice shall be accompanied by a statement of the reasons why the promotion was denied.

ARTICLE 15
TENURE

15.1 A tenured employee may be terminated only for cause in accordance with the provisions of Article 16, Termination and Other Actions, or laid off in accordance with the provisions of Article 13, Layoff and Recall.

15.2 The decision to award tenure to an employee shall take into account the annual performance evaluations as well as the assessment by appropriate employees and administrators of the contribution the employee may be expected to make to the institution, and the needs of the department, college, and university. The university shall give a copy of the criteria for tenure to employees eligible for tenure, and each such employee shall be apprised in writing once each year of the employee's progress toward tenure. The purpose of the appraisal is to provide assistance and counseling to candidates to help them to qualify themselves for tenure. The appraisals are not binding upon the university.

15.3 The Board or its representatives may modify the criteria for tenure so long as the UFF Chapter President (in the case of Board criteria, UFF) has been notified of the proposed changes and offered an opportunity to discuss such changes in consultation with the university President or representative (in the case of Board criteria, the Board or its representative). Changes in criteria shall not become effective until one full year following adoption of the changes, unless mutually agreed to in writing by the UFF Chapter President and the university President or representative (in the case of Board criteria, the Board or representative). In the event the criteria for tenure are developed or modified after the effective date of this Agreement, copies of such criteria shall be available for discussion by members of the affected departments or equivalent units.

15.4 Employees with the rank of Assistant Professor, Associate Professor, Professor, and other employees the Board may designate (such as Assistant Librarians, Associate Librarians and Librarians at the University of Florida), shall be eligible for tenure. Universities may, by rule, make Assistant Professors ineligible for tenure. The universities' rule-making power to make Assistant Professors ineligible for tenure shall apply only to employees appointed after January 1, 1982. Other employees shall be governed by the agreement in force at the time of their original appointment. The Board may designate other positions as tenure-earning and shall notify the employee of such status at the time of initial appointment. Tenure shall be in a department or other appropriate unit. Tenure shall not extend to administrative appointments in the General Faculty or Administrative and Professional classification plans.

15.5 Except for employees who, by virtue of prior service credited at time of appointment, are eligible for consideration earlier, an employee shall normally be considered for tenure during the fifth year of continuous service in a tenure-earning position or, at the option of the employee and with the concurrence of the appropriate administrative officials, during the sixth such year in a tenure-earning position. Part-time service of an employee employed at least one full semester in any 12 month period shall be accumulated. For example, two semesters of half-time service shall be considered one-half year of service for purposes of tenure eligibility. By the end of six full years of service within the State University System, an employee eligible for tenure shall either be awarded tenure by the Board or given notice that further employment will not be offered. The notice shall be accompanied by a statement of reasons by the President or representative why tenure was not granted.

15.6 The decision of the Board to award or deny tenure shall be made by September 15th and the employee shall be notified in writing by the President or representative within five days of the decision of the Board. An employee being considered for tenure prior to the sixth year may withdraw from consideration on or before March 15th without prejudice.

15.7 Recommendations for the awarding of tenure shall be made by the employee's supervisor and shall include a poll by secret ballot of the

Appendix III

tenured members of the employee's department or equivalent unit. The performance of an employee during the entire term of employment at the institution shall be given consideration in determining whether to grant tenure. Recommendations regarding tenure shall include a copy of applicable tenure criteria and, if the employee chooses, the employee's tenure apprisals. The reviewers at any stage in the review may request to review the apprisals. Prior to the consideration of the employee's candidacy, the employee shall have the right to review the contents of the tenure file and may attach a brief and concise response to any materials therein. It shall be the responsibility of the employee to see that the file is complete. If any material is added to the file after the commencement of consideration, a copy shall be sent to the employee who, within five days thereafter, may attach a brief and concise response thereto.

15.8 Tenure may be granted by the Board at the time of initial appointment. Administrators are encouraged to review such recommendations with tenured employees in the department prior to making the final tenure recommendation.

15.9 Tenured SUS employees who transfer within an SUS university or to another SUS university, and who are employed in the same or similar discipline, may transfer their tenure if a vacancy exists and they are offered employment through the normal hiring process. The amount of prior SUS service creditable toward tenure at another university may, by mutual agreement, be all or part of such service. In the absence of mutual agreement, all such service shall be credited.

15.10 Permanent Status for Developmental Research School Employees. By the end of three full years of full-time, or equivalent part-time, service within the State University System in a permanent status-earning position, employees in developmental research schools operated under the Board, excluding supervisors and administrative personnel, shall be granted permanent status by the President or President's representative, or given notice that further employment will not be offered. This provision shall apply only to employees appointed after January 1, 1982. Other employees shall be governed by the agreement in force at the time of their original appointment. Permanent status shall be earned and held as a ranked employee in an academic position and shall not extend to an administrative or supervisory position. An employee with permanent status may be disciplined only for cause in accordance with the provisions of Article 16, Termination and Other Actions, or laid off only in accordance with the provisions of Article 13, Layoff and Recall.

15.11 Authorized leaves of absence may, under the provisions of Article 17, Leaves, be credited toward eligibility for tenure.

ARTICLE 16
TERMINATION AND OTHER ACTION

16.1 Just cause shall be defined as:

(a) incompetence, or

(b) misconduct. An employee's activities which fall outside the scope of employment shall constitute misconduct only if such activities adversely affect the legitimate interests of the university or Board.

16.2 Termination. A tenured appointment or any appointment of definite duration may be terminated during its term for just cause. An employee shall be given written notice of termination at least six months in advance of the effective date of such termination, except that in cases where the President or representative determines that an employee's actions adversely affect the functioning of the university or jeopardize the safety or welfare of the employee, colleagues, or students, the President or representative may give less than six months notice.

16.3 Disciplinary Action Other Than Termination. The Board, or its representative, retains its right to impose other disciplinary action for just cause including, but not limited to, suspension with or without pay. Counseling shall not be considered disciplinary action.

16.4 The President or representative may place an employee on leave pending investigation under Article 17.8.

16.5 All notices of disciplinary action shall include a statement of the reasons therefor. Any disciplinary action taken under provisions of this Article shall be subject to Article 20, Grievance Procedure.

16.6 When the President or representative has reason to believe that disciplinary action should be imposed, the President or representative shall provide the employee with a written notice of proposed discipline and the reasons therefor. The employee shall be given at least ten days in which to respond in writing and/or orally to the President or representative before the proposed disciplinary action is taken. The President or representative then may issue a notice of discipline under Article 16.5.

16.7 Both parties endorse the principle of progressive discipline as applied to professional employees.

ARTICLE 17
LEAVES

17.1-17.9 Compensated Leaves.

17.1 Accrual During Leave with Pay. Employees shall accrue normal leave credits while on compensated leave in full pay status, or while participating in the sabbatical or professional development programs. If an employee is on compensated leave in less than full pay status for other than sabbaticals or professional development programs, the employee shall accrue leave in proportion to the pay status. Academic terms during which the employee is on compensated leave for more than 50 percent of the time shall not be creditable for the purpose of

Appendix III

determining eligibility for tenure unless the employee elects otherwise at the time the leave is requested, whenever possible.

17.2 Holidays. Employees shall be entitled to observe all official holidays designated by statute for State employees and other holidays designated by the Department of Administration for State employees. No classes shall be scheduled on holidays. Classes not held because of a holiday shall not be rescheduled. Supervisors are encouraged not to require employees to perform duties on holidays; however, those employees required to perform duties on holidays shall have their schedules adjusted to provide equivalent time off, up to a maximum of eight hours for each holiday worked. If an employee who has performed duties on a holiday terminates employment prior to being given time off, the employee shall be paid, upon termination, for the holiday hours worked within the previous 12-month period.

17.3 Sick Leave.

    (a) Earning of Sick Leave.

        (1) Full-time employees shall earn four hours of sick leave for each biweekly pay period, or the number of hours that are directly proportionate to the number of days worked during less than a full pay period, without limitation as to the total number of hours that may be accrued.

        (2) Part-time employees shall accrue sick leave at a rate directly proportionate to the percent of time employed, effective December 1, 1980.

    (b) Uses of Sick Leave.

        (1) Sick leave shall be earned before being taken, provided that employees who participate in sick leave pools shall not be prohibited from using sick leave otherwise available to them through the sick leave pool.

        (2) A "disability" is defined as any physical or mental impairment of health, including such an impairment proximately resulting from pregnancy, which disables an employee from the full and proper performance of duty.

        (3) An employee must take sick leave when the employee, due to disability, is unable to be present to perform classroom teaching or other scheduled activities, or is unavailable to perform other professional responsibilities. An employee who is unable to perform duties because of a disability shall use any and all accrued sick leave credits unless granted a leave of absence without pay; however, annual leave may be used for such purposes after sick leave credits are exhausted, and for personal appointments with a doctor, dentist, or other recognized medical practitioner.

(4) A continuous period of sick leave commences with the first day of absence and includes all subsequent days until the employee returns to work. For this purpose, Saturdays, Sundays, and official holidays observed by the State shall not be counted unless the employee is scheduled to perform services on such days. During any seven day period, the maximum number of days of sick leave charged against any employee shall be five.

(5) An employee who suffers a disability necessitating the use of sick leave should notify the supervisor as soon as practicable.

(6) An employee who becomes disabled while on approved annual leave shall, upon notifying the supervisor, substitute the use of accrued sick leave to cover the period of disability.

(7) At the discretion of the supervisor, an employee may use sick leave in reasonable amounts for absences resulting from illness or injury of the employee's immediate family.

(8) At the discretion of the supervisor, an employee may use sick leave in reasonable amounts for absences resulting from the death of a member of the employee's family.

(c) Verification. If an employee's absence due to disability exceeds four consecutive days, or if a pattern of absences is documented, the university may require an employee to furnish verification of a disability in the form of a written statement from an attending licensed physician. If the medical certification furnished by the employee is not acceptable, the employee may be required to submit to a medical examination which shall be paid for by the university.

(d) Transfer of Credits.

(1) When an SUS employee moves from one State University System university to another within 100 days, the full balance of accrued sick leave shall accompany the employee.

(2) When an employee moves from a position in State government outside the SUS to a leave earning position within the SUS, all unused sick leave may accompany the employee as governed by applicable State law.

(3) When an SUS employee moves to a position in State government outside the General Faculty and Administrative and Professional Classification Plans, the transfer of unused sick leave credits shall be governed by the rules of the plan to which the employee is transferring.

Appendix III

- (4) The transfer of unused sick leave from a local government to an SUS position is not permitted unless a reciprocal agreement in writing between the Board or its representative and the previous employing entity is in effect.

(e) Payment for Unused Sick Leave.

- (1) An employee with less than ten years of State service who separates from State government shall not be paid for any unused sick leave.

- (2) An employee who has completed ten or more years of State service, has not been found guilty or has not admitted to being guilty of committing, aiding, or abetting any embezzlement, theft, or bribery in connection with State government, or has not been found guilty by a court of competent jurisdiction of having violated any State law against or prohibiting strikes by public employees, or has not been dismissed for cause pursuant to the provisions of Section 110.122, Florida Statutes, and separates from State government because of retirement for other than disability reasons, termination, or death, shall be compensated at the employee's current regular hourly rate of pay for one-eighth of all unused sick leave accrued prior to October 1, 1973, plus one-fourth of all unused sick leave accrued after October 1, 1973; provided that one-fourth of the unused sick leave since 1973 does not exceed 480 hours.

- (3) Upon layoff, an employee with ten or more years of State service shall be paid for unused sick leave as described in paragraph 2. above, unless the employee requests in writing that sick leave credits be retained pending reemployment. For employees who are reemployed by the university within 12 calendar months following layoff, all unused sick leave shall be restored to the employee, provided the employee requests such action in writing and repays the full amount of any lump sum leave payments received at the time of layoff. Employees who are not reemployed within 12 calendar months following layoff shall be paid for sick leave in accordance with Section 110.122, Florida Statutes.

- (4) All payments for unused sick leave authorized by Section 110.122, Florida Statutes, shall be made in lump sum and shall not be used in determining the average final compensation of an employee in any State administered retirement system. An employee shall not be carried on the payroll beyond the last official day of employment, except that an employee who is unable to perform duties because of a disability may be continued on the payroll until all sick leave is exhausted.

(5) In the event of the death of an employee, payment for unused sick leave at the time of death shall be made to the employee's beneficiary, estate, or as provided by law.

17.4 Job-Related Disability. An employee who sustains a job-connected disability that is compensable under the Workers' Compensation Law shall be carried in full pay status for a period not to exceed seven calendar days without being required to use accrued sick or annual leave credits. If the employee is unable to resume work at the end of the seven calendar-day period, the employee shall normally be placed on leave without pay. If the President or representative determines that special circumstances warrant, however, the employee may be placed on leave with pay. The disability leave with or without pay shall be for a period not to exceed the duration of the disability or one year, whichever is less, provided that the employee may during such period use accrued leave credits, but in no case shall the sum of such salary payments and Workers' Compensation benefits exceed the amount of regular salary earned prior to the occurrence of the disability. If at the end of the one-year leave period the employee is still unable to return to work, the President or representative may, based upon a current medical certification by a licensed physician, and taking the university's needs into account, (a) extend the employee's leave-without-pay status for a specified period, (b) request the employee's resignation, (c) offer the employee a part-time appointment, (d) release the employee from employment, notwithstanding the provisions of Article 15.1 and 15.10 or, (e) if the employee is eligible, place the employee on disability retirement.

17.5 Annual Leave.

(a) Earning of Annual Leave.

(1) Full-time calendar year employees shall earn annual leave at the rate of 14.667 hours per month, or a number of hours that is directly proportionate to the number of days worked during less than a full pay period for full-time employees. Up to 44 days (352 hours) of annual leave may be accumulated; after 352 hours of annual leave have been earned, no further annual leave shall be earned until the balance credited falls below 352 hours.

(2) Part-time calendar year employees shall accrue annual leave at a rate directly proportionate to the percent of time employed.

(3) Effective September 1, 1985, full-time employees who are appointed for less than 12 months but more than nine months, other than employees appointed to academic year (39 weeks) appointments and Developmental Research School employees, shall earn annual leave at the rate of 6.769 hours biweekly or 14.667 hours per month of employment (or a number of hours that is directly

Appendix III

proportionate to the the number of days worked during less than a full pay period for full-time employees), and the hours earned shall be credited at the conclusion of each pay period or, upon termination, at the effective date of termination.

(4) Effective September 1, 1985, part-time employees who are appointed for less than 12 months but more than nine months, other than employees appointed to academic year (39 weeks) appointments and Developmental Research School employees, shall earn annual leave at a rate directly proportionate to the percent of time employed.

(5) Academic year (39 weeks) employees, Developmental Research School employees, employees appointed for less than nine months, and OPS employees shall not earn annual leave.

(b) Use and Transfer of Annual Leave.

(1) Annual leave shall be earned before being taken except in those instances where the President or representative may authorize the advancing of annual leave. When leave has been advanced and employment is terminated prior to the employee earning sufficient annual leave to credit against the leave that was advanced, the State shall deduct from the employee's warrant the cost of any annual leave advanced under this provision. All requests for annual leave shall be submitted by the employee to the supervisor as far in advance as possible and appropriate. Approval of the dates on which an employee wishes to take annual leave shall be at the discretion of the supervisor and shall be subject to the consideration of departmental and organizational scheduling.

(2) Upon transfer of a calendar year employee, or other annual leave accruing employee, from one institution to another within the State University System within 100 days, the employee may choose to:

a. transfer up to 44 days of unused annual leave or,

b. make an irrevocable decision to receive a lump sum payment for up to 30 days of annual leave, thereby forfeiting the right to any unused annual leave in excess of 30 days. Such leave payment shall not constitute a break-in-service.

(3) When a calendar year employee, or other annual leave accruing employee, moves from a position in State government outside the SUS to a leave-earning position within the SUS within 30 days, up to 44 days of unused

annual leave may accompany the employee if not prohibited by the previous employer.

(4) When a calendar year SUS employee, or other annual leave accruing employee, moves to a position in State government outside the General Faculty and Administrative and Professional Classification Plans, the transfer of leave shall be governed by the rules of the plan to which the employee is transferring. Should all unused leave not be transferable, up to 30 days (240 hours) of the remaining balance shall be paid in lump sum, effective the last day of SUS employment, without affecting other leave benefits.

(5) The transfer of unused annual leave from a local government to an SUS position is not permitted unless a reciprocal agreement in writing between the Board or its representative and the previous employing entity is in effect.

(c) Payment for Unused Annual Leave.

(1) Upon termination from a calendar year or other annual leave accruing contract, or transfer from an annual leave accruing contract to an academic year or Developmental Research School contract, and unless the employee requests the option in (3) below, the university shall pay the employee for up to 30 days (240 hours) of unused annual leave at the calendar year rate the employee was earning as of the employee's last day of work, provided that a determination has been made by the President or representative that the employee was unable to reduce the unused annual leave balance prior to reassignment to an academic year or Developmental Research School contract. All unused annual leave in excess of 30 days shall be forfeited by the employee.

(2) Upon transfer from a calendar year or other annual leave accruing contract to an academic year or Developmental Research School contract within the SUS, the employee may elect to retain all unused annual leave until such time, not to exceed two years, as the employee transfers back to an annual leave accruing contract or terminates employment with the SUS. Upon such termination or at the end of two years, whichever comes first, the unused leave balance shall be paid lump sum for up to 30 days at the annual rate the employee was earning as of the employee's last day of work on an annual leave accruing contract.

(3) Upon layoff, an employee shall be paid for up to 30 days (240 hours) of unused annual leave in lump sum, unless the employee requests in writing that annual leave credits be retained pending reemployment. For employees

Appendix III 241

who are reemployed by the university within 12 calendar months following layoff, all unused annual leave shall be restored to the employee, provided the employee requests such action in writing and repays the full amount of any lump sum leave payment received at the time of layoff. Employees who are not reemployed within 12 calendar months following layoff and who elected to retain their annual leave credit pending reemployment shall be paid for up to 30 days (240 hours) of unused annual leave at the calendar rate the employee was earning as of the employee's last day of work.

(4) In the event of the death of an employee, payment for all unused annual leave credits at the time of death, up to 352 hours, shall be made to the employee's beneficiary, estate, or as provided by law.

17.6 Jury Duty and Court Appearances. An employee who is summoned as a member of a jury panel or subpoenaed as a witness in a matter not involving the employee's personal interests, shall be granted leave with pay and any jury or witness fees shall be retained by the employee; leave granted hereunder shall not affect an employee's annual or sick leave balance. No employee shall be given leave with pay, nor shall the employee be excused from scheduled professional responsibilities, for the purpose of appearing as an expert professional witness when the employee receives the usual and customary professional compensation for the appearance; such activities fall under the universities' policies and rules relative to outside employment. If an employee is required, as a direct result of the employee's employment, to appear as an official witness to testify in the course of any action as defined in Section 92.142(2), Florida Statutes, such duty shall be considered a part of the employee's job assignment, and the employee shall be paid per diem and travel expenses and shall turn over to the university any fees received.

17.7 Military Leave.

(a) Short-term Military Training. An employee who is a member of the United States Armed Forces Reserve, including the National Guard, upon presentation of a copy of the employee's official orders or appropriate military certification, shall be granted leave with pay during periods in which the employee is engaged in annual field training or other active duty for training exercises. Such leave with pay shall not exceed 17 work days in any one calendar year.

(b) National Guard State Service. An employee who is a member of the Florida National Guard shall be granted leave with pay on all days when ordered to active service by the State. Such leave with pay shall not exceed 17 work days at any one time.

(c) Other Military Leave. Other military leave, with or without pay, will be granted in accordance with applicable provisions of law. Military leave granted under this Article shall not affect an employee's annual or sick leave balance.

17.8 Leave Pending Investigation. When the President or representative has reason to believe that the employee's presence on the job will adversely affect the operation of the university, the President or representative may immediately place the employee on leave pending investigation of the event(s) leading to that belief. The leave pending investigation shall commence immediately upon the President or representative providing the employee with a written notice of the reasons therefor. The leave shall be with pay, with no reduction of accrued leave.

17.9 Personal Leave Days. A Developmental Research School employee may be granted one day (non-cumulative) of leave per year for emergencies or for other personal reasons. Except in the case of emergency, the employee shall provide at least two days notice of the intended leave. Such leave shall not be used on the day immediately preceding or following a holiday or vacation without the approval of the President or representative.

17.10 Uncompensated Leave. Upon request of an employee, the President or representative shall grant a leave without pay for a period not to exceed one year, unless the President or representative determines that granting such leave would be inconsistent with the best interests of the university. Such leave may be extended upon mutual agreement. Upon return, the salary of the employee shall be adjusted to reflect all nondiscretionary increases distributed during the period of leave. Retirement credit for such periods of leave without pay shall be governed by the rules and regulations of the Division of Retirement and the provisions of Florida Statutes, Chapter 121. While on leave without pay, the employee shall retain accumulated sick leave and annual leave, but shall not earn sick leave or annual leave nor be entitled to holiday pay. Time spent on uncompensated leave shall not be creditable for the purpose of determining eligibility for tenure, except by mutual agreement of the employee and the university. In deciding whether to credit leave without pay toward tenure eligibility, the President or representative shall consider the relevance of the employee's activities while on such leave to the employee's professional development and to the employee's field of employment, the benefits, if any, which accrue to the university by virtue of placing the employee on such leave, and other appropriate factors.

17.11 Compulsory Disability Leave. If the President or representative believes that an employee is unable to perform assigned duties due to illness, disability, or injury, the President or representative may require the employee to submit to a medical examination by a licensed physician chosen and paid by the university, or by a licensed physician chosen and paid by the employee, and who is acceptable to the President or representative and who shall submit a report to the university. If the university agrees to accept the employee's choice of licensed physician, the university may not then require another university-paid examination. If the medical examination confirms that the employee is unable to perform assigned duties, the President or representative

Appendix III

shall place the employee on compulsory disability leave, at which time the employee shall be notified in writing of the duration of the compulsory leave period and the conditions under which the employee may return to work. These conditions may include the requirement of the successful completion of, or participation in, a program of rehabilitation or treatment. If the employee fulfills the terms and conditions of the compulsory disability leave and receives a current medical certification that the employee is able to perform assigned duties, the President or representative shall return the employee to the employee's previous duties, if possible, or to equivalent duties. An employee who is placed on compulsory disability leave shall be required to exhaust all earned leave credits prior to being placed on leave without pay.

If the employee fails to fulfill the terms and conditions of the compulsory disability leave and/or is unable to return to work and perform assigned duties at the end of a compulsory leave period, the President or representative may, based upon the university's needs:

(a) extend the leave without pay;

(b) offer the employee part-time employment;

(c) request the employee's resignation; or

(d) release the employee from employment, notwithstanding the provisions of Article 15.1 and 15.10.

17.12 Child Care Leave. The university President or representative shall approve an employee's written request for leave of absence without pay when the employee becomes a biological parent or a child is placed in the home pending adoption. Such leave without pay may not normally exceed six months but may be extended at the discretion of the President or representative. The leave without pay may begin no more than two weeks before the expected date of the child's arrival. Accrued annual leave may be used prior to the employee being placed on leave without pay. Any illness caused or contributed by pregnancy shall be treated as a temporary disability, and the employee shall be allowed to use accrued sick leave credits when certified by a licensed physician. At the end of the approved child care leave without pay and at the employee's request, the President or representative shall grant part-time leave without pay for a period not to exceed one year, unless the President or representative determines that granting such leave would be inconsistent with the best interests of the university. Should any portion of this leave be paid leave, the employee shall be entitled to accumulate all benefits granted under paid leave status. Compensated or uncompensated leave taken under this article shall be creditable toward tenure eligibility in accordance with the provisions of Articles 17.1 and 17.10.

17.13 The President or President's representative may close the university, or portions of the university, in the event conditions are such that it is not appropriate for employees to be on campus or to travel to the university. Such closings will be only for the period of time it takes to restore normal working conditions. Such leave shall not reduce employees' leave balances.

ARTICLE 18
COPYRIGHTS AND PATENTS

Copyrights

18.1 An employee may procure copyrights, and receive the royalties resulting therefrom, for the employee's products, provided (a) the ideas came from the employee, (b) the products were the result of the employee's independent labors, and (c) the university was not held responsible for any opinions expressed therein. If the products were in any way supported by university funds, personnel, facilities, equipment, or materials, the employee shall report to the President or representative the employee's interest in having the product copyrighted.

Within 30 days after receiving such report, the President or representative will inform the employee whether the university seeks an interest in the copyright, and a written contract shall thereafter be negotiated to reflect the interest of both parties. All such agreements shall comport with and satisfy any preexisting commitments to outside sponsoring agencies, but the employee and the university shall not commit any act which would tend to defeat the university's or employee's interest in the matter and shall take any necessary steps to protect such interests.

Patents

18.2 An employee shall disclose all patentable inventions and technological developments which the employee may develop or discover while an employee of the State University System. With respect to discoveries or inventions made during the course of approved outside employment, the employee may delay such disclosure, when necessary to protect the outside employer's interests, until the decision has been made whether to seek a patent.

18.3 All discoveries or inventions made outside the field in which the discoverer or inventor is employed by the institution and for which the university has provided no support are the private property of the inventor. The employee and the President or representative may agree that the patent for such discovery and invention be pursued by the university and the proceeds shared.

18.4 Except for discoveries or inventions made during the course of approved outside employment, a discovery or invention which is made in the field in which the investigator is employed by the university or by using university funds, facilities, materials, equipment, personnel, or proprietary technological information, is the property of the university and the inventor shall share in the proceeds therefrom.

Appendix III

While an employee may, in accordance with Article 19, Conflict of Interest/Outside Activity, engage in outside employment pursuant to a consulting agreement, requirements that an employee waive the employee's or university's rights to any patentable inventions or discoveries which arise during the course of such outside employment must be approved by the President or representative. An employee who proposes to engage in such outside employment shall furnish a copy of this Article and the university's patents policy to the outside employer prior to or at the time the consulting agreement is executed.

18.5 Reporting Procedures. The employee shall report to the President or representative the nature of the discovery or invention, together with an outline of the project and the conditions under which it was done. If the university wishes to assert its interest in the patent, the President or representative shall inform the employee within 30 days. The President or representative shall conduct an investigation which shall assess the respective equities of the employee and the university in the invention or technological development, and determine its importance and the extent to which the university should be involved in its protection, development and promotion. The President or representative shall inform the employee of the university's decision to apply for the patent within a reasonable time, not to exceed 135 days from the date of the disclosure to the President or representative. The division, between the university and the employee, of proceeds generated by the licensing or assignment of patent rights or trade secrets, shall be negotiated and reflected in a written contract between the university and the employee. All such agreements shall comport with and satisfy any preexisting commitments to outside sponsoring agencies, but the employee shall not commit any act which would tend to defeat the university's interest in the matter, and the university shall take any necessary steps to protect such interest.

18.6 In the event a contractor has been offered the option to apply for the patent, the university will use its good offices in an effort to obtain such a decision within 120 days. At any stage of making the patent applications, or in the development of a patent secured, if it has not otherwise assigned to a third party the right to pursue its interests, the President or representative may withdraw and shall return the patent rights to the employee, in which case the patent shall be the employee's property, and none of the costs incurred by the university or on its behalf shall be assessed against the inventor.

All assignments of or release of patents rights by the President or representative to the employee shall contain the provision that such invention and/or process, if patented by the employee, shall be available royalty-free for governmental purposes of the State of Florida.

ARTICLE 19
CONFLICT OF INTEREST/OUTSIDE ACTIVITY

It is the policy of the Board to insure that employees are aware of their obligations and responsibilities as public employees of the State University System. An employee is bound to observe, in all official acts, the highest standards of ethics consistent with the code of ethics of the State of Florida (Chapter 112, Part III, Florida Statutes) and the advisory opinions rendered with respect thereto. Other provisions of State law govern obligations and responsibilities of employees who receive State compensation in addition to their annual salary (see Section 240.283. Florida Statutes).

19.1 An employee shall not engage in any outside activity which interferes with the full performance of the employee's professional responsibilities or other institutional obligations. Nothing in this Article is intended to discourage an employee from engaging in outside activity in order to increase the employee's professional reputation, service to the community, or income, subject to the conditions stated herein.

"Outside Activity" shall mean any private practice, private consulting, additional teaching or research, or other activity, compensated or uncompensated, which is not part of the employee's assigned duties and for which the university has provided no compensation.

19.2 Conflict of Interest. Any employee who proposes to engage in any outside activity which the employee should reasonably conclude may create a conflict of interest, or which may otherwise interfere with the full performance of the employee's professional or institutional responsibilities, shall notify the employee's supervisor, in writing, of the details of such proposed activity prior to engaging therein.

19.3 Compensated Professional Activity. Any employee who proposes to engage in any outside compensated professional activity shall notify the employee's supervisor, in writing, of the details of such proposed activity prior to engaging therein.

19.4 Written notification, as described in 19.2 and 19.3, above, shall include, where applicable, the name of the employer or other recipient of services, and the funding source; the location where such activity shall be performed; the nature and extent of the activity; and any intended use of university facilities, equipment, or services. The reporting provisions of this section shall not apply to activities performed wholly during a period in which the employee has no appointment with the State University System.

19.5 In the event the proposed outside activity is determined to constitute a conflict of interest or other interference with the employee's institutional responsibilities, the supervisor shall discuss the matter with the employee within two weeks of receipt of the employee's written notification.

If the matter is unresolved following this discussion, the employee may refer the matter to the President or representative, who shall determine whether the outside activity creates a conflict of interest or otherwise interferes with the employee's professional or institutional responsibilities. The employee shall be notified of the university's determination no later than three weeks from the date the matter was referred to the President or representative. If the employee desires

Appendix III   247

to challenge the university's determination, the employee may request an expedited arbitration hearing under Article 20, Grievance Procedure. Under this proceeding, the arbitrator shall be selected from the grievance arbitration panel within three days, shall hear the matter within one week, and shall issue a decision orally or in writing at the conclusion of the hearing or as soon thereafter as is practicable, but not later than three days following the close of the hearing.

The employee may engage in such outside activity pending the decision of the arbitrator. If the arbitrator determines that there is a conflict of interest or other interference with the employee's professional or institutional responsibilities, the employee shall cease such activity immediately and turn over to the university any compensation earned therefrom.

19.6 Any outside activity currently engaged in, falling under the provisions of this Article but not previously reported, shall be reported within 60 days of the execution of this Agreement and shall conform to the provisions of this Article.

19.7 An employee engaging in any outside activity shall not use the facilities, equipment, or services of the university in connection with such outside activity without prior approval of the President or representative. Such approval may be conditioned upon reimbursement for the use thereof.

19.8 An employee engaging in outside activity shall take reasonable precautions to ensure that the outside employer or other recipient of services understands that the employee is engaging in such outside activity as a private citizen and not as an employee, agent, or spokesperson of the university.

ARTICLE 20
GRIEVANCE PROCEDURE AND ARBITRATION

20.1 Purpose. The parties agree that all problems should be resolved, whenever possible, before the filing of a grievance but within the time limits for filing grievances stated elsewhere in this Article, and encourage open communications between administrators and employees so that resort to the formal grievance procedure will not normally be necessary. The parties further encourage the informal resolution of grievances whenever possible. At each step in the grievance process, participants are encouraged to pursue appropriate modes of conflict resolution. The purpose of this Article is to promote a prompt and efficient procedure for the investigation and resolution of grievances. The procedures hereinafter set forth shall be the sole and exclusive method for resolving the grievances of employees as defined herein.

20.2 Resort to Other Procedures. If prior to seeking resolution of a dispute by filing a grievance hereunder, or while the grievance proceeding is in progress, an employee seeks resolution of the matter in any other forum, whether administrative or judicial, the Board or representative shall have no obligation to entertain or proceed further with the matter pursuant to this grievance procedure. Further, since the parties do not intend that this grievance procedure be a device for appellate review, the President's response to a recommendation of a hearing officer or other individual or group having appropriate jurisdiction in any other procedure shall not be an act or omission giving rise to a grievance under this procedure.

20.3 Definitions. As used herein:

    (a) The term "grievance" shall mean a dispute filed on a form appended to this Agreement concerning the interpretation or application of a specific term or provision of this Agreement, subject to those exclusions appearing in other Articles of this Agreement.

    (b) The term "grievant" shall mean an employee or group of employees who have filed a grievance in a dispute over a provision of this Agreement which confers rights upon them, or UFF which has filed a grievance in a dispute over a provision of this Agreement which confers rights upon UFF. A grievance filed by a chapter of UFF which alleges a violation of its rights by a university shall be initiated at Step 1. A grievance filed by UFF which alleges a violation of its rights by the Board or two or more universities shall be initiated at Step 2. A grievance which involves grievants at two or more universities may be initiated by UFF at Step 2.

20.4 Representation. UFF shall have the exclusive right to represent any employee in grievances filed hereunder, provided employees may represent themselves or be represented by legal counsel. If an employee elects not to be represented by UFF, the Board or representative shall promptly inform UFF in writing of the grievance. No resolution of any individually processed grievance shall be inconsistent with the terms of this Agreement and for this purpose UFF shall have the right to have an observer present at all meetings called for the purpose of discussing grievances.

20.5 Grievance Representatives. UFF shall annually furnish to the Board or representative, and to the President or representative, a list of all persons authorized to act as grievance representatives and shall update the list as needed. The UFF grievance representative shall have the responsibility to meet all classes, office hours, and other duties and responsibilities incidental to the assigned workload. Some of these activities are scheduled to be performed at particular times. Such representative shall have the right during times outside of those hours scheduled for these activities to investigate, consult, and prepare grievance presentations and attend grievance hearings and meetings. Should any hearings or meetings with the President, Board, or their representatives necessitate rescheduling of assigned duties, the representative may, with the approval of the appropriate administrator, arrange for the rescheduling of such duties or their coverage by colleagues. Such approval shall not be unreasonably withheld.

Appendix III

20.6 Appearances. When an employee participates during working hours in arbitration proceedings or in a grievance conference or meetings between the grievant or representative and the President or Board or either of their representatives, that employee's compensation shall neither be reduced nor increased for time spent in those activities.

Prior to participation in any such proceedings, conferences, or meetings, the employee shall make arrangements acceptable to the appropriate supervisor for the performance of the employee's duties. Approval of such arrangements shall not be unreasonably withheld. Time spent in such activities outside regular working hours shall not be counted as time worked.

20.7 Grievance Forms. All grievances, requests for review, and arbitration notices must be submitted in writing on forms attached to this Agreement as Appendices "C", "D", and "E", respectively, and shall be signed by the grievant. Except for the initial filing of the grievance, if there is difficulty in meeting any time limit, the UFF representative may sign such documents for the grievant. The President or Chancellor, or their representatives, may refuse consideration of a grievance not filed or processed in accordance with this Article.

Formal Grievance Procedure

20.8 Step 1. All grievances shall be filed with the President or represent-ative, or in case of grievances initiated at Step 2 with the Chancellor or representative, within 25 days following the act or omission giving rise thereto, or the date on which the employee knew or reasonably should have known of such act or omission if that date is later.

The filing of a grievance constitutes a waiver of any rights to judicial review of agency action pursuant to Florida Statutes, Chapter 120, or to the review of such actions under university or Board procedures which may otherwise be available to address such matters. Only those acts or omissions and sections of the Agreement identified at Step 1 may be considered at subsequent steps. The grievant may, in the written grievance which is filed, request the postponement of any action in processing the grievances formally for a period of up to 25 days, during which period efforts to resolve the grievance informally shall be made. The initial such request shall be granted. Upon the grievant's written request, additional 25-day extensions should be liberally granted unless to do so would impede resolution of the grievance. Upon request, the President or representative shall, during such postponement period(s), arrange an informal conference between the appropriate administrator and the grievant. The grievant shall have the right to representation by UFF during attempts at informal resolution of the grievance. The grievant may at any time terminate the postponement period by giving written notice to the President or representative that the grievant wishes to proceed with the Step 1 meeting provided for below. If the postponement period, or any extension thereof, expires without such written notice, the grievance shall be deemed informally resolved to the grievant's satisfaction and need not be processed further. The President or representative shall conduct a meeting with the grievant and the UFF representative no sooner than seven and no later than 15 days following (a) receipt of the grievance if no postponement is requested, or (b) receipt of written notice that the grievant wishes to proceed with the Step 1 meeting.

In advance of the Step 1 meeting, the grievant shall have the right, upon request, to a copy of any identifiable documents relevant to the grievance. At the Step 1 meeting, the grievant shall have the right to present any evidence in support of the grievance and the grievant, and/or the UFF representative, and the President or representative shall discuss the grievance. The President or representative shall issue a written decision, stating the reasons therefor, within 25 days following the conclusion of the meeting. Where practicable, the Step I reviewer shall make available to the grievant, or grievance representative, documentation referenced in the Step I decision, prior to its issuance. All documents referred to in the decision and any additional documents presented by the grievant shall be attached to the decision together with a list of these documents.

20.9 Step 2. If the grievance is not satisfactorily resolved at Step 1, the grievant may file a written request for review with the Chancellor or representative within 25 days following receipt of the Step 1 decision. The Chancellor, or representative, and the representative of the grievant shall schedule a conference in Tallahassee for the purpose of reviewing the matter no sooner than seven and no later than 15 days following receipt of the request for review. The Chancellor or representative shall issue a written decision, stating the reasons therefor, within 25 days following the conclusion of the review conference.

20.10 Step 3. If the grievance has not been satisfactorily resolved at Step 2, UFF may, upon the request of the grievant, proceed to arbitration by filing a written notice of intent to do so. Notice of intent to proceed to arbitration must be filed with the Chancellor or representative within 25 days after receipt of the Step 2 decision and shall be signed by the grievant and the UFF President or representative. The grievance may be withdrawn at any time by the grievant or by the UFF representative at any point during Step 3.

20.11 Selection of Arbitrator. Representatives of the Board and UFF shall meet within 90 days after the execution of this Agreement for the purpose of selecting a fifteen-member Arbitration Panel. Within 14 days after receipt of a notice of intent to arbitrate, representatives of the Board and UFF shall meet for the purpose of selecting an arbitrator from the Panel. Selection shall be by mutual agreement or by alternately striking names from the Arbitration Panel list until one name remains. The right of the first choice to strike from the list shall be determined by the flip of a coin. If the parties are unable to agree to a panel of arbitrators, they shall follow the normal American Arbitration Association procedure for the selection an arbitrator. The parties may mutually select as the arbitrator an individual who is not a member of the Arbitration Panel. The arbitration shall be held within 90 days following the selection of the arbitrator.

Appendix III   251

20.12 Authority of the Arbitrator. The arbitrator shall neither add to, subtract from, modify, or alter the terms or provisions of this Agreement. Arbitration shall be confined solely to the application and/or interpretation of this Agreement and the precise issues(s) submitted for arbitration. The arbitrator shall refrain from issuing any statements of opinion or conclusions not essential to the determination of the issues submitted.

Where an administrator has made a judgment involving the exercise of discretion, such as decisions regarding tenure or promotion, the arbitrator shall not substitute the arbitrator's judgment for that of the administrator. Nor shall the arbitrator review such decision except for the purpose of determining whether the decision has violated this Agreement. If the arbitrator determines that the Agreement has been violated, the arbitrator shall direct the university to take appropriate action. An arbitrator may award back salary where the arbitrator determines that the employee is not receiving the appropriate salary from the university, but the arbitrator may not award other monetary damages or penalties. If notice that further employment will not be offered is not given on time, the arbitrator may direct the university to renew the appointment only upon a finding that no other remedy is adequate, and that the notice was given so late that (a) the employee was deprived of reasonable opportunity to seek other employment, or (b) the employee actually rejected an offer of comparable employment which the employee otherwise would have accepted.

An arbitrator's decision awarding employment beyond the sixth year shall not entitle the employee to tenure. In such cases the employee shall serve during the seventh year without further right to notice that the employee will not be offered employment thereafter. If an employee is reappointed at the direction of an arbitrator, the President or representative may reassign the employee during such reappointment.

In all grievances except disciplinary grievances in accordance with Article 16, Termination and Other Actions, the burden of proof shall be on the employee. In disciplinary grievances, the burden of proof shall be on the Board.

20.13   Arbitrability. In any proceeding, the first matter to be decided is the arbitrator's jurisdiction to act, which decision the arbitrator shall announce. Upon concluding that the arbitrator has no such power, the arbitrator shall make no decision or recommendation as to the merits of the grievance. Upon concluding that the issue is arbitrable, the arbitrator shall normally proceed with the hearing at that time, provided that either party may seek judicial review of the arbitrator's decision as to jurisdiction and have the hearing on the merits of the grievance delayed until such review is completed, pursuant to Florida Statutes, Section 682.03.

20.14   Conduct of Hearing. The arbitrator shall hold the hearing in the city where the grievant is employed, unless otherwise agreed by the parties. The hearing shall commence within 25 days of the arbitrator's acceptance of selection, or as soon thereafter as is practicable, and the arbitrator shall issue the decision within 60 days of the close of the hearing or the submission of briefs, whichever is later, unless additional time is agreed to by the parties. The decision shall be in writing and shall set forth findings of fact, reasoning, and conclusions on the issues submitted. Except as expressly specified in this Article, the provisions of the Florida Arbitration Code, Florida Statutes, Chapter 682, shall not apply. Except as modified by the provisions of this Agreement, arbitration proceedings shall be conducted in accordance with the rules and procedures of the American Arbitration Association.

20.15   Effect of Decision. The decision or award of the arbitrator shall be final and binding upon the Board, UFF, and the grievant, provided that either party may appeal to an appropriate court of law a decision that was rendered by the arbitrator acting outside of or beyond the arbitrator's jurisdiction, pursuant to Florida Statutes, Section 682.13.

20.16   Fees and Expenses. All fees and expenses of the arbitrator shall be divided equally between the parties. Each party shall bear the cost of preparing and presenting its own case. The party desiring a transcript of the arbitration proceedings shall provide written notice to the other party of its intention to have a transcript of the arbitration made at least one week prior to the date of the arbitration. The party desiring such transcript shall be responsible for scheduling a stenotype reporter to record the proceedings. The parties shall share equally the appearance fee of the stenotype reporter and the cost of obtaining an original transcript and one copy for the party originally requesting a transcript of the proceedings. The requesting party shall, at its expense, photocopy the copy of the transcript received from the reporter and deliver the photocopy to the other party within five days after receiving the copy of the transcript from the reporter.

20.17   Time Limits. All time limits contained in this Article may be extended by mutual agreement of the parties, except that the time limits for the initial filing of a grievance may be extended only by agreement between the Board and UFF. Upon failure of the Board or its representatives to provide a decision within the time limits provided in this Article, the grievant or UFF, where appropriate, may appeal to the next step. Upon the failure of the grievant or UFF, where appropriate, to file an appeal within the time limits provided in this Article, the grievance shall be deemed to have been resolved by the decision at the prior step.

20.18   Notification. All grievances, requests for review, notices, and decisions shall be transmitted in person or by certified or registered mail, restricted delivery, return receipt requested. In the event of a question as to the timeliness of any grievance, request for review, notice, or decision, the date of receipt shall be determinative. In the event that any action falls due on a Saturday, Sunday, or holiday (as referred to in Article 17.2) the action will be considered timely if it is accomplished by 5:00 p.m. on the following business day.

Appendix III

20.19 Precedent. No complaint informally resolved, or grievance resolved at either Step 1 or 2, shall constitute a precedent for any purpose unless agreed to in writing by the Chancellor or representative and UFF acting through its President or representative.

20.20 Retroactivity. An arbitrator's award may or may not be retroactive as the equities of each case may demand, but in no case shall an award be retroactive to a date earlier than 30 days prior to the date the grievance was initially filed in accordance with this Article or the date on which the act or omission occurred, whichever is later.

20.21 Processing. The filing or pendency of any grievance or arbitration proceedings under this Article shall not operate to impede, preclude, or delay the Board from taking the action complained of. Reasonable efforts, including the shortening of time limits when practical, shall be made to conclude the processing of a grievance prior to the expiration of the grievant's employment, whether by termination or failure to reappoint. In no event shall any employee, as a result of a pending grievance, receive compensation following cessation of employment.

20.22 Reprisal. No reprisal of any kind will be made by the Board or UFF against any grievant, any witness, any UFF representative, or any other participant in the grievance procedure by reason of such participation.

20.23 Records. All written materials pertinent to a grievance shall be filed separately from the evaluation file of the grievant or witnesses, except decisions resulting from arbitration or settlement.

ARTICLE 21
OTHER EMPLOYEE RIGHTS

21.1 Professional Meetings. Employees should be encouraged to and may, with the approval of the supervisor, attend professional meetings, conferences, and activities. Subject to the availability of funds, the employee's expenses in connection with such meetings, conferences, or activities shall be reimbursed in accordance with the applicable provisions of State law and rules and regulations having the force and effect of law.

21.2 Office Space. Each employee shall be provided with office space which may be on a shared basis. The parties recognize the desirability of providing each employee with enclosed office space with a door lock, office equipment commensurate with assigned responsibilities, and ready access to a telephone. Each employee shall, consistent with building security, have reasonable access to the employee's office space and laboratories, studios, music rooms, and the like used in connection with assigned responsibilities; this provision may require that campus security provide access on an individual basis.

21.3 Safe Conditions. Whenever an employee reports a condition which the employee feels represents a violation of safety or health rules and regulations or which is an unreasonable hazard to persons or property, such conditions shall be promptly investigated. The appropriate administrator shall reply to the concern, in writing, if the employee's concern is communicated in writing.

21.4 Tuition-free Courses. Subject to the approval of the receiving university, a permanent full-time employee, including those employees on sabbaticals or on professional development or grants-in-aid leave, with at least six months of service, may take up to six credit hours of on-campus instruction per term tuition-free at any university within the State University System on a space available basis, limited to courses that do not increase the direct cost to the university. For purposes of this paragraph, the word "term" is defined as one of the two semesters in the academic year or the period of approximately 13 weeks between the end of the spring semester and beginning of the fall semester.

21.5 Limitation on Personal Liability

    (a) In the event an employee is sued for an act, event, or omission which may fall within the scope of Florida Statutes, Section 768.28, the employee should notify the President's office as soon as possible after receipt of the summons commencing the action in order that the Board may fulfill its obligation. Failure to notify the employer promptly may affect the rights of the parties.

    (b) For information purposes, the following pertinent language of Florida Statutes, Section 768.28(9) is reproduced herein.

    "No officer, employee, or agent of the state or its subdivisions shall be held personally liable in tort for any injuries or damages suffered as a result of any act, event or omission of action in the scope of his employment or function unless such officer, employee or agent acted in bad faith or with malicious purpose or in a manner exhibiting wanton or willful disregard of human rights, safety or property."

21.6 The universities will, to the extent permitted by State regulation and law, provide travel advances, upon request, of up to 80 percent of budgeted expenses for authorized travel of longer than five consecutive days.

21.7 Consistent with law, the provisions of Article 18, and the legitimate interests of the university, employees shall have the right to and control of their personal correspondence, notes, raw data, and other working papers.

Appendix III

ARTICLE 22
PROFESSIONAL DEVELOPMENT PROGRAM AND SABBATICALS

22.1 Professional Development Leave.

(a) Policy: Professional development leave shall be made available to employees who meet the requirements set forth below. Such leaves are granted to increase an employee's value to the university through enhanced opportunities for professional renewal, educational travel, study, formal education, research, writing, or other experience of professional value, not as a reward for service.

(b) Types of Professional Development Leave.

Each year, the university or its representatives will make available at least one professional development leave at full pay for one semester for each 20 eligible employees, subject to the conditions set forth below.

(c) Eligibility for Professional Development Leave.

Employees with three or more years of service, except those who are serving in tenure-earning or tenured positions, shall be eligible for professional development leaves if the terms of a contract and grant through which an employee may be compensated allow for such leave.

(d) Application and Selection.

(1) Application for professional development leave shall contain an appropriate outline of the project or work to be accomplished during the leave.

(2) The university or its representative shall select applicants when the university believes that completion of the project or work would improve the productivity of the department or function of which the employee is a part. Criteria for selection of professional development leave applicants shall be specified by the university, and made available to eligible employees.

(3) Upon return to work, the employee shall submit a brief written report of activities during such leave.

(4) No more than one employee in each department or other professional unit need be granted leave at the same time.

(e) Terms of Professional Development Leave.

(1) The employee must return to university employment for at least one academic year following the conclusion of such leave. Agreements to the contrary must be reduced to

writing prior to participation. Return to the university of salary received during the program may be required in those instances where neither of the above is satisfied.

 (2) An employee who fails to spend the time as stated in the application shall reimburse the university for the salary received during such leave.

 (3) Employees shall not normally be eligible for a second professional development leave until three years of continuous service are completed following the previous leave.

22.2 Other Study Leave.

 (a) Job-Required. An employee required to take academic course work as part of assigned duties shall not be required to charge time spent attending classes during the work day to accrued leave.

 (b) Job-Related. An employee may, at the discretion of the supervisor, be permitted to attend up to six credits of course work per semester during work, provided that:

  (1) the course work is directly related to the employee's professional responsibilities;

  (2) the supervisor determines that the absence will not interfere with the proper operation of the work unit;

  (3) the supervisor believes that completion of the course work would improve the productivity of the department or function of which the employee is a part; and

  (4) the employee's work schedule can be adjusted to accommodate such job-related study without reduction in the total number of work hours required per pay period.

 (c) Employees may, in accordance with this Article, use accrued annual leave for job-related study.

22.3 Sabbaticals.

 (a) Policy. Sabbaticals for professional development are to be made available to employees who meet the requirements set forth below. Such sabbaticals are granted to increase an employee's value to the university through enhanced opportunities for professional renewal, planned travel, study, formal education, research, writing, or other experience of professional value, not as a reward for service.

 (b) Types of Sabbaticals.

Appendix III

(1) The Board or representative will make available to each employee who applies, subject to the conditions set forth below, a sabbatical for two semesters (i.e., one academic year) at half pay.

(2) The Board or representative will make available, subject to the conditions set forth below, at least 60 sabbaticals for one semester at full pay. These full-pay sabbaticals shall be distributed to each university in proportion to the number of eligible employees.

(c) Eligibility for Sabbaticals.

Full-time tenured employees with at least six years of full-time service within the State University System shall be eligible for sabbaticals, if the terms of a contract or grant through which such an employee may be compensated allow for such sabbaticals.

(d) Application and Selection.

(1) Applications for sabbaticals shall be submitted to the President of the university or representative in accordance with procedures established through the consultation process (Article 2) at each university. Each application shall include a statement describing the program to be followed while on sabbatical, the expected increase in value of the employee to the university, any anticipated supplementary income, and a statement that the applicant agrees to comply with the conditions of the sabbatical program as described in 22.3(e).

(2) Sabbaticals at half-pay shall be granted upon application, subject to the conditions set forth in this Article.

(3) If there are more applicants for one semester sabbaticals at full pay than available sabbaticals, a committee shall rank the applicants. The committee members shall be tenured employees elected by tenured employees. The committee chair-person shall be selected by the President or representative. The committee, in ranking the applicants, shall consider the benefits of the proposed program to the employee, the university, and the profession; an equitable distribution of sabbaticals among colleges, divisions, schools, departments, and disciplines within the university; and the length of time since the employee was relieved of teaching duties for the purpose of research and other scholarly activities. The committee shall submit a ranked list of recommended employees to the President or representative. The President or representative shall make appointments from the list and consult with the committee prior to an

appointment that does not follow the committee's ranking.

(4) No more than one employee in a department or other professional unit need be awarded a sabbatical at the same time.

(e) Terms of Sabbatical Program.

(1) While on sabbatical, the employee's salary shall be one-half pay for two semesters (one academic year), or full pay for one semester.

(2) The employee must return to the university for at least one academic year following participation in the program. Agreements to the contrary must be reduced to writing prior to participation. Return to the university of salary received during the program may be required in those instances where neither of the above is satisfied.

(3) The employee must provide a brief written report of the employee's accomplishments during the sabbatical to the President or representative upon return to the university.

(4) Employees shall not normally be eligible for a second sabbatical until six years of continuous service is completed following the first.

(5) Contributions normally made by the Board to retirement and social security programs shall be continued on a basis proportional to the salary received. Board contributions normally made to employee insurance programs and any other employee benefit programs shall be continued during the sabbatical.

(6) Eligible employees shall continue to accrue annual and sick leave on a full-time basis during the sabbatical.

(7) While on leave, an employee shall be permitted to receive travel and living expenses, fellowships, grants-in-aid, contracts or grants, or other financial assistance from sources other than the university to assist in accomplishing the purposes of the sabbatical. If such financial assistance is received, the university salary shall normally be reduced by the amount necessary to bring the total income of the sabbatical period to a level comparable to the employee's normal salary. Employment unrelated to the purpose of the sabbatical is governed by the provisions of Article 19, Conflict of Interest/Outside Activity.

Appendix III   259

22.4 Retraining. A university may, at its discretion, provide opportunities for retraining of employees when it is in the university's best
interests. Such opportunities may be provided to employees who are
laid off, to those who are reassigned, or in other appropriate circumstances. These retraining opportunities may include enrollment in
tuition-free courses under the provisions of Article 21.4, and Sabbatical or Professional Development Leave under this Article.

                            Article 23
                            SALARIES

Salaries for the 1985-86 academic year are governed by this Article.
Salaries in subsequent years shall be negotiated according to the
provisions of Article 30.1.

23.1(a)   The annual salary rate of all full-time employees shall
          correspond to a salary rate contained in the salary table.
          Part-time employees shall be paid at a salary rate repre-
          senting a proportion of a step contained in the salary table
          as determined by their fractional F.T.E. appointment. All
          salary increases shall be distributed in a manner which
          results in an employee's salary rate remaining on a salary
          table step or half-step. If an employee's salary rate should
          for any reason not correspond to a salary rate on the salary
          table, the employee's salary rate shall be adjusted to the
          next higher step or half-step.

   (b)   1985-86 Salary Table. The amounts in the salary table have
          been increased 3.0% (see Articles 23.2(a), 23.3(a), and
          23.4(b)(1) and (c)(1)).

23.2 From a total fund of 5% of the June 30, 1985, annual salary rate
of employees, the Board shall provide salary increases as follows:

   (a)   General Salary Table Increase. The annual salary rate for
          each half-step in the 1984-85 salary table shall be increased
          2.00% for 1985-86. All eligible employees, as described in
          Section 23.10, below, shall receive this increase.

   (b)   Salary Table Incremental Step. After the implementation of
          general salary table increases, as described in 23.2(a),
          above, has been provided, funds at an annual rate of .25% of
          the June 30, 1985 annual salary rate of employees shall be
          used to provide a one-half step increase (1.75%) to employees
          on Step 23.5 or below at each university. Any funds remain-
          ing at a university after such increases are provided shall
          be distributed pursuant to Article 23.2(d).

   (c)   Discretionary Increases. Funds at an annual rate of 1.50% of
          the June 30, 1985, salary rate of employees shall be distrib-
          uted to employees for the following purposes:

(1) Salary adjustments required by Section 240.247, Florida Statutes. The procedures for conducting the Salary Equity Study shall include:

   a. By September 15, each university President shall notify eligible employees of the procedures adopted by the university to conduct the salary study. The notification shall include the following statement: "In any year, an employee may seek to resolve a salary inequity due to discrimination based on race or sex either by filing a grievance under Article 6--Nondiscrimination--or by conducting a salary equity study according to this procedure. But the employee cannot do both."

   b. Pursuant to notification, as provided in a. above, an employee who perceives that the factors of race or sex may have affected the employee's salary may request a meeting with the department chair (or dean or director where an administrative unit is not organized along departmental lines) to review salary data and to request assistance in preparing the employee's salary study. This meeting shall be scheduled by October 15. The employee may be assisted by a colleague at this and all subsequent meetings. The administrator shall provide reasonable assistance to the employee, including copies of available documents that the employee may request, excluding those documents that are evaluative in nature and thereby protected from access under Article 11 of this Agreement and Section 240.253, Florida Statutes.

   c. In accordance with university procedures, employees will be afforded an opportunity to present the results of their completed studies to the appropriate chairperson, dean, or director who will review the studies and indicate in writing to the employees whether a salary adjustment is recommended. This notification shall be provided within 30 days following the receipt of employees' completed studies.

   d. If an employee does not agree with the recommendation of the chairperson, dean, or director, the employee may request that the matter be referred to the appropriate vice president or to a review panel established by the university.

   e. The employee's self study, the recommendation of the chairperson, dean, or director, and any recommendation of the vice president or review panel, must be submitted to the university President or President's designee. In all cases, the President

Appendix III   261

   or designee shall make the final decision to
   approve or deny a salary adjustment.

f. The President shall report the results of the study
   to the Board of Regents on or before February 15,
   or as soon thereafter as possible.

g. A salary equity adjustment awarded an employee
   shall be effective on the same date as other salary
   increases awarded the employee for the next academic year. The amount of the salary equity adjustment shall be to remedy an inequity based on race
   or sex existing during the academic year in which
   the employee's self study is submitted.

h. In any year, as an alternative to participating in
   the Salary Equity Study, an employee may seek
   redress of salary discrimination under Article 6.2
   of this Agreement by filing a grievance pursuant to
   Article 20, no later than 25 days after the date of
   the notification issued under paragraph a., above.
   Pursuant to Article 20.2 of this Agreement, the
   results of the Salary Equity Study shall not be an
   act or omission giving rise to a grievance under
   Article 20, nor shall the above procedures be
   grievable.

(2) Promotion Increases. Prior to making allocations of
promotion awards, the appropriate administrator should
consider recommendations which may have been made
through the collegial system of shared governance.
Promotion increases shall be granted to full-time
employees in the following amounts (proportional increases shall be granted to part-time employees):

To Assistant Professor, Assistant University School
Professor, Associate in _____, and Assistant
University Librarian -- one salary table step;

To Associate Professor, Associate University School
Professor, Research Associate (9166), Associate Curator
(9151), Associate Research Scholar/Scientist, Associate
Engineer, and Associate University Librarian -- 1½
salary table steps; and

To Professor, University School Professor, Curator
(9150), Research Scholar/Scientist, Engineer, and
University Librarian -- 2½ salary table steps.

(3) Developmental Research School Supplements.

a. Employees in Developmental Research Schools shall receive salary supplements for the approved activities, and in the amounts, described in b., below, under the following conditions:

1. The activity must be assigned by the Director, who shall determine which activities are to be performed and to whom they will be offered; provided that such activity must be offered in sufficient time to allow voluntary acceptance or rejection.

2. The activity must involve duties which extend beyond the normal workday, or duties for which an appropriate reduction in regular professional duties assigned during the normal work day has not been made, consistent with Article 9.9;

3. Employees shall receive a separate salary supplement for each assigned activity listed in b., below;

4. The amount of the annual salary supplements described in b., below, shall be paid over the period each year for which the activity is assigned;

5. Notwithstanding the provisions of Article 23.1(a), salary supplements may be paid in a manner that results in an employee's salary rate not corresponding with a salary rate in the salary table; and

6. Salary supplements are not to be included in the base salary rate upon which future salary increases are calculated.

b. Salary supplements shall be provided as follows:

1. A $500 supplement shall be provided for the following activities:

   Department chair (three or more 1.0 FTE members in a department)
   Student council/government advisor
   Drama coach
   Literary magazine sponsor
   Faculty sponsor
   Assistant coach
   Division director/chair

2. An $800 supplement shall be provided for the following activities:

Appendix III

                Cheerleader sponsor/coach
                Newspaper sponsor
                Yearbook sponsor
                Head coach, junior varsity sports
                Head coach, minor sports
                Choral director

          3. A $1,100 supplement shall be provided for the following activities:

                Athletic director
                Band Director
                Head coach, major sports

          4. A salary supplement for an activity may be paid at the next higher rate than those described above if, in the judgment of the Director, such higher rate is justified by the extent of the duties involved; however, no supplement shall exceed $1,100.

      c. Supplements for activities other than those described above may be provided at the discretion of the university.

   (4) Other Discretionary Increases.

      a. Prior to making allocations of discretionary increases, the appropriate administrator should consider recommendations which may have been made through the collegial system of shared governance. The administrator retains the right to make the final decision concerning the allocations of such increases.

      b. Complaints with respect to the amount of, and procedures leading to, the allocation of salary increases under Section 23.2(c)(4) and (d) shall not be grievable, except as they pertain to allegations of unlawful discrimination under Article 6.

      c. These funds shall not be used to provide increases to employees in Developmental Research Schools.

(d) Merit Salary Increases. Funds at an annual rate of 1.25% of the June 30, 1985 salary rate of employees shall be distributed to eligible employees pursuant to Article 23.5. In addition, funds which may be available subsequent to the distribution of increases under Article 23.2(b) shall also be distributed pursuant to this section.

23.3 Top Quartile Increases. In partial implementation of the State Board of Education's goal of raising the average salaries of State University System faculty members into the top quartile of the states, the Board shall provide salary increase funds of 2.0% of the June 30, 1985, annual salary rate of employees in classification codes 9001, 9002, 9003, 9004, 9005, 9006, 9007, 9009, 9060, 9061, 9062, 9063, 9064, 9065, 9066, 9067, 9068, 9069, 9070, 9071, 9072, 9115, 9116, 9117, 9118, 9119, 9120, 9121, 9126, 9127, 9128, 9129, 9130, 9160, 9161, 9162, 9166, 9167, 9168, 9169, 9170, 9401, 9420, and 9475. These salary increase funds shall be distributed to these employees as follows:

(a) The annual salary rate for each half-step in the salary table shall be increased 1.0%, thereby providing such an increase to these eligible employees,

(b) Funds in the amount of .50% of the annual salary rate of the employees listed above shall be distributed to eligible employees pursuant to Article 23.5, and

(c) The remainder of these salary increase funds (approximately .50% of the annual salary rate of the employees listed above) shall be distributed to eligible employees at the discretion of the Board.

23.4 Competitive Salary Adjustments.

(a) The Board shall distribute, in addition to other salary increases for which the following employees may be eligible, the salary increase funds described below in the 1985-86 fiscal years. These salary increase funds are provided to ensure that the salaries of these employees are as competitive in their respective markets as the salaries of SUS ranked faculty are in theirs.

(b) The Board shall provide salary increase funds of 6.75% of the June 30, 1985, annual salary rate of employees in classification codes 9016, 9017, 9018, and 9019 as follows:

(1) The annual salary rate for each half-step in the salary table shall be increased 1.0%, thereby providing such an increase to these eligible employees,

(2) The salaries of these employees shall be increased one-half step (1.75%) on the salary table, and

(3) The remainder of these funds (approximately 4.0%) shall be distributed to ensure that the 1985-86 salaries of each of these employees are not less than the salaries provided to individuals by the county within which each Developmental Research School is located, based on degree and years of experience on the county's 1984-85 schedule.

(c) The Board shall provide salary increase funds of 4.5% of the June 30, 1985, annual salary rate of employees in classification codes 9150, 9151, 9152, 9163, 9164, 9165, 9380, 9381, 9382, 9383, 9395, 9396, 9480, 9481, 9482, 9484, 9485, and

Appendix III 265

9486. These salary funds shall be distributed to these employees as follows:

(1) The annual salary rate for each half-step in the salary table shall be increased 1.0%, thereby providing such an increase to these eligible employees, and

(2) The salaries of these employees shall be increased two half-steps (3.5%) on the salary table.

(d) In distributing the funds available under 23.2(d) for 1985-86, each university shall ensure that the June 30, 1985, total salary rate of employees in the position classifications listed in 23.4(b) and (c), above, is increased by a percentage amount equal to at least the percentage increase in the June 30, 1985 total employee salary rate represented by the funds in 23.2(d). Each university shall also apply these same provisions to the funds available under 23.2(c)(4) for employees in the position classifications listed in 23.4(c), above.

23.5 Merit Criteria.

(a) The employees of each academic department or equivalent academic unit, and of administrative units within the library, shall develop and recommend written criteria and related evaluative procedures to be used by each university for the distribution of salary increase funds which the Board shall make available for the purpose of rewarding meritorious performance.

(1) The process by which merit criteria and related evaluative procedures are to be developed or revised shall be initiated upon a majority vote of the employees in a department or equivalent academic unit, or of the employees in administrative units within the library, or upon the initiation of the appropriate administrator.

(2) The appropriate administrator shall discuss these procedures, and the mission and goals of the department/unit and the university, with the department/unit employees who are to participate in the process.

(3) Each department/unit shall recommend merit criteria and related evaluative procedures by a secret ballot vote of at least a majority of the employees eligible to participate in departmental/unit governance. These criteria shall be written standards of performance and shall be the sole basis upon which administrators shall award merit salary increases.

(4) Departments/units are encouraged to exchange and discuss drafts of their merit criteria and related evaluative procedures during the formulation process.

(5) The proposed merit criteria and related evaluative procedures shall be reviewed by the university President or representative to ensure that they meet the following conditions:

    a. Compliance with the provisions of the BOR/UFF Agreement, State and Federal law, and the Florida Administrative Code. A copy of the relevant portions of State law and the Code shall be provided to each department/unit at the outset of the process. A copy of the BOR/UFF Agreement shall also be available at the outset for reference by the department/unit.

    b. Consistency with the mission and goals of the university, the college, and the department/unit.

    c. Consistency with the department's/unit's annual evaluation process, which shall be based upon assigned duties that may differ among employees.

If the university President or representative determines that the recommended criteria do not meet these conditions, the proposal shall be referred back to the department/unit within one month of receipt for reconsideration, with a written statement of reasons for non-approval. No merit salary increase funds shall be provided to a department/unit until its criteria have been approved by the university President or representative.

(b) Approved merit criteria and related evaluative procedures shall be kept on file in the department/unit office, and at the college and university levels. Additionally, employees in each department/unit shall be provided with a copy of that department's/unit's merit criteria and related evaluative procedures.

(c) The procedures, recommendations, and decisions made pursuant to this Article are not grievable. Complaints regarding the review and approval of proposed merit criteria and related evaluative procedures under 23.5(a)(1) and (5), above, may be filed by UFF with the President or representative within 30 days following the date on which UFF knew or reasonably should have known of the act or omission giving rise to the complaint. The President or representative shall seek resolution of the complaint and shall respond in writing to the complaint within 30 days after it is filed. If the complaint is not satisfactorily resolved by the procedure described herein, UFF may file the complaint with the

Appendix III

Chancellor or representative. The Chancellor or representative shall seek resolution of the complaint and shall respond in writing to the complaint within 30 days of its filing.

(d) Employees who wish to discuss the initial recommendation for their merit salary increase may do so under the provisions of Appendix "F" of this Agreement. A review of the implementation of this section of the Agreement shall be the subject of a consultation at each university pursuant to Article 2.2 of the Agreement.

23.6 Notification Procedures. All salary increases shall be allocated in accordance with the provisions of the notice contained in Appendix "F" of the Agreement. This notice shall be posted in all departments or other appropriate work locations for at least two weeks prior to the date on which the initial recommendation regarding salary increases is made. Upon request, employees shall be provided the opportunity to consult with the person or committee which makes the initial recommendations regarding salary increases.

23.7 Report to Employees. Each employee shall be sent a report, on the form prescribed in Appendix "G", not later than two weeks prior to the implementation of the salary increase.

23.8 Report to UFF.

(a) Two reports of the distribution of all salary increases arranged by university (one alphabetically and one by discipline), identifying the employee and the amount received in each of the categories, shall be made available to UFF no later than November 15th of each year. A copy of the reports for each university shall be placed in the main library along with the documents prescribed in Article 7.

(b) In addition to the reports described in 23.8(a), no later than two weeks after the beginning of the academic year or of the first pay period in which any salary increases are reflected, whichever is later, each university shall furnish the campus UFF Chapter with a copy of a report of the distribution of all employee salary increases, arranged by department or equivalent unit, identifying each employee and the amount received in each salary increase category, and specifying the mean and median merit salary increases for each department or equivalent unit, college, and for the university. A copy of each department's portion of the report shall be placed on file in the department, available upon request to any employee of the department.

23.9 The Board or its representative shall provide UFF, and post in each department or equivalent unit, a listing of the top quartile goals, by rank, for the State University System faculty.

23.10 Eligibility for Salary Increases.

(a) Only those employees hired before July 1, 1985, shall receive salary increases specified in Article 23.2(a) and (b), 23.3(a), and 23.4(b)(1) and (c)(1). Employees hired after that date shall receive only those increases that are necessary to maintain their salaries at the next higher salary rate contained in the salary table established in 23.1(b).

(b) Employees otherwise eligible for salary increases under the provisions of Article 23.2(c) and (d), 23.3(b) and (c), 23.4(b)(2) and (3), and 23.4(c)(2), shall receive such salary increases only if they were employed on or before January 31, 1985, with the exception of increases under 23.2(c)(3) for which employees are eligible regardless of hiring date.

23.11 Effective Date for Salary Increases. Salary increases shall be effective at the beginning of an employee's 1985-86 appointment, but not before August 7, 1985.

23.12 Nothing contained herein shall prevent the Board from providing salary increases beyond the increases specified above, provided that all such increases shall be in the form of incremental steps or half-steps.

23.13 Contract and Grant Funded Increases.

(a) Nothing contained herein shall prevent employees whose salaries are funded by grant agencies from being allotted raises higher than those provided in this Agreement.

(b) Employees on contracts or grants shall receive non-discretionary salary increases equivalent to similar employees on regular funding, provided that such salary increases are permitted by the terms of the contract or grant. In the event such salary increases are not permitted by the terms of the contract or grant, or in the event adequate funds are not available, the Board or its representatives shall seek to have the contract or grant modified to permit such increases.

(c) Employees on contracts or grants shall be eligible for consideration for discretionary salary increases equivalent to similar employees on regular funding, provided that such salary increases are permitted by the terms of the contract or grant and provided further that adequate funds are available for this purpose in the contract or grant. In the event adequate funds are not available, the Board or its representatives shall seek to have the contract or grant modified to permit such increase.

23.14 Order of Salary Increases. To arrive at a full-time employee's 1985-86 salary rate, begin with the employee's June 30, 1985, salary rate and add increases in the following order:

Appendix III

(a) Salary Equity 23.2(c)(1).
(b) DRS County Schedule 23.4(b)(3).
(c) General Salary Table Increases 23.2(a), 23.3(a), 23.4(b)(1) and (c)(1).
(d) Competitive Salary Table Step Increases 23.4(b)(2) and (c)(2).
(e) Salary Table Incremental Step Increases 23.2(b).
(f) Promotion Increases 23.2(c)(2).
(g) Merit Salary Increase 23.2(d) and 23.3(b).
(h) Discretionary Increases 23.2(c)(4) and 23.3(c).
(i) Developmental Research School Supplements 23.2(c)(3).

ARTICLE 24
FRINGE BENEFITS

The provisions of this Article are subject to renegotiation for the 1986-87 and 1987-88 years as provided in Article 30.1

24.1 The Board shall provide improvement in existing State-sponsored fringe benefits for employees to the extent authorized and funded by the State Legislature.

24.2 The parties agree to review the fringe benefits program available to employees. This review shall consider: a "cafeteria" benefits program, a child care program, and an employee assistance program. This review shall be completed by November 30, 1985, and funding shall be sought, if necessary, for those programs agreed to by the parties. The Board remains committed to regularly review and seek improvements in the fringe benefits program for employees, and will include UFF participation in this review process.

24.3 Part-time employees, except those in positions funded from Other Personal Services funds, are entitled to employer-funded fringe benefits under the provisions of State Law and the rules of the Department of Administration and the Division of Retirement. Part-time employees should contact the personnel office at their university to determine the nature and extent of the benefits for which they are eligible.

24.4 Retirement credit for employees who are authorized to take uncompensated or partially compensated leaves of absence shall be granted in accordance with State law and the rules of the Division of Retirement as they may exist at the time leave is granted. The rules, as of July, 1985, limit retirement credit for such leaves to 12 months at one time and a total of 24 months during the employee's entire period of State employment. The current rules also require that to receive retirement credit, the employee on uncompensated or partially compensated leave must make payment of the retirement contribution that would otherwise be made by the university. Employees who are to take such a leave of absence should contact the personnel office at their university for complete information prior to taking the leave.

24.5 Retired employees with at least ten years service with the university shall be eligible, upon request, on the same basis as other employees to receive the following benefits at the university from which they retired, subject to local regulations:

  (a) retired employee identification card;
  (b) use of the university library (i.e. public rooms, lending and research service);
  (c) listing in the university directory; and
  (d) placement on designated university mailing lists.

In addition, fees may be charged retired employees for the following, and/or access granted to them on a space available basis:

  (e) use of university recreational facilities; and
  (f) a university parking decal.

At the option of the university, and in accordance with local policy, retired employees may, upon request, be given office space.

24.6 Optional Retirement Program.

  (a) An Optional Retirement Program will be provided including at least the following provisions:

  (1) Eligibility for all full-time faculty, and those A&P employees who meet the criteria listed below, who are in the collective bargaining unit, and who are otherwise eligible for membership in the Florida Retirement System. A&P employees serving in positions which the Division of Retirement determines meet the following criteria shall be eligible for the Optional Retirement Program: the duties and responsibilities of the position must include either the formulation, interpretation, or implementation of academic policies, or the direct support of the academic program of the university; and recruiting to fill vacancies in the position must be conducted within the national or regional market;

  (2) A reasonable period of at least 90 days in which an eligible employee may decide whether to participate in the Optional Retirement Program;

  (3) No loss of accrued service credit or vested retirement benefits in the Florida Retirement System if an employee elects to participate in the Optional Retirement Program, provided however, that any employee participating in the Optional Retirement Program at the time of the employee's retirement shall not be eligible to participate nor accrue retirement credit in any State retirement system, including the Florida Retirement System, subsequent to retirement, whether or not the employee is reemployed by the State University System after retirement;

Appendix III

- (4) Benefits under the Optional Retirement Program shall be fully and immediately vested in the participating employees;

- (5) The employer shall contribute to the Optional Retirement Program, on behalf of each employee participating in the program, an amount equal to the normal cost portion of the employer's contribution to the Florida Retirement System, less a reasonable and necessary amount, as determined by the Legislature, which shall be provided to the Division of Retirement for administering the program;

- (6) A participating employee may contribute to the Optional Retirement Program, by salary reduction or deduction, a percentage amount of the employee's gross compensation not to exceed the percentage amount contributed by the employer to the Optional Retirement Program.

(b) The parties agree to inform eligible employees regarding the existence and impact of the Optional Retirement Program upon their retirement benefits.

24.7 Phased Retirement Program.

(a) Eligibility.

- (1) Employees who have accrued at least ten years of creditable service in the Florida or Teachers Retirement System or Optional Retirement Program and have attained at least 62 years of age are eligible to participate in the Phased Retirement Program. Employees who choose to participate must provide written notice to the university of their decision to participate not later than 180 days after the date upon which they become eligible, or thereafter forfeit such eligibility. Employees who choose to participate must retire with an effective date not later than 180 days, nor less than 90 days, after they submit such written notice.

- (2) Employees who have accrued at least ten years of creditable service in the Florida or Teachers Retirement System or Optional Retirement Program, but have not attained 62 years of age, are eligible to participate in the Phased Retirement Program until such eligibility ends in accordance with the eligibility provisions of paragraph (1), above. Employees who choose to participate under the provisions of this paragraph must provide the university with written notice of their decision to participate not later than 180 days prior to their effective date of retirement.

- (3) Employees who are reemployed by the State University System subsequent to their retirement shall not be eligible to participate nor accrue retirement credit in any State retirement system, including the Florida Retirement System, subsequent to their retirement.

The decision to participate in the Phased Retirement Program is irrevocable.

    (b) Program Provisions.

        (1) All participants must retire and thereby relinquish all rights to tenure as described in Article 15, except as stated otherwise in this Article. Participants' retirement benefits shall be determined as provided under Florida Statutes and the rules of the Division of Retirement.

        (2) Participants shall, upon retirement, receive payment for any unused annual leave or sick leave to which they are entitled.

        (3)

            a. Participants on academic year appointments, or those who are employed for more than nine months, shall be offered reemployment by the university for one-half (.5 FTE) of the academic year (780 hours, or 19½ weeks), at a salary proportional to their salary prior to retirement. The assignment shall be scheduled within one semester unless the participant and the university agree otherwise. Participants shall also be offered the option of continuing their pre-retirement appointment during the year next following the date of retirement. If the employee accepts reemployment by the university during any portion of the 12 month period following the employee's effective date of retirement, the employee shall not receive retirement benefits during such reemployment in accordance with Section 121.091(9)(b), Florida Statutes (1984).

            b. Participants on appointments of less than nine months, or less than 1.0 FTE, shall be reemployed for one-half of their pre-retirement appointment, not to exceed 19½ weeks, and at a proportional salary.[3] These participants may exercise the option of continuing their pre-retirement appointment during the year following retirement, subject to the conditions outlined in (3)a. above, and (5).

---

3   For example, an employee serving on a six-month appointment prior to retirement would be eligible for a 13 contiguous week appointment (6/9 of a 19 1/2 contiguous week appointment.)

Appendix III

(4) Upon reemployment, participants shall accrue sick leave at a rate directly proportionate to the percent of time employed. Participants will not be reimbursed for unused sick leave at the termination of their post-retirement reemployment period.

(5) The period of reemployment obligation shall extend over five consecutive years, beginning with the academic year next following the date of retirement, except that for those participants who exercise the option of continuing their pre-retirement appointment the year following retirement (as described in (3) above), the period of reemployment obligation shall extend over four consecutive years beginning with the academic year next following the date of retirement.

The period of reemployment obligation shall not be shortened by the university except under the provisions of Article 16 of the Agreement. During the period of reemployment, participants are to be treated as tenured or as having five or more years of continuous service, as appropriate, for purposes of Article 13.1(a) and (b) of the Agreement.

(6) A participant may decline an offer of reemployment, with reasonable notice to the university. Such a decision shall not extend the period of reemployment beyond the period described above. At the conclusion of the reemployment period, the university may, at its option, continue to reemploy participants in this program on a year-to-year basis.

(7) Participants shall receive all across-the-board salary adjustments available to employees, in an amount proportional to their part-time appointment, and shall be eligible for discretionary salary increases on the same basis as other employees.

(8) Participants may participate in all fringe benefit programs for which they are otherwise eligible as part-time employees and retirees.

(9) Participants shall retain all rights, privileges, and benefits of employment, as provided in laws, rules, the BOR/UFF Agreement, and university policies, subject to the conditions contained in this Article.

(10) Nothing shall prevent the employer or the participant, consistent with law and rule, from supplementing the participant's employment with contracts or grants.

ARTICLE 25
INSURANCE DEDUCTION

The Board agrees to provide one payroll deduction per employee per pay period for the UFF voluntary economic services programs. It is understood that all such programs and deductions will meet requirements of State and Board rules and regulations.

ARTICLE 26
PAYROLL DEDUCTION

Pursuant to the provisions of Section 447.303, Florida Statutes, the Board and UFF hereby agree to the following procedure for the deduction and remittance of UFF membership dues and uniform assessments.

26.1 Deductions. During the term of this Agreement, the Board, by and through the respective universities, agrees to deduct UFF membership dues and uniform assessments, if any, in an amount established by UFF and certified in writing by the UFF State President to the Board, from the pay of those employees in the bargaining unit who individually and voluntarily make such request on a written checkoff authorization form as contained in Appendix "B" to this Agreement.

Deductions will be made biweekly beginning with the first full pay period commencing at least seven full days following receipt by the university of checkoff authorization. UFF shall give written notice to the Board of any changes in its dues or uniform assessments at least 45 days prior to the effective date of any such change.

26.2 Remittance. The dues and uniform assessments deducted, if any, shall be remitted by the Board to the UFF State President on a biweekly basis, within 30 days following the end of the pay period. Accompanying each remittance shall be a list of the employees from whose salaries such deductions were made and the amounts deducted.

26.3 Termination of Deduction. The Board's responsibility for deducting dues and uniform assessments, if any, from an employee's salary shall terminate automatically upon either (a) 30 days written notice from the employee to the Board, the university personnel office, and to UFF revoking that employee's prior checkoff authorization, or (b) the transfer or promotion of the authorizing employee out of the bargaining unit. An employee who has a valid dues checkoff authorization filed with the university and whose dues checkoff is discontinued because of a leave without pay, shall have the dues checkoff resumed upon return to pay status within the bargaining unit.

26.4 Indemnification. UFF assumes responsibility for (a) all claims against the Board and the universities, including the cost of defending such actions, arising from their compliance with this Article, and for (b) all monies deducted under this Article and remitted to UFF. UFF shall promptly refund to the Board excess monies received under this Article.

Appendix III

26.5 Exceptions. The Board will not deduct any UFF fines, penalties, or special assessments from the pay of any employee.

26.6 Termination of Agreement. The Board's responsibilities under this Article shall terminate automatically upon (a) decertification of UFF or the suspension or revocation of its certification by the Florida Public Employees Relations Commission, or (b) revocation of UFF's checkoff privilege by the Florida Public Employees Relations Commission.

ARTICLE 27
MAINTENANCE OF BENEFITS

No employee may be required to waive the benefits provided by the terms of this Agreement. No employee shall, as a result of the establishment of a level of rights or benefits in this Agreement, suffer a loss or diminution of any such rights or benefits for which otherwise eligible.

ARTICLE 28
MISCELLANEOUS PROVISIONS

28.1 No Strike or Lockout. The Board agrees that there will be no lockout systemwide or at any of the universities during the term of this Agreement. UFF agrees that there will be no strike by itself or by any employees during the term of this Agreement.

28.2 Effect of Passage of Law. Any provision of this Agreement which is contrary to law, but becomes legal during the term of this Agreement, shall take immediate effect upon the enactment of such legislation.

28.3 Legislative Action. The Board and UFF agree that neither will attempt to influence or support changes in existing statutes or legislation which would change the terms of this Agreement.

28.4 Venue. For purposes of venue in any judicial review of an arbitrator's decision, the parties elect to submit themselves to the jurisdiction of the courts in Leon County, Florida. In an action commenced in Leon County, neither the Board nor UFF will move for a change of venue based upon the defendant's residence in fact if other than Leon County.

28.5 Copies of Agreement. The Board agrees to provide 8,000 copies of the ratified Agreement to UFF for distribution to employees, to make additional copies of the Agreement available for examination at designated places at each university, and to provide a copy to each new employee upon hiring. If the employee does not receive a copy from the university as part of the hiring process, the employee may obtain one from the UFF chapter. UFF agrees to distribute copies of the Agreement to current employees in the unit when the Agreement is ratified.

28.6 Class Titles.

(a) Whenever the Board creates a new class, it shall designate such class as being either within or outside the bargaining unit and shall notify UFF. Further, if the Board revises the specifications of an existing class so that its bargaining unit designation is changed, it shall notify UFF of such new designation. Within ten days following such notification, UFF may request a meeting with the Board or its representative for the purpose of discussing the designation. If, following such discussion, UFF disagrees with the designation, it may request the Florida Public Employees Relations Commission to resolve the dispute through unit clarification proceedings.

(b) An employee may request a review of the appropriateness of the employee's classification by the appropriate university office. In case of disagreement with the results of the review, the matter shall be discussed in accordance with Article 2, Consultation, but shall not be subject to Article 20, Grievance Procedure.

28.7 Salary Rate Calculation and Payment.

The biweekly salary rate of employees serving on 12 month (calendar year) appointments shall be calculated by dividing the calendar year salary rate by the number of work days in the appointment year (260 to 262)[4] and shall be paid over the term of the appointment.

ARTICLE 29
SEVERABILITY

In the event that any provision of this Agreement (a) is found to be invalid or unenforceable by final decision of a tribunal of competent jurisdiction, or (b) is rendered invalid by reason of subsequently enacted legislation, or (c) shall have the effect of a loss to the State of Florida or to the State University System of funds, property, or services made available through federal law, or (d) pursuant to Florida Statutes, Section 447.309(3), can take effect only upon the amendment of a law, rule, or regulation and the governmental body having such amendatory powers fails to take appropriate legislative action, then that provision shall be of no force or effect, but the remainder of the Agreement shall continue in full force and effect. If a provision of this Agreement fails for reason (a), (b), or (c) above, the parties shall enter into immediate negotiations for the purpose of arriving at a mutually satisfactory replacement for such provision.

---

[4] The actual number of work days in any calendar year is affected by such factors as leap-year and may vary from year to year.

Appendix III

ARTICLE 30
AMENDMENT AND DURATION

30.1 The Agreement shall become effective on the date it is signed and remain in effect through June 30, 1988, with the following exceptions:

- (a) Salaries (Article 23) and Fringe Benefits (Article 24) shall be subject to renegotiation as follows:

    (1) Renegotiations for salaries and fringe benefits for the 1986-87 year shall begin no later than October 15, 1985. Additionally, these renegotiations shall include issues related to the study to be conducted under Article 9.10.

    (2) Renegotiations for salaries and fringe benefits for the 1987-88 year shall begin no later than October 15, 1986.

- (b) Other subjects may be subject to negotiation or renegotiation upon the agreement of the parties.

- (c) Negotiations for a successor agreement shall begin no later than October 1, 1987.

- (d) The dates for renegotiations, or negotiations as specified above, may be changed by agreement of the parties. If the Board and UFF fail to secure a successor agreement prior to the date upon which this Agreement expires, the parties may agree to extend this Agreement for any period of time.

30.2 In the event the Board and UFF negotiate a mutually acceptable amendment to this Agreement, such amendment shall be put in writing and become part of this Agreement upon ratification by both parties.

ARTICLE 31
TOTALITY OF AGREEMENT

The parties acknowledge that during the negotiations which resulted in the Agreement, UFF had the unlimited right and opportunity to present demands and proposals with respect to any and all matters lawfully subject to collective bargaining, and that all of the understandings and agreements arrived at thereby are set forth in this Agreement, and that it shall constitute the entire and sole Agreement between the parties for its duration.

Therefore, the Board and UFF, during the term of this Agreement, voluntarily and unqualifiedly waive the right, and agree that the other shall not be obligated, to bargain collectively with respect to any subject or matter, whether or not referred to or covered by this Agreement, even though such subject or matter may not have been within the knowledge or contemplation of the parties at the time they negotiated or signed this Agreement.

Nothing herein shall, however, preclude the parties from mutually agreeing to alter, amend, supplement, delete, enlarge, or modify any of the provisions of this Agreement in writing.

ARTICLE 32
DEFINITIONS

As used in this Agreement, the term:

32.1 "bargaining unit" means those employees, collectively, represented for collective bargaining purposes by UFF pursuant to the certification of the Florida Public Employees Relations Commission dated November 21, 1984, wherein the Commission ordered that Certification number 218, previously issued to UFF, remain in effect, and Order number 84-E-112, dated June 14, 1984, wherein the Commission adopted the bargaining unit agreed to by the Board of Regents and UFF, as amended.

32.2 "Board" or "Board of Regents" means the body established by Florida Statutes, Chapter 240.

32.3 "break in service" means those absences following which the employee is treated as a new employee for purposes of computing seniority and years of service.

32.4 "continuous service" means employment uninterrupted by a break in service.

32.5 "days" means calendar days and "months" means calendar months.

32.6 "employee" means a member of the bargaining unit.

32.7 "supervisor" means an individual identified by the President or representative as having immediate administrative authority over bargaining unit employees.

32.8 "SUS" or "State University System" means the system of institutions and agencies within the jurisdiction of the Board of Regents.

32.9 "UFF" means United Faculty of Florida.

32.10 "university" means one of the nine institutions in the State University System and its staff.

32.11 Number--The singular includes the plural.

32.12 Titles and Headings--The titles of Articles and headings which precede text are inserted solely for convenience of reference and shall not be deemed to limit or affect the meaning, construction, or effect of any provision of this Agreement.

32.13 "equitable" means fair and reasonable under the circumstances.

Appendix III

IN WITNESS WHEREOF, the parties, by their duly authorized officers and agents, have affixed their signatures this 26th day of July, 1985.

FOR THE BOARD OF REGENTS:

Robin Gibson
Robin Gibson, Chairman

Barbara W. Newell
Barbara W. Newell, Chancellor

James J. Parry
James J. Parry, Chief Negotiator

Art Adams
Marian Alves
Robert Bryan
Gary Fane
Paul Gallagher
Albert Hartley
Frank Juge
John Martin
Emoryette McDonald
Kenneth Michels
Nancy Stepina
Augustus Turnbull
Paul Zeigler

j1/204

FOR THE UNITED FACULTY OF FLORIDA

Roy C. Weatherford
Roy Weatherford, President

Phyllis Hudson
Phyllis Hudson, Chief Negotiator

Harry Goldman
Thelman Gorham
Jeanene McNair
Cary Mills
Clay Steinman
Dan Ward
Butler Waugh

APPENDIX A

The parties agree that the bargaining unit class titles listed below shall be amended to conform to the changes resulting from the transfer of positions between the Faculty and Administrative and Professional classification and pay plans pursuant to the authorization contained in the 1985 Appropriations Act.

All employees in the following positions holding regular, visiting, provisional, research, affiliate, or joint appointments are included in the bargaining unit certified by PERC:

```
9001 - Professor
9002 - Associate Professor
9003 - Assistant Professor
9004 - Instructor
9005 - Lecturer
9006 - Graduate Research Professor
9007 - Distinguished Service Professor
9009 - Eminent Scholar
9016 - University School Professor
9017 - University School Associate Professor
9018 - University School Assistant Professor
9019 - University School Instructor
9063 - Associate Chairperson and Professor
9064 - Associate Chairperson and Associate Professor
9065 - Associate Chairperson and Assistant Professor
9066 - Assistant Chairperson and Professor
9067 - Assistant Chairperson and Associate Professor
9068 - Assistant Chairperson and Assistant Professor
9069 - Assistant Chairperson and Instructor
9070 - Area Chairperson and Professor
9071 - Area Chairperson and Associate Professor
9072 - Area Chairperson and Assistant Professor
9115 - Coordinator
9116 - Coordinator and Professor
9117 - Coordinator and Associate Professor
9118 - Coordinator and Assistant Professor
9119 - Coordinator and Instructor
9120 - Associate in _____
9121 - Assistant in _____
9126 - Program Director
9127 - Program Director and Professor
9128 - Program Director and Associate Professor
9129 - Program Director and Assistant Professor
9130 - Program Director and Instructor
9144 - Athletic Head Coach
9145 - Athletic Coach
9147 - Assistant Athletic Coach
9148 - Athletic Trainer
9150 - Curator
```

Appendix III

```
9151 - Associate Curator
9152 - Assistant Curator
9160 - Research Scholar/Scientist
9161 - Associate Research Scholar/Scientist
9162 - Assistant Research Scholar/Scientist
9163 - Engineer
9164 - Associate Engineer
9165 - Assistant Engineer
9166 - Research Associate
9167 - Counselor/Advisor and Professor
9168 - Counselor/Advisor and Associate Professor
9169 - Counselor/Advisor and Assistant Professor
9170 - Counselor/Advisor and Instructor
9172 - Physician's Assistant in _____
9173 - Counselor/Advisor
9334 - Computer Research Specialist
9380 - University Librarian
9381 - Associate University Librarian
9382 - Assistant University Librarian
9383 - Instructor Librarian
9394 - Cooperative Education Coordinator
9395 - Curator
9396 - Associate Curator
9401 - Instructional Specialist
9410 - Assistant Radio/Television News Director
9419 - University Research Editor
9420 - Research Associate
9433 - Staff Musician
9434 - University Counseling Psychologist
9435 - Counselor to Students
9460 - University Psychiatrist
9461 - Clinical Psychologist
9462 - University Physician
9463 - University Veterinarian
9464 - Physician's Assistant
9475 - Staff Physicist
9480 - Department Head and University Librarian
9481 - Department Head and Associate University Librarian
9482 - Department Head and Assistant University Librarian
9484 - Assistant Department Head and University Librarian
9485 - Assistant Department Head and Associate University Librarian
9486 - Assistant Department Head and Assistant University Librarian
9490 - University Dentist
9495 - Student Counseling Specialist
```

Together with chairpersons (9060-9062) in the following universities, divisions, schools, or colleges:

Florida Atlantic University

Florida International University
    College of Arts and Sciences
    School of Education
    School of Public Affairs and Services

Florida State University
    College of Arts and Sciences
    College of Business
    College of Communication
    College of Social Sciences
    College of Visual Arts

University of Florida
    College of Liberal Arts and Sciences
    College of Education
    College of Business Administration
    College of Fine Arts
    College of Physical Education, Health and Recreation

University of South Florida
    College of Arts and Letters
    College of Natural Sciences
    College of Social and Behavioral Sciences
    College of Education

All other employees of the Board of Regents are excluded from this bargaining unit.

APPENDIX B

DUES CHECK-OFF AUTHORIZATION FORM

I authorize the Florida Board of Regents, through the university, to deduct from my pay, biweekly starting with the pay for the first full pay period commencing not earlier than seven full days from the date this authorization is received by the university, membership dues and uniform assessments of the United Faculty of Florida in such amount as may be established from time to time in accordance with the constitution and bylaws of the UFF and certified in writing to the Florida Board of Regents by the UFF, and I direct that the sum or sums so deducted be paid over to the UFF.

This authorization shall continue until either (1) revoked by me at any time upon thirty days written notice to the Florida Board of Regents, University Personnel Office, and to UFF, or (2) my transfer or promotion out of this bargaining unit.

Date:_____   _____
                                   (Employee's Signature)

_____   _____
(Social Security Number)   (Name-printed)

_____   _____
(Department)   (University)

Effective date if later than above _____

Please return to your chapter treasurer or UFF State Office, 213 S. Adams Street, Tallahassee, Florida 32301.

STATE UNIVERSITY SYSTEM OF FLORIDA
Board of Regents/United Faculty of Florida

APPENDIX C
GRIEVANCE

I.   Date (Received by University)

_____

GRIEVANT   STEP 1 GRIEVANCE REPRESENTATIVE

NAME:_____   NAME:_____

UNIVERSITY:_____   MAILING ADDRESS:

COLLEGE:_____   _____
                                                _____
DEPT:_____   _____

OFFICE PHONE:_____   OFFICE PHONE:_____

If grievant is represented by UFF or legal counsel, all university communications should go to the grievant's representative.

Other address to which university mailings pertaining to grievance shall be sent:

_____
_____
_____
_____

II. GRIEVANCE

Provisions of Agreement allegedly violated (specify Articles and Sections):
_____
_____
_____

Statement of grievance (must include <u>date</u> of acts or omissions complained of):

Remedy Sought:

Appendix III

III. <u>AUTHORIZATION</u>

I will be represented in this grievance by: (check one - representative must sign on appropriate line):

____ UFF   _____

____ Legal Counsel _____

____ Myself   _____

I (do)____(do not)____ want a postponement for up to 25 days to seek informal resolution of this grievance.

I UNDERSTAND AND AGREE THAT BY FILING THIS GRIEVANCE, I WAIVE WHATEVER RIGHTS I MAY HAVE UNDER CHAPTER 120 OF THE FLORIDA STATUTES WITH REGARD TO THE MATTERS I HAVE RAISED HEREIN AND UNDER ALL OTHER UNIVERSITY PROCEDURES WHICH MAY BE AVAILABLE TO ADDRESS THESE MATTERS.

This grievance was filed with the President's Office on _____
by (check one) mail (certified or registered, restricted delivery, return receipt requested) ____; personal delivery ____.

_____
Signature of Grievant

(Grievant must sign if grievance is to be processed.)

Copies of the Step 1 Decision shall be sent to: Grievant
                                                  Step 1 Representative
                                                  OHR, BOR

STATE UNIVERSITY SYSTEM OF FLORIDA
Board of Regents/United Faculty of Florida

APPENDIX D
REQUEST FOR REVIEW OF STEP 1 DECISION

GRIEVANT   STEP 1 REPRESENTATIVE

NAME:_____   NAME:_____

UNIVERSITY:_____   MAILING ADDRESS:_____

OFFICE ADDRESS:_____   _____
_____   _____
_____   _____

DATE OF STEP 1 DECISION:
_____

Provisions of Agreement allegedly violated (as specified at Step 1): _____
_____

I hereby request that the Chancellor or representative review the attached decision made in connection with the attached grievance because:

Grievant received the decision on _____, and filed this request for review with the Chancellor's office on _____, by (check one): mail (certified or registered, restricted delivery, return receipt requested) _____; personal delivery _____.
DATE OF RECEIPT BY CHANCELLOR'S OFFICE:_____

_____
Signature of Grievant

I am represented in this grievance by (check one - representative should sign on appropriate line):
_____ UFF
_____ Legal Counsel   _____
_____ Myself   _____

A copy of the following documents must be attached to this Request at the time of its filing with the Chancellor or representative:

1. Appendix C - Original grievance form filed with the University.
2. Step 1 Decision, if issued by University.
3. All attachments to Step 1 Decision, as required in Article 20.8, Grievance Procedure.

Appendix III

This request should be sent to:

> OFFICE OF HUMAN RESOURCES
> BOARD OF REGENTS, STATE UNIVERSITY SYSTEM OF FLORIDA
> 107 W. Gaines St., Collins Bldg., Rm. 210-F
> Tallahassee, Florida 32301

Copies of Step 2 Decision shall be sent to: Grievant, Step 1 Representative and Step 1 Reviewer.

STATE UNIVERSITY SYSTEM OF FLORIDA
Board Of Regents/United Faculty Of Florida

APPENDIX E

NOTICE OF ARBITRATION

The United Faculty of Florida hereby gives notice of its intent to proceed to arbitration in connection with the decision of the Chancellor's office dated _____ and received by UFF-Tallahassee on _____ in this grievance of:

      NAME: _____
      BOR FILE NO: _____

The following statement of issue(s) before the Arbitrator is proposed:

This notice was filed with the Chancellor's office on _____ by (check one): mail (certified or registered, restricted delivery, return receipt requested) _____ ; personal delivery _____ .

Date of receipt by Chancellor's office: _____

_____
Signature of UFF Representative

I hereby authorize UFF to proceed to arbitration with my grievance. I also authorize UFF and the Board of Regents or its representatives to use, during the arbitration proceedings, copies of any materials in my evaluation file pertinent to this grievance and to furnish copies of the same to the arbitrator.

_____
Signature of Grievant

This notice should be sent to:

      OFFICE OF HUMAN RESOURCES
      BOARD OF REGENTS, STATE UNIVERSITY SYSTEM OF FLORIDA
      107 W. Gaines St., Collins Bldg., Rm. 210-F
      Tallahassee, Florida 32301

Appendix III

APPENDIX F

SALARY INCREASES--198_-8_

I. In accordance with provisions of the 198_-8_ negotiated Agreement between the Board of Regents and the United Faculty of Florida, the following salary increases shall be provided:

A. _____

B. _____

C. _____

D. _____

E. _____

F. _____

G. _____

II. Order of Salary Increases:

   A. _____

   B. _____

   C. _____

   D. _____

   E. _____

   F. _____

   G. _____

III. Eligibility for Salary Increases:

Appendix III

IV. Effective Date for Increases:

V. The person(s) making the initial recommendation for this area is (are):

Name(s):

Office(s):

If you wish to consult with the person(s) regarding the recommendation for salary increases, please contact him or her prior to ___(Date)___ .

All employees have the right to consult with the person(s) making the initial recommendation regarding salary increases. All employees will be notified two weeks prior to the implementation of the salary increase of the amount of increase and the categories in which the salary increase is distributed.

THIS NOTICE MUST BE POSTED AT LEAST TWO WEEKS PRIOR TO THE DATE ON WHICH THE INITIAL RECOMMENDATION REGARDING SALARY INCREASES IS MADE.

APPENDIX G
SALARY INCREASE NOTIFICATION
198_-8_

In accordance with the provisions of the Agreement negotiated between the Board of Regents and the United Faculty of Florida, your salary increase is:

Current (198_-8_) Salary: $_____

                                                                                $_____

                                                                                $_____

                                                                                $_____

                                                                                $_____

                                                                                $_____

                                                                                $_____

                                                                                $_____

                                                                                $_____

New Salary (198_-8_) $_____

The recommendation for your salary increase was prepared by:

_____

You may request a conference to discuss this increase.

Appendix III

APPENDIX H

MEMORANDUM OF UNDERSTANDING

BOARD OF REGENTS AND UNITED FACULTY OF FLORIDA
EXCLUSIVE ASSIGNMENT DISPUTE RESOLUTION PROCEDURE

The Board of Regents and United Faculty of Florida agree to the following procedure as the exclusive method of resolving disputes which allege that an employee's assignment has been imposed arbitrarily or unreasonably.

The dispute shall not be processed unless it is filed prior to the effective date of the employee's assignment. If the employee's assignment begins prior to final resolution of the dispute, the employee shall perform the assignment until the matter is finally resolved by the Neutral Umpire.

All time limits contained herein may be extended by mutual agreement of the President's representative and the UFF representative. Upon failure of the employee's UFF representative to comply with the time limits herein, the dispute shall be deemed to have been finally determined at the prior step.

All references to "days" herein refers to "calendar days". The "end of the day" shall refer to the end of the business day, i.e., the day ends at 5:00 p.m.

An employee who alleges that the assignment has been imposed arbitrarily or unreasonably may file a grievance under Article 20 of the BOR/UFF Agreement only to enforce the exclusive Assignment Dispute Resolution (ADR) procedure delineated below, not to seek a determination as to whether an assignment has been arbitrarily and unreasonably imposed.

(a) An employee who believes that the assignment has been imposed arbitrarily or unreasonably shall, no later than six weeks prior to the starting date of the assignment or within seven days of receipt of the assignment, whichever is the later date, notify the individual responsible for making the assignment of that belief. Within four days of receipt of such notification, the individual responsible for making the assignment shall meet with the employee and discuss the dispute.

(b) If the employee continues to be aggrieved following the initial conference, the employee shall complete Part 1 of the Assignment Dispute Resolution (ADR) Form and present it to the Dean or other appropriate administrator no later than four days after the initial conference.

(c) The UFF representative shall schedule a meeting with the Dean or other appropriate administrator to be held no later than four days after delivery of the ADR Form to the Dean or other appropriate administrator. At this meeting, the employee, UFF representative, and the Dean or appropriate administrator shall discuss the dispute and attempt to resolve it. At the conclusion of this meeting, the Dean or appropriate administrator and the UFF representative shall complete Part 2 of the ADR Form. Both shall retain a copy thereof.

(d) If consultation with the Dean or appropriate administrator does not resolve the matter, the UFF representative may file, within four days of that meeting, Part 3 of the ADR Form with the President's designee, indicating an intention to submit the dispute to a Neutral Umpire. The filing of the Form may be accompanied by a brief and concise statement of the employee's arguments, a list of witnesses expected to be called should the matter proceed to a Neutral Umpire, a copy of Parts 1 and 2 of the ADR Form, and any relevant documentation supporting the employee's position. This documentation shall be placed in a file entitled "Employee's Assignment Dispute Resolution File", which shall be kept separate from the employee's personnel evaluation file.

(e) Upon receipt of the completed ADR Form and other documentation, the President's designee may place a written explanation, brief statement of the University's position, a list of expected witnesses, and other relevant documentation in the employee's ADR File. A copy of all documents placed in the employee's ADR File shall be presented to the UFF representative.

(f) Following the filing of the completed ADR Form with the President's designee, the UFF representative shall schedule a meeting with the President's designee for the purpose of selecting a Neutral Umpire from the Neutral Umpire Panel. This meeting shall be scheduled for no later than seven days after filing of the completed ADR Form. Selection of the Neutral Umpire shall be by mutual agreement or by alternatively striking names from the Neutral Umpire Panel list until one name remains. The right of first choice to strike from the list shall be determined by the toss of a coin. The right to strike first shall alternate in any subsequent Neutral Umpire selection.

(g) The President's designee shall contact the selected Umpire no later than three days following the selection. Should the Umpire selected be unable to serve, the President's designee shall contact the UFF representative as soon as practicable, and schedule another selection meeting.

(h) Upon the agreement of the Neutral Umpire to participate, the President's designee and the UFF representative shall have three days in which they may add further documentation to the employee's ADR File. A copy of any documents added to the ADR File shall be provided to the other party, i.e., the President's designee or UFF representative. On the fourth day after the Umpire agrees to hear the dispute, the President's designee shall provide the Umpire with the employee's ADR File.

(i) The ADR Meeting shall be scheduled as soon as practicable after the Neutral Umpire has received the employee's ADR File. The President's designee shall notify the UFF representative of the time and place of the ADR Meeting no later than 48 hours prior to it being convened.

(j) The ADR Meeting shall be conducted as follows:

  (1) The employee, or UFF representative, and a representative of the President shall be the sole representatives of the parties. Each representative may present documentary evidence from the

employee's ADR File, interrogate witnesses, and offer arguments. Each representative shall have the right of cross-examination.

(2) The Neutral Umpire will conduct and have total authority at the ADR Meeting. The Neutral Umpire may conduct the ADR Meeting in whatever fashion, consistent with this Agreement, that will aid in arriving at a just decision. Immediately after the presentation of all evidence or arguments, the Umpire shall be left alone to review the evidence and write the decision. Upon completing the decision, the Umpire will reconvene the ADR Meeting and submit to all parties the formal written decision on Part 4 of the ADR Form.

(3) Should the Neutral Umpire determine that the employee's assignment was imposed arbitrarily or unreasonably, the written decision shall indicate the reasons for that determination to aid the President or President's designee in fashioning an appropriate remedy. The Neutral Umpire shall not, however, make or suggest an assignment.

(4) The decision of the Neutral Umpire shall be final and binding on both parties.

(k) No person concerned with or involved in the assignment dispute shall attempt to lobby or otherwise influence the decision of the Umpire.

(l) The President's representative and the UFF representative shall meet within two weeks of the signing of this Memorandum for the purpose of selecting an odd-numbered Neutral Umpire Panel. The Panel shall consist of no less than five and no more than nine individuals, not employed by the SUS, who meet the following qualifications:

(1) familiarity with academic assignments;

(2) an ability to serve as Neutral Umpire on short notice;

(3) a willingness to serve on the Panel for one academic year; and

(4) acceptability to both the University and UFF.

The President's designee and the UFF representative are encouraged to select educators from other non-SUS institutions in the area, fully retired faculty and administrators, and professional mediators and arbitrators, to be on the Neutral Umpire Panel. In the event the parties cannot reach agreement on Panel membership, a representative of the Board and a UFF member holding a statewide office or position shall select the Panel.

Panel membership may be reviewed, at the initiation of the University or UFF, through written notice provided before the end of the preceding fiscal year.

(m) All fees and costs of the neutral umpire shall be borne equally by the University and UFF.

ARTICLE 9.5 EXCLUSIVE ASSIGNMENT DISPUTE RESOLUTION FORM

PART 1: STATEMENT OF DISPUTE

_____
Employee's Name

_____
Department

_____
Employee's Address

_____
Person Making Assignment

_____
Date Assignment Made

_____
Date Assignment to Begin

Was the assignment discussed with the person making the assignment?
_____
yes/no

Date assignment was discussed with person making assignment. _____

I believe the assignment was arbitrarily or unreasonably imposed because:

_____
_____
_____

Submitted to _____
             Name of Dean or Appropriate Administrator

on _____
   Date Submitted

_____   _____
Employee's Signature   UFF Representative's Signature

Appendix III

PART 2: DECISION OF DEAN OR APPROPRIATE ADMINISTRATOR

_____
Date Dispute Discussed with Employee

DECISION: _____ The Disputed Assignment was not arbitrarily or unreasonably imposed.

_____ The Disputed Assignment has been resolved in the following manner:

Decision Issued on _____ by _____
                              Date of Decision   Signature and Title

_____
UFF Representative's Signature

PART 3: UFF NOTICE OF INTENT TO REFER ASSIGNMENT DISPUTE TO NEUTRAL UMPIRE

The decision of the Dean or other appropriate administrator is not satisfactory and UFF hereby gives notice of its intent to refer the dispute to a Neutral Umpire.

_____   _____
Employee's Name   Date of Receipt by President's
                                    Designee

_____
UFF Representative

                                    _____
                                    Receipt Acknowledged by President's Designee

PART 4: NEUTRAL UMPIRE'S DECISION

The disputed assignment was _____/was not _____ arbitrarily or unreasonably imposed.

Reasons for the determination that the assignment was arbitrarily or unreasonably imposed are:

_____   _____
   Neutral Umpire's Name   Employee's Name

_____   _____
   Neutral Umpire's Signature   Date Decision Issued

INDEX

Abortion leave 29
Absenteeism 32
Academic calendar 71
Academic freedom 70, 214
Academic librarians 4, 10, 11, 18, 25
Academic library employees 4
Adoption leave 29, 243
Affirmative action 17, 35
Age Discrimination Act of 1978 32
Agency shop 26, 101
American Association of University Professors 25
Arbitration 17, 36, 37, 106, 177, 250-253
Arkansas Gazette 12

Barber-Scotia College 10
Bargaining unit recognition 7, 60, 69, 100, 145, 208
Bereavement leave 28, 125
Berry, John 45
Bilingual salary increment 44
Billings, Montana 7
Black librarians 35, 49
Boston Public Library 34, 55-59, 61, 97-140
Boston University 10, 13, 19
Bradford College 12
Brandeis University 4, 10, 12, 19, 25, 61, 62, 63, 65
Bristol Public Library 49
Brooklyn Public Library 19
Buffalo and Erie county library 8, 19, 30
Bulletin boards 129, 155, 210
Bumping 17, 24

Capital Times 12
Catalogers 10
Catholic University Law School 12
Central Michigan University 34
Certification elections 8
Child care leave 29, 243
Child care program 269
Childbearing leave 29
Citizenship discrimination 34, 61
City University of New York 72
Civil Rights Act of 1964 32, 48
Claremont Colleges 4, 10, 12
Clause finders 3
Closed shop 26
Columbia Teachers' College 10
Community college librarians 10, 11
Comparable worth 45, 46, 48
Compulsory disability leave 242
Connecticut, bargaining units 8
Consumer Price Index 45
Contra Costa County library 19, 29, 30
Contracting out 27, 52, 56, 102
Copyrights and patents 75, 244, 245
Cost of living adjustment 45
Court leave 125, 161

Delaware (Pa.) Community

College 12
Department heads 12
Detroit Public Library 29
Discipline and discharge 31, 56, 64, 74, 75, 103, 104, 168-171, 233, 234

East Detroit Public Library 49
Educational leave 18, 124
Emergency leave 161, 243
Equity pay 44
Evaluation 72, 224

Faculty 10, 11, 13, 18, 23
Firemen 9
Florida Southern College 12
Fordham University 12
Fresno county library 27

Galveston, Texas 8
Gladstone, Ore., library 29, 30
Governance 191-194
Government service leave 161
Grievance 37, 38, 56, 66, 76, 104-106, 171-176

Handicap discrimination 33
Health insurance 136, 158
Heat and humidity relief 132
Holidays 20, 21, 30, 115, 166
Hours 110, 222, 223
Huntington Beach, California 19

Immigration Act of 1986 34

Jennings, Sir William Ivor 9
Job-related disability leave 238
Jury leave 27, 126, 160, 241
Just cause 31, 104

Labor Relations Act of 1935 32
Language proficiency 72, 225
Layoff and recall 17, 24, 26, 63, 74, 108-110, 151

Leave pending investigation 242
Leaves 75, 116-128, 160-166, 234
Librarians' Association of University of California 68, 180, 192
Library technicians 10
Longevity pay 134
Los Angeles county library 27

Madison Heights, Wisconsin 19, 30
Management rights 56, 64, 70, 102, 159, 213
Managerial employees 3, 13
Marital status discrimination 71
Market for librarians 51
Marternity leave 127, 243
Media specialists 10
Medical condition discrimination 61
Medical separation 198
Mental handicap discrimination 33, 61
Merit pay 44, 265, 266
Military leave 28, 126, 160, 241
Mount Vernon College 12
Municipal employees 9, 10, 17, 20

National Labor Relations Board 7, 8, 9, 10, 13
National origin discrimination 35
Negotiation team 130, 156
New York City Library 8
New York University 12
No-strike clause 56, 66, 76, 107, 178, 275
Non-discrimination 32, 33, 34, 59, 61, 70, 101, 146, 214
Northeastern University 12
Norwalk Public Library 39

Oakland, California 19

Index

Occupational Safety and Health Act of 1970 36
Occupational assault leave 28
Outside activity 75, 245-247
Overtime 58, 110-111

Paternal leave 29, 128, 243
Peer review 62, 148, 180
Personal leave 28, 242
Personnel files 62, 63, 130, 149, 227
Picketing 56, 107
Point Park College 12
Police officers 9
Political activity discrimination 71
Pre-professionals 103
Pregnancy Discrimination Act of 1978 30, 31, 32
Pregnancy leave 29
Probation 103
Professional conduct 180
Professional development 19, 21, 22, 61, 76
Professional development leave 61, 76, 147, 180, 195, 255
Professional employees 10, 11
Progressive discipline 32
Promotion 17, 62, 74, 113, 148, 230, 231
Public librarians 4, 9, 20
Public library employees 4, 9, 17

Rapid City public library 30
Ratification 1
Rehabilitation Act of 1973 32
Rensselaer Polytechnic Institute 12
Retirement programs 269-273
Retraining 26
Retrenchment 23, 24
Right to Know 36
Rosenberg library 8

Sabbaticals 76, 256-259
Safety 35, 63, 76, 154, 254
Salaries, librarians' placement 47
Salaries, union effect on 49, 50

Salary 133, 158, 196, 200, 217-220, 259-269
San Jose library 49
Santa Ana library 30
School librarians 10, 11
Scituate library 49
Second master's pay 134
Seniority 17, 20, 21, 23, 24, 25, 35, 42, 104, 115, 153
Sex discrimination 32, 33
Sexual harassment 33, 71, 175
Sexual preference 34
Sick leave 28, 118-123, 164, 235
Special librarians 4, 9
Staff-management committee 59, 128
Strikes 2, 107
Student assistants 60
Study leave 256
Supervisors 1, 10, 11, 12, 20

Tenure 23, 25, 74, 232-233
Texas, public employees 8
Training 18
Transfer 151
Tuition waiver 137, 158, 254

U.S. Naval Academy 27
Union activity discrimination 32
Union dues 26, 51, 64, 101, 156, 274
Union rights 154-156, 208-213
Union security 26
Union shop 26
Unions 7
United Faculty of Florida 70
University of California 4, 10, 11, 25, 33, 34, 60-68
University of Chicago 4, 12, 25
University of Florida 69-78
University of New Hampshire 10
University of San Francisco 12

Vacancies 112, 114
Vacations 20, 116, 165
Veteran status discrimination 71
Video display terminals 36
Voting leave 124

Washington formula 223

Wayne County, Michigan 7
Wild-cat strike 56
Wisconsin teachers 29, 30
Women librarians 35

Yale University 53
Yeshiva University 12, 13

SOUTHEASTERN MASSACHUSETTS UNIVERSITY
Z682.2.U5 W4 1988
Librarians' agreements

3 2922 00036 514 5

309473